D1268748

JUL -- 2002

Gregory I. Stevens, Editor

Assisted by Sarah Parker Scotchmer

VIDEOS
for Understanding
DIVERSITY

A Core Selection
and Evaluative Guide

American Library Association
Chicago and London 1993

LC
1099.3
S 74
1993

Designed by Ellen Scanlon

Composed by Publishing Services Inc.
in Century Light and Symbol on
Xyvision/Cg8600

Printed on 50-pound Glatfelter, a
pH-neutral stock, and bound in
10-point C1S cover stock by
McNaughton & Gunn, Inc.

The paper used in this publication meets the minimum requirements of American National Standard for Information Sciences—
Permanence of Paper for Printed Library Materials, ANSI Z39.48-
1984.∞

Library of Congress Cataloging-in-Publication Data

Stevens, Gregory I.
    Videos for understanding diversity : a core selection and
evaluative guide / by Gregory I. Stevens.
        p.   cm.
    Includes bibliographical references and index.
    ISBN 0-8389-0612-5 (alk. paper)
    1. Intercultural education—United States—Video tape catalogs.
    2. Pluralism (Social sciences)—United States—Video tape catalogs.
    I. Title.
    LC1099.3.S74 1993
    370.19′6′0208—dc20   93-2662

Copyright © 1993 by the American Library Association. All rights
reserved except those which may be granted by Sections 107 and
108 of the Copyright Revision Act of 1976.

Printed in the United States of America.

97 96 95 94 93   5 4 3 2 1

#27338612
6/28/94 OH

Contents

Acknowledgments

This guide could never have been done without the keen interest and trenchant expertise of faculty from the University at Albany, State University of New York, committed to this endeavor, a group of scholars representing an array of diverse cultural backgrounds. Each review, signed by the author, is to me a lasting tribute to their caring and generosity.

A complex project such as ours had its challenges; fortunately, there were many who pitched in to meet them. The former vice president for academic affairs, Warren Ilchman, and Jeanne Gullahorn, vice president for research, provided additional funding to complement the New York State/United University Professions (NYS/UUP) grant, as did deans Francine Frank and John Webb.

Meredith Butler, dean of University Libraries, gave us access to the wisdom of her colleagues, especially Deborah Curry of the University Library's collection development department, who provided essential services in the painstaking process of locating and obtaining materials for review. We are thankful also to Kate Skelton of the NYS/UUP Joint Labor-Management Committee for her instrumental assistance and guidance.

Finally, special thanks and recognition must go to Sara Parker Scotchmer, a doctoral student in communication at the time we compiled the guide. Without her persistence and unflagging attention to detail, the completion of this project would have been impossible. Sara gathered catalogs, monitored faculty progress, facilitated the inevitable flow of paperwork, and provided the overall savoir faire to stitch it all together.

Introduction

This evaluative guide to 126 videos derives from an escalating awareness in the United States of human diversity, an awareness in both our institutional and personal lives. This increasing sensitivity to cultural differences finds varied expression; the undeniable fact is that one's conception of world, culture, and self is enriched by an understanding of how others—"different" others—conceive of themselves and how, in turn, they are conceived of.

As several institutions have now done, the University at Albany, State University of New York (SUNY), has introduced a graduation requirement in Human Diversity within its General Education program. The intent is to give students a way to compare their experiences to those of people in different cultures. Courses were created to compare and relate aspects of racial and ethnic diversity, including gender-related concerns, to various course topics. Within this comparative approach, students are expected to gain a substantial knowledge of diversity as expressed through social, political, ideological, and aesthetic aspects of human endeavor.

However, not all means of portraying these aspects are equal in terms of student attention, especially when audiences today are so attuned to visual stimuli. Taking advantage of a funding opportunity, we decided to make greater use of videos and to assemble critical evaluations—expert reviews—into a videography to be distributed campus-wide. The American Library Association edition is an expanded, revised, and updated publication of that videography.

Funding for the original compilation came from the New York State/United University Professions Joint Labor Management's Affirmative Action Committee, enabling us to enlist, as selectors and reviewers, thirty scholars with specializations in various aspects of human diversity. Out of the hundreds of feature and documentary videotapes available, these scholars selected those most clearly associated with facets of multicultural education, as well as those best illustrating the range of topics within the subject areas.

The reviews themselves provide several access points for instructional purposes, broadly conceived. The approach taken offers instructors, programmers, and audiences a stimulating perspective on how diverse cultural groups have contributed to the social and historical development of the United States. Users of the guide and audiences can be encouraged to recognize how their perceptions of "reality" have been molded by the norms of their dominant society.

The Power of Video

Video represents an immediate and easily accessible medium for conveying information. Not only are people used to receiving information through this technology, but the medium also has a way of shaping belief systems and values. Understanding of how knowledge can be acquired through the critical use of video becomes all the more important.

Video extends our experience with human diversity with an immediacy and imagery that a written text cannot achieve. Video allows viewers to study how human communication works: how our understandings—and misunderstandings—of one another are affected by such factors as appearances, speech styles, postures, and intensity of expression. Video permits us to look at the ways people and events are captured and represented in images, how the medium itself represents a reality, and how it speaks to that representation. There is much truth in John Berger's statement in *Ways of Seeing* (Penguin, 1977) that "seeing comes before words."

Considering video's ability to provide substantial knowledge about human diversity, programmers have an ideal opportunity to distinguish objective information from video's intentional impact on our ideas and perspectives. Videos have a point of view, a perspective, a comment, or a slant that may be subtle or quite overt. The reviews here seek to give a frame of reference to the videos, to provide access points, and to supply a responsible critical analysis. Of course, there will be differences in interpretations, even among experts in the field. The subject of human diversity evokes variations in assessment owing to differences in starting points and subsequent goals. For this reason, two parallel reviews are included for "James Baldwin: The Price of the Ticket" and for "Affirmative Action versus Reverse Discrimination" (part of the series, The Constitution: That Delicate Balance). The use of these materials requires an awareness of the existence of multiple perspectives.

Our reviews give particular attention to the points of view implicitly couched in the videos or explicitly stated. Several of the videos are useful in demonstrating how commercial exploitations of underrepresented groups have led to negative stereotyping of these groups.

While definitions and discussions of human diversity or multiculturalism abound, two articles in the July-August 1991 *Change* magazine succinctly identify the major aspects. "Multi-culturalism: The Crucial Philosophical and Organizational Issues" by Patrick J. Hill (pp. 38–47) and "Diversity and Community: Right Objectives and Wrong Arguments" by Frank F. Wong (pp. 48–54) are good places to start. These essays will help situate the topic within larger intellectual, educational, and social milieux.

How to Use This Guide

The selections and comments of our knowledgeable reviewers will inform a wide range of video consumers, whether building library collections, supporting academic curricula or staff development programs, or independently acquiring videos for specific classroom use. The guide was initially prepared for use by college instructors, but as a whole it offers themes appropriate for all public audiences and for students from young adults up. In considering individual videos, however, users of the guide will want to make their own judgments of audience level.

Specifically, those planning to use a particular tape should preview it privately or in an evaluation group to assure the material's suitability for intended purpose and audience. In a group preview, it might be emphasized that the video is to be used for an examination or exploration of a topic through which an open discussion of ideas can be facilitated.

The guide provides ample assistance to those conducting discussions in human diversity, whether in schools and colleges, public programs, or personnel training. Guided use of the videos can encourage viewers to understand differing perspectives. In a communications context, the videos can evoke discussion of how visual media affect values and beliefs.

In fact, the guide can inform activities as wide-ranging as the themes treated in the ''Key to Themes and Categories'' that follows—from race relations and gender to religion, politics, and immigration, topics within the arts, humanities, and social sciences. Social studies and language arts teachers will find sources for complementary instructional use. Those planning public programs, especially in public libraries, will find stimulating material for creating NEH-funded ''Let's Talk about It'' or young adult humanities programs. (State humanities councils can assist in finding appropriate scholars for interpretive public programs based on video representations.)

Finding Aids

Three thematic indexing aids and a directory of video distributors will help users get the most out of this guide.

The Key to Themes and Categories explains a simple abbreviation code used to describe the coverage of the videos. The first two letters of the code indicate whether the video's major concern is the United States (US) or global (GL). The next six letters represent the two most prominent diversity themes in the material (each diversity theme has three letters). For example, the code US-GENSTE indicates that the video deals with gender (GEN) stereotyping (STE) in the United States (US).

The Title-Theme Index offers an alphabetical listing of the 126 titles reviewed, with a brief description and thematic code (see above) for each.

For searching by topic, the Categorical Index groups appropriate titles under thematic categories and sub-categories. For example, there are twelve sub-categories under Ethnicity to indicate the broad range of possibilities. The eight-letter thematic code is also given here for each video.

The entry for each video consists of two main parts. Videographic information, as readily obtainable by the compilers, is given first: title, series, producer, director, distributor, date of release, technical (running time, color or black-and-white, in English or another language), rental information, purchase price (subject to change and exclusive of shipping and handling), type of presentation, awards received or ratings given, and availability of transcript or study guide.*

---

*Further rental information may be obtained from the reference series, *Educational Film and Video Locator* (Bowker), published irregularly (1st edition in 1978; 4th in 1990–91), which includes in its locations the video-lending institutions of the Consortium of College and University Media Centers. Many of the videos in this guide are held by these institutions. Another standard reference on available videos is the *Video Source Book* (Gale), published annually with a semi-annual supplement.

The second part, the heart of this guide, contains the critical analyses of the videos by specialist reviewers. The analyses may contain all or several of these elements:

- Suggested viewer and subject level for classroom uses and programming;
- Reliability of the group perspectives/experiences represented;
- Special considerations, for example:
  —does the video require special introduction for some viewers?
  —of what limitations or biases should the viewer be aware?
- Application of subject area to the study of diversity
  —central focus (arts, production, civil rights, social roles, etc.);
  —additional (obvious or potential) applications;
- Suitability for use in classes or programs in Human Diversity or Multiculturalism;
- Theoretical assumptions implicit/explicit in the video representation;
- Other information useful for planning, such as historical background and other resources.

In the context of the reviews themselves, the term *film* is often used as an alternative to *video*. The format is always video, however, except for two productions apparently available in film only, but important to include.

On Classroom Use and Public Performance of Videos

In the classroom, a copyrighted "home-use only" video may be legally shown, without special licensing, *if* the following conditions are met (Source: Section 110(1) of the Revised Copyright Act of 1976 [Title 17 of the U.S. Code, Sections 101–810], and the *Copyright Primer for Librarians and Educators*, by Mary Hutchings Reed [American Library Association/National Education Association, 1987]):

1. The use must be by instructors (including guest lecturers) or by pupils;
2. The use is in connection with face-to-face teaching activities;
3. The entire audience is involved with the teaching activity;
4. The entire audience is in the same room or general area;
5. The teaching activities are conducted by a nonprofit education institution (the law does not include public libraries within this category);
6. The showing takes place in a classroom or similar

place devoted to instruction, such as school library, gym, auditorium, or workshop; and
7. The videotape is lawfully made; the person responsible had no reason to believe that the videotape was unlawfully made.

Outside these classroom conditions, however, "performance" or showing of copyrighted videos to a public audience usually requires permission in the form of licensing, which generally involves fees. The law defines "public performance" as a performance taking place anywhere "open to the public or at any place where a substantial number of persons outside of a normal circle of a family and its social acquaintances is gathered." The American Library Association's copyright analysts believe that "to the extent a videotape is used in an educational program conducted in a library's public room, that performance will not be infringing if the requirements for classroom use [above] are met." Most showings of a copyrighted videotape in a public room as part of an entertainment or cultural program would, however, require performance licensing.

According to *Video Policies and Procedures for Libraries* by James C. Scholtz, videocassette producers generally provide two licensing options: blanket licenses covering unlimited showings of specific items from specific producers, or public performance rights on a per-title (per-copy) basis, paid for when the video is purchased. Sometimes single-showing and per-title public performance rights can be obtained through written agreement with the producer.

Users, other than in home and classroom situations, are advised to inquire at the time of purchasing or renting a copyrighted video as to the licensing and fees required for public showing. With some videos, the availability and costs of public-performance licensing are clearly delineated by the distributor, though these items are subject to change. (Also, videos with public-performance rights will generally state such rights on the case or container or pre-title frame.) Often, however, there is some uncertainty as to which rights the distributor or even the producer can license. "When in doubt," suggests Scholtz, "contact the *copyright holder* for permission (in writing).

Selected sources on legal use of videos

Galvin, Thomas, and Mason, Sally, eds. "Video, Libraries, and the Law: Finding the Balance." (A forum.) *American Libraries* 20 (1989):110–19.

Miller, Jerome K. *Using Copyrighted Videocassettes in Classrooms, Libraries, and Training Centers*. 2nd ed. Friday Harbor, Wash.: Copyright Information Service, 1988.

Reed, Mary Hutchings. *The Copyright Primer for Librarians and Educators.* Chicago/Washington: American Library Association, National Education Association, 1987.

Scholtz, James C. *Developing and Maintaining Video Collections in Libraries.* Santa Barbara, Calif.: ABC-CLIO, 1988.

—— *Video Policies and Procedures for Libraries.* Santa Barbara, Calif.: ABC-CLIO, 1991.

Hotline

Association for Media Information and Equipment: (800) 444-4203 (to clarify issues concerning the right to show purchased, borrowed, or rented videotapes in classrooms and to the public).

A Final Note

In using the guide as a selection tool, it should be remembered that expert faculty considered hundreds of videos dealing with issues of human diversity to come up with the broadest coverage of diversity topics, including race, gender, age, language, sexual orientation, marital status, national origin, religion, lifestyle, ethnicity, appearance, and geographical location. One would be hard put to find a more carefully considered "core" video collection for institutions addressing human diversity.

We allowed a wide range in the length of reviews, encouraging our reviewers to run with their ideas and discouraging them from fleshing out to a required length when it seemed unnecessary. While these considerable discrepancies may disappoint on a few occasions, we felt it was a fair trade for the diversity of styles and expert opinions we have gathered. In any case, it should be remembered that the length of reviews does not necessarily reflect the relative values of the videos.

Unlike other subject areas that might be more objective, external, or theoretical, human diversity is a special case: it is subjective, immediate, and visible. The development of this guide was based on a clear understanding of and deep commitment to the need of all peoples to create ties that bind rather than divide. In the words of Senator J. William Fulbright, "The rapprochement of peoples is only possible when differences of culture and outlook are respected and appreciated rather than feared or condemned, when the common bond of human dignity is recognized as the essential bond for a peaceful world."

We hope you find the guide useful. Your comments would be most welcome.

Key to Themes and Categories

As a shorthand clue to scope and theme, we have assigned each video a composite, eight-letter code, as follows:

1. First two letters: United States (US) or global (GL) focus

2. Next three letters: A diversity theme central to the video (see list below)

3. Final three letters: A second diversity theme, usually subordinate to the first.

Thus, the code for ''Back Inside Herself,'' about an African American's search for identity, is USETHGEN —US meaning United States focus, ETH for ethnicity as central theme, and GEN for gender as second theme.

These codes offer quick snapshots of the videos as one searches the guide's two indexes: the Title-Theme Index is arranged alphabetically by title, and the Categorical Index by subject. Videos thus identified as candidates for acquisition, teaching, or programming can then be evaluated with the help of our extensive reviews.

Relevant Populations

United States only, or including US	US
Global (other than US)	GL

Video Themes

Race, race relations	RAC
Ethnicity	ETH
Civil Rights	
African American	
Africana global	
Latino American	
Latino global	
Jewish American	
Jewish global	
Native American	
Native Cultures of Americas	
Gender	GEN
Women's concerns, (her)stories	
Men's concerns, (his)stories	
Gay and lesbian concerns, stories	
Religion, values	REL
Class	CLA
Economics, work	ECO
Politics, action	POL
Culture	CUL
Expression (artistic, musical, poetic, etc.)	EXP
Lifestages	AGE
Social relationships (family, friends, etc.)	SOC
Communication (Interaction, language, media)	COM
Immigration	IMM
Law	LAW
Social stereotypes, social identity	STE

Title-Theme Index

TITLE	CATEGORY	PAGE
Maggie Kuhn, Wrinkled Radical Issues of aging and public policy; women; founder of Gray Panthers	USAGEGEN	129
A Man When He Is a Man Latin America (Costa Rica); gender roles and machismo	GLGENSOC	130
Martha Mitchell of Possum Walk Road Women; quilting as creative expression by an older generation	USGENCLA	131
Master Harold . . . and the Boys South Africa; apartheid 1950; drama; pathology of racism	GLRACCLA	132
Men's Lives Contemporary; male identity in American culture	USGENSOC	133
Miles from the Border Mexican immigration and acculturation from the perspective of a family	USIMMRAC	135
Minor Altercation Race relations; contemporary racial conflict in public schools	USRACCOM	137
Mitsuye and Nellie Asian American; emerging social identity of two women (Japanese, Chinese)	USETHGEN	138
Mr. Ludwig's Tropical Dreamland Brazil; the Jari Project, development of Amazon rainforest	GLECOPOL	139
Music of the Devil, the Bear, and the Condor Latin America (Bolivia): Aymara religion, ritual, music	GLCULREL	140
Never Turn Back: The Life of Fannie Lou Hamer African American; women in social reform, 1964–1977	USRACGEN	141
New Puritans: The Sikhs of Yuba City Asian American; history of immigration, contemporary cultural identity	USIMMETH	143
Northern Lights Anglo American; Norwegian farmers in North Dakota, 1915–1917	USETHECO	144
Orfeu do Carnaval (Black Orpheus) Latin America; Afro-Brazilians in 1950s at carnival time	GLCULEXP	146
Our Hispanic Heritage Hispanic American; history of Spanish cultural influence in Americas	USETHCUL	148

TITLE	CATEGORY	PAGE
Out in Suburbia Gender; lesbian experiences, lifestyles; first-person accounts	USGENSOC	149
Picking Tribes African American, Native American; social identity	USETHSOC	150
Place of the Falling Waters Native American (Flathead, Montana); land rights, cultural implications	USETHECO	151
Pockets of Hate Contemporary U.S. urban racial violence	USRACIMM	153
Portrait of Teresa Latin America (Cuba); equality vs. sexism, post-Revolutionary Cuba	GLGENPOL	155
Price You Pay Asian-American refugees (p 1975); discrimination; stereotypes	USIMMRAC	156
Puerto Rico Latin America; Spanish, African, Indian influences on dance	GLCULEXP	157
Quilombo Brazil; history of democratic communities for runaway slaves	GLETHCLA	159
Race against Prime Time U.S. urban race riots in Miami; critique of media coverage	USRACCOM	161
Racism in America Resurgence of racial violence in 1980s; major issues	USRACETH	162
Raisin in the Sun African-American drama, 1950s; dreams of respect, equal rights	USRACECO	164
Raoni: The Fight for the Amazon Brazil; Mekroniti Indians and white settlers in Amazon region	GLETHECO	165
Ribbon Starts Here Textile and needle arts; grassroots protest of nuclear arms	USCULEXP	167
Rice Ladle: The Changing Role of Women in Japan Japan; women; contemporary work pressure, challenges to stereotypes	GLGENECO	169
Right to Be Mohawk Native American; political and social identity at Akwesasne	USETHPOL	170
Rise in Campus Racism Racism; higher education; 1991 teleconference	USRACSOC	171

TITLE	CATEGORY	PAGE

Touring Mexico
Latin America (Mexico); five centuries of history encoded in ancient ruins

GLCULEXP   192

Town Meeting in South Africa
South Africa; discussions on apartheid; public communication hosted by Ted Koppel

GLRACCOM   194

Triumph of the Spirit
Europe; story of Salamo Arouch, survivor of the Holocaust

GLRACREL   196

Trouble Behind: Roots of Racism
Contemporary white racism in small Kentucky town

USRACCLA   197

Two Dollars and a Dream
African American; women; self-determination; racial solidarity

USETHGEN   198

Variety Is the Spice of Life
Gender; contemporary representations

USGENEXP   200

Weapons of the Spirit
France; WW II Jewish refugees sheltered by people of Le Chambon

GLRACREL   201

West of Hester Street
Jewish American; immigration; Galveston Movement, 1906–1916

USETHIMM   203

When You Think of Mexico
Hispanic American; commercial images, stereotypes of Mexicans in the United States

USETHSTE   205

With Babies and Banners
Women's struggle for job fairness; 1936–7 GM sit-down strikes

USGENCLA   207

With Silk Wings
Asian American; women; life histories; challenging stereotypes

USETHGEN   208

Witnesses: Anti-Semitism in Poland, 1946
Europe; interviews with survivors of a post-Holocaust massacre

GLRACREL   210

Wobblies
History; workers' union of 1905–1920

USCLAECO   211

Yanco
Latin America (Mexico); clash of cultures; artistic expression

GLCULEXP   213

Categorical Index

Note: Many videos address several themes of diversity, often more than the two indicated in our abbreviated codes. Therefore, in the following list, a single video title may appear under several thematic categories that apply.

GENERAL CATEGORIES	CODE
Race, Race Relations	
Autobiography of Miss Jane Pittman	USRACPOL
Back Inside Herself	USETHGEN
Birthwrite: Growing Up Hispanic	USETHRAC
Civil War: The Cause, 1861	USPOLRAC
Do the Right Thing	USRACETH
Ethnic Notions: Black People in White Minds	USRACSTE
Eyes on the Prize	USPOLRAC
Freedom Bags	USRACECO
Ida B. Wells: A Passion for Justice	USRACGEN
James Baldwin: The Price of the Ticket	USRACGEN
Los Vendidos	USETHSTE
Master Harold . . . and the Boys	GLRACCLA
Miles from the Border	USIMMRAC
A Minor Altercation	USRACCOM
Never Turn Back: The Life of Fannie Lou Hamer	USRACGEN
Orfeu do Carnaval (Black Orpheus)	GLCULEXP
Pockets of Hate	USRACIMM
Race against Prime Time	USRACCOM
Racism in America	USRACETH
A Raisin in the Sun	USRACECO
Rise in Campus Racism	USRACSOC
Road to Brown	USRACLAW
To Kill a Mockingbird	USRACCUL
Trouble Behind: Roots of Racism	USRACCLA
Ethnicity: Civil Rights	
Affirmative Action verus Reverse Discrimination	USPOLLAW
Civil War: The Cause, 1861	USPOLRAC
Eyes on the Prize	USPOLRAC
Never Turn Back: The Life of Fannie Lou Hamer	USRACGEN

GENERAL CATEGORIES	CODE
Pockets of Hate	USRACIMM
A Raisin in the Sun	USRACECO
Road to Brown	USRACLAW
Ethnicity: African-American	
Autobiography of Miss Jane Pittman	USRACPOL
Back Inside Herself	USETHGEN
Civil War: The Cause, 1861	USPOLRAC
Do the Right Thing	USRACETH
Ethnic Notions: Black People in White Minds	USRACSTE
Eyes on the Prize	USPOLRAC
Freedom Bags	USRACECO
Ida B. Wells: A Passion for Justice	USRACGEN
James Baldwin: The Price of the Ticket	USRACGEN
Life and Times of Rosie the Riveter	USGENCLA
Minor Altercation	USRACCOM
Never Turn Back: The Life of Fannie Lou Hamer	USRACGEN
Picking Tribes	USETHSOC
Pockets of Hate	USRACIMM
Race against Prime Time	USRACCOM
Racism in America	USRACETH
A Raisin in the Sun	USRACECO
Rise in Campus Racism	USRACSOC
Road to Brown	USRACLAW
That's Black Entertainment	USETHEXP
To Kill a Mockingbird	USRACCUL
Trouble Behind: Roots of Racism	USRACCLA
Two Dollars and a Dream	USETHGEN
Ethnicity: Africana, global	
A Clash of Cultures	GLETHCUL
Bahia: Africa in the Americas	GLRELCUL
Five Pillars of Islam	GLRELCUL
Hail Umbanda	GLRELCUL

GENERAL CATEGORIES	CODE
Haiti: Dreams of Democracy	GLCULCLA
Land of Look Behind	GLCULEXP
Master Harold . . . and the Boys	GLRACCLA
Orfeu do Carnaval (Black Orpheus)	GLCULEXP
Quilombo	GLETHCLA
Selbe: One among Many	GLGENECO
Town Meeting in South Africa	GLRACCOM

Ethnicity: Latino-American

Ballad of Gregorio Cortéz	USETHPOL
Birthwrite: Growing Up Hispanic	USETHRAC
Bronx: A Cry for Help	USETHCLA
El Mojado (The Wetback)	USIMMLAW
El Norte	USIMMECO
El Otro Lado (The Other Side)	USIMMLAW
Flight of the Dove	USETHREL
Los Sures	USETHCLA
Los Vendidos	USETHSTE
Our Hispanic Heritage	USETHCUL
When You Think of Mexico	USETHSTE

Ethnicity: Latino, global

Bahia: Africa in the Americas	GLRACCUL
Blood Wedding	GLETHGEN
Brazil: Heart of South America	GLCULPOL
Christians, Jews and Muslims in Medieval Spain	GLRELCUL
Double Day	GLGENECO
Frida Kahlo (1910–1954)	GLGENEXP
Haiti: Dreams of Democracy	GLCULCLA
Hour of the Star	GLGENCLA
La Operacion (The Operation)	GLECOGEN
Land of Look Behind	GLCULEXP
Life and Poetry of Julia de Burgos	GLGENEXP
A Man When He Is a Man	GLGENSOC
Miles from the Border	USIMMRAC
Portrait of Teresa	GLGENPOL
Puerto Rico: Folk Dances	GLCULEXP
Quilombo	GLETHCUL
Simplemente Jenny	GLGENCLA
Touring Mexico	GLCULEXP
Yanco	GLCULEXP

Ethnicity: Asian-American

Asianization of America	USETHECO
Becoming American	USIMMETH
Carved in Silence	USIMMRAC
Mitsuye and Nellie	USETHGEN
New Puritans: The Sikhs of Yuba City	USIMMETH
Pockets of Hate	USRACIMM
Price You Pay	USIMMRAC
Slaying the Dragon	USETHSTE

GENERAL CATEGORIES	CODE
With Silk Wings	USETHGEN

Ethnicity: Asian, global

Rice Ladle: The Changing Role of Women in Japan	GLGENECO
Small Happiness: Women of a Chinese Village	GLGENECO

Ethnicity: European-American

America and Lewis Hine	USETHCLA
American Tongues	USETHCOM
Les Tisserands (The Mills of Power)	USETHCLA
Northern Lights	USETHECO

Ethnicity: European, global

Canada: True North—A Song for Québec	GLPOLCUL
Christians, Jews and Muslims in Medieval Spain	GLRELCUL

Ethnicity: Jewish-American

Biggest Jewish City in the World	USETHREL
Exiles	USETHCUL
Gefilte Fish	USCULETH
Half the Kingdom	USGENREL
Pockets of Hate	USRACIMM
West of Hester Street	USETHIMM

Ethnicity: Jewish, global

Christians, Jews and Muslims in Medieval Spain	GLRELCUL
Triumph of the Spirit	GLRACREL
Weapons of the Spirit	GLRACREL
Witnesses	GLRACREL

Ethnicity: Native-American

Beyond Tradition	USETHEXP
Geronimo and the Apache Resistance	USETHSTE
Heathen Injuns and the Hollywood Gospel	USETHSTE
Honored by the Moon	USETHGEN
How Hollywood Wins the West	USETHCOM
I'isaw: Hopi Coyote Stories	USETHCUL
Itam Hakim, Hopiit	USETHEXP
Place of the Falling Waters	USETHECO
Right to Be Mohawk	USETHPOL
Ritual Clowns	USETHEXP
Running on the Edge of the Rainbow	USETHCUL
Sun, Moon, and Feather	USETHSTE

GENERAL CATEGORIES	CODE	GENERAL CATEGORIES	CODE

GENERAL CATEGORIES	CODE
Martha Mitchell of Possum Walk Road	USGENCLA
Master Harold . . . and the Boys	GLRACCLA
Miles from the Border	USIMMRAC
Never Turn Back: The Life of Fannie Lou Hamer	USRACGEN
Northern Lights	USETHECO
Racism in America	USRACETH
Simplemente Jenny	GLGENCLA
That's Black Entertainment	USETHEXP
To Kill a Mockingbird	USRACCUL
Trouble Behind: Roots of Racism	USRACCLA
With Babies and Banners	USGENCLA
Wobblies	USCLAECO

Economics

Asianization of America	USETHECO
Bronx: A Cry for Help	USETHCLA
Contact: The Yanomami Indians of Brazil	GLRACECO
Crystal Lee Jordan	USGENCLA
Double Day	GLGENECO
El Mojado (The Wetback)	USIMMLAW
El Norte	USIMMECO
El Otro Lado (The Other Side)	USIMMLAW
Freedom Bags	USRACECO
La Operacion (The Operation)	GLECOGEN
Les Tisserands (The Mills of Power)	USETHCLA
Life and Times of Rosie the Riveter	USGENCLA
Los Sures	USETHCLA
Maggie Kuhn, Wrinkled Radical	USGENAGE
Mr. Ludwig's Tropical Dreamland	GLECOPOL
Never Turn Back: The Life of Fannie Lou Hamer	USRACGEN
New Puritans: The Sikhs of Yuba City	USIMMETH
Northern Lights	USETHECO
Place of the Falling Waters	USETHECO
Portrait of Teresa	GLGENPOL
Quilombo	GLETHCLA
A Raisin in the Sun	USRACECO
Raoni: The Fight for the Amazon	GLETHECO
Rice Ladle: The Changing Role of Women in Japan	GLGENECO
Selbe: One among Many	GLGENECO
Simplemente Jenny	GLGENCLA
Small Happiness: Women of a Chinese Village	GLGENECO
Still Killing Us Softly	USGENCOM
Two Dollars and a Dream	USETHGEN
With Silk Wings	USETHGEN
Wobblies	USCLAECO

GENERAL CATEGORIES	CODE

Politics

Affirmative Action versus Reverse Discrimination	USPOLLAW
Autobiography of Miss Jane Pittman	USRACPOL
Ballad of Gregorio Cortéz	USETHPOL
Before Stonewall	USGENSTE
Black and White in Color	GLRACPOL
Brazil: Heart of South America	GLCULPOL
Bronx: A Cry for Help	USETHCLA
Canada: True North—A Song for Québec	GLPOLCUL
Carved in Silence	USIMMRAC
Civil War: The Cause, 1861	USPOLRAC
Clash of Cultures	GLETHCUL
Do the Right Thing	USETHSTE
El Mojado (The Wetback)	USIMMLAW
El Norte	USIMMECO
El Otro Lado (The Other Side)	USIMMLAW
Ethnic Notions: Black People in White Minds	USRACSTE
Eyes on the Prize	USPOLRAC
Geronimo and the Apache Resistance	USETHSTE
Haiti: Dreams of Democracy	GLCULCLA
How Hollywood Wins the West	USETHCOM
Ida B. Wells: A Passion for Justice	USRACGEN
La Operacion (The Operation)	GLECOGEN
Life and Poetry of Julia de Burgos	GLGENEXP
Los Vendidos	USETHSTE
Maggie Kuhn, Wrinkled Radical	USAGEGEN
Mr. Ludwig's Tropical Dreamland	GLECOPOL
Northern Lights	USETHECO
Place of the Falling Waters	USETHECO
Portrait of Teresa	GLGENPOL
Price you Pay	USIMMRAC
Racism in America	USRACETH
A Raisin in the Sun	USRACECO
Ribbon Starts Here	USCULEXP
Right to Be Mohawk	USETHPOL
Road to Brown	USRACLAW
Slaying the Dragon	USETHSTE
Style Wars!	USCLAEXP
Town Meeting in South Africa	GLRACCOM

Culture

Bahia: Africa in the Americas	GLCULREL
Becoming American	USIMMETH
Beyond Tradition	USETHEXP
Birthwrite: Growing Up Hispanic	USETHRAC
Brazil: Heart of South America	GLCULPOL
Canada: True North—A Song for Québec	GLPOLCUL

GENERAL CATEGORIES	**CODE**
Christians, Jews and Muslims in Medieval Spain	GLRELCUL
A Clash of Cultures	GLETHCUL
Common Threads	USGENSOC
Contact: The Yanomami Indians of Brazil	GLRACECO
Do the Right Thing	USRACETH
Ethnic Notions: Black People in White Minds	USRACSTE
Exiles	USETHCUL
Five Pillars of Islam	GLRELCUL
Flight of the Dove	USETHREL
Foster Child	GLETHSOC
Frida Kahlo (1910–1954)	GLCULEXP
Gefilte Fish	USCULETH
Hail Umbanda	GLRELCUL
Haiti: Dreams of Democracy	GLCULCLA
Half the Kingdom	USGENREL
Hearts and Hands	USGENEXP
I'isaw: Hopi Coyote Stories	USETHCUL
Itam Hakim, Hopiit	USETHPOL
Land of Look Behind	GLCULEXP
Machu Picchu	GLCULREL
Martha Mitchell of Possum Walk Road	USGENCLA
Music of the Devil, Bear, Condor	GLCULREL
Orfeu do Carnaval (Black Orpheus)	GLCULEXP
Our Hispanic Heritage	USETHCUL
Puerto Rico: Folk Dances	GLCULEXP
Ribbon Starts Here	USCULEXP
Rice Ladle: The Changing Role of Women in Japan	GLGENECO
Right to Be Mohawk	USETHPOL
Ritual Clowns	USETHEXP
Running on the Edge of the Rainbow	USETHCUL
Small Happiness: Women of a Chinese Village	GLGENECO
Still Killing Us Softly	USGENCOM
Style Wars!	USCLAEXP
Teotihuacán: City of the Gods	GLCULREL
That's Black Entertainment	USETHEXP
Touring Mexico	GLCULEXP
Yanco	GLCULEXP

Expression (artistic, musical, poetic, dramatic, etc., including videos of performances related to diversity themes)

America and Lewis Hine	USETHCLA
Autobiography of Miss Jane Pittman	USRACPOL
Back Inside Herself	USETHGEN

GENERAL CATEGORIES	**CODE**
Ballad of Gregorio Cortéz	USETHPOL
Beyond Tradition	USETHEXP
Birthwrite: Growing Up Hispanic	USETHRAC
Blood Wedding	GLETHGEN
Common Threads	USGENSOC
Do the Right Thing	USRACETH
Ethnic Notions: Black People in White Minds	USRACSTE
Frida Kahlo (1910–1954)	GLCULEXP
Hearts and Hands	USGENEXP
Hour of the Star	GLGENCLA
I'isaw: Hopi Coyote Stories	USETHCUL
Itam Hakim, Hopiit	USETHEXP
James Baldwin: The Price of the Ticket	USRACGEN
Land of Look Behind	GLCULEXP
Les Bon Debarras (Good Riddance)	GLCLAGEN
Life and Poetry of Julia de Burgos	GLGENEXP
Los Vendidos	USETHSTE
Machu Picchu	GLCULREL
Martha Mitchell of Possum Walk Road	USGENCLA
Master Harold . . . and the Boys	GLRACCLA
Music of the Devil, Bear, Condor	GLCULREL
Orfeu do Carnaval (Black Orpheus)	GLCULEXP
Our Hispanic Heritage	USETHCUL
Puerto Rico: Folk Dances	GLCULEXP
Quilombo	GLETHCLA
A Raisin in the Sun	USRACECO
Ribbon Starts Here	USCULEXP
Ritual Clowns	USETHEXP
Running on the Edge of the Rainbow	USETHCUL
Slaying the Dragon	USETHSTE
Still Killing Us Softly	USGENCOM
Style Wars!	USCLAEXP
Sun, Moon, and Feather	USETHSTE
Teotihuacán: City of the Gods	GLCULREL
That's Black Entertainment	USETHEXP
To Kill a Mockingbird	USRACCUL
Torch Song Trilogy	USGENSOC
Touring Mexico	GLCULEXP
Variety Is the Spice of Life	USGENEXP
Yanco	GLCULEXP

Age: Lifestages

Coming of Age	USAGESOC
Foster Child	GLETHSOC
Gefilte Fish	USCULETH
Maggie Kuhn, Wrinkled Radical	USAGEGEN
Men's Lives	USGENSOC

GENERAL CATEGORIES	CODE
New Puritans: The Sikhs of Yuba City	USIMMECO
Northern Lights	USETHECO
Pockets of Hate	USRACIMM
Price You Pay	USIMMRAC
West of Hester Street	USETHIMM
With Silk Wings	USETHGEN

Law

Affirmative Action versus Reverse Discrimination	USPOLLAW
Ballad of Gregorio Cortéz	USETHPOL
Carved in Silence	USIMMRAC
El Mojado (The Wetback)	USIMMLAW
El Otro Lado (The Other Side)	USIMMLAW
Eyes on the Prize	USPOLRAC
Ida B. Wells: A Passion for Justice	USRACGEN
Right to Be Mohawk	USETHPOL
Road to Brown	USRACLAW
Style Wars!	USCLAEXP
To Kill a Mockingbird	USRACCUL
Town Meeting in South Africa	GLRACPOL

Social Stereotypes: Social identity

American Tongues	USETHCOM
Asianization of America	USETHECO
Back Inside Herself	USETHGEN

GENERAL CATEGORIES	CODE
Ballad of Gregorio Cortéz	USETHPOL
Before Stonewall	USGENSTE
Birthwrite: Growing Up Hispanic	USETHSTE
Coming of Age	USAGESOC
Do the Right Thing	USRACETH
Ethnic Notions: Black People in White Minds	USRACSTE
Geronimo and the Apache Resistance	USETHSTE
Heathen Injuns and the Hollywood Gospel	USETHSTE
Honored by the Moon	USETHGEN
How Hollywood Wins the West	USETHSTE
Just Because of Who We Are	USGENSTE
Los Vendidos	USETHSTE
Men's Lives	USGENSOC
Pockets of Hate	USRACIMM
Price You Pay	USIMMRAC
Race against Prime Time	USRACCOM
Slaying the Dragon	USETHSTE
Still Killing Us Softly	USGENCOM
Sun, Moon, and Feather	USETHSTE
That's Black Entertainment	USETHEXP
To Kill a Mockingbird	USRACCUL
Trouble Behind: Roots of Racism	USRACCLA
Variety Is the Spice of Life	USGENEXP
When You Think of Mexico	USETHSTE

The Reviews

(in alphabetical order)

Written by Faculty of
the University at Albany,
State University of New York

USPOLLAW

Title:	## Affirmative Action versus Reverse Discrimination
Series:	The Constitution, That Delicate Balance (no. 12), part of Annenberg/CPB Collection
Producer:	Jude Dratt, Columbia University Graduate School of Journalism Media & Society Seminars
Distributor:	Intellimation
Release Date:	1984
Technical:	60 min. / color / English
Purchase Price:	$29.95
Rental:	varies (available from Penn State Audio Visual Services)
Presentation:	Seminar format wherein a group of distinguished Americans from the bar (including retired Supreme Court justice Potter Stewart), broadcast and print journalism, education, and government are questioned by Washington attorney and former head of the Federal Communications Commission, Tyrone Brown; filmed in 1982
Study Guide:	Text and program guides available through Intellimation: "A Guide to the Constitution, That Delicate Balance," $12.25

Following is the first of two reviews of *Affirmative Action versus Reverse Discrimination*.

Content: In response to federal legislation, many employers and institutions have been required to implement affirmative action plans. The 1978 Supreme Court ruling in the Bakke case raised questions about affirmative action resulting in reverse discrimination. Debate continues about affirmative action as a strategy for redressing the history of discrimination against protected classes in the United States. Several prominent national figures discuss a hypothetical case in which a white male, a white female, and an African-American male are being considered for tenure at a university where only one such position is available. The discussion illustrates a wide variety of perspectives and well-articulated arguments for and against affirmative action.

Panel members represent a broad range of perspectives, including educators (e.g., Dr. Alvin Pouissant), legislators (e.g., Rep. Charles Rangel of New York), members of the Supreme Court (e.g., Justice Potter Stewart), current and past members of the executive branch of government (e.g., Joseph Califano of the Health, Education and Welfare Department, Eleanor Holmes Norton of the Equal Employment Opportunity Commission), journalists, and others. Social groups represented: African Americans, women, white males.

Classroom Use: This is an excellent video that illuminates the complexities of implementing affirmative action in the United States. The issues are discussed from a historical, political, economic, and legal perspective. The arguments are well-articulated, and divergent viewpoints are presented. Undergraduate and graduate students, as well as faculty, would benefit from viewing and discussing this video.

Critical Comments: Theoretical assumptions of the video's presentation: (1) Affirmative action is a social policy that has been and will continue to be debated. (2) Dialogue among people from diverse groups is beneficial to understanding the multifaceted and complex nature of implementing social policies such as affirmative action.

In communication, this video could be used to demonstrate how discourse constructs social reality and influences attitudes and beliefs (e.g., the video discussed how it was possible for the Supreme Court to interpret the concept of "equal protection" to uphold racial segregation in *Plessy* vs. *Ferguson*, 1896, and later to abolish racial segregation in *Brown* vs. *Board of Education*, 1954, using the same concept). The video provides excellent examples of argumentation that would be useful in a debate class.

Also, a class that examined political discourse and social movements or social policy would be enriched by the inclusion of this video in course materials. Beyond communication applications, this video could be used in history, sociology, political science, women's studies, and African-American studies to explore the issue of affirmative action as applicable to those disciplines.

Salome Raheim, Department of Communication

See also below.

Content: As the subtitle of this seminar presentation reminds us, there has been—since its promulgation in the mid-1960s—and there remains today, a profound division of mind in America about whether affirmative action—preferential treatment based on race, gender, ethnicity, or some other classification—is ethically justifiable, legally permissable or even pragmatically useful as a solution for redressing the nation's long history of past discrimination. Because the 13-part series on the Constitution was produced to commemorate its bicentennial and because a majority of the participants in this program are lawyers, the hour concentrates on the constitutionality of affirmative action; of specific concern is whether group-based preference is permissible under the Fourteenth Amendment's Equal Protection clause. Implicit throughout the discussion is the conundrum which asks: How can a society that has historically professed to believe that the goal of equality is best reached by giving everyone an equal opportunity come to grips with the opposite notion that the equality of some may well require the denial of opportunity to the many?

Classroom Use: As a backdrop to viewing, a review of three Supreme Court cases will prove helpful. These are *Plessy* vs. *Ferguson* (1896, including the lone dissent of John Harlan, who said that the Constitution was colorblind); *Brown* vs. *Board of Education* (1954); and *Regents of the Univ. of California* vs. *Allan Bakke* (1978). Indirectly, and for that reason perhaps more effectively, the broadcast underscores the centrality of the black experience for understanding American history including currently controversial subjects like race, racism, gender, meritocracy, and others. References to Jefferson, the Founders, slavery, the Constitution, the Civil War, the Civil War amendments, and the Jim Crow era help students understand that racial attitudes and patterns of race relations are the product of a complex evolution over a period of centuries.

Critical Comments: Under federal pressure in the mid-1970s, Dalton State University, a fictitious—though prestigious—midwestern institution, initiated affirmative action measures for the recruitment and promotion of its faculty personnel. A three-member faculty tenure committee made up of its chairman, (Judge) Robert Bork (former Secretary of Education), Shirley M. Hufstedler, and Albert Shanker (president, American Federation of Teachers), has convened to consider its recommendations for the promotion, with tenure, of one of three candidates—a middle-aged black professor named William Raspberry (columnist for the *Washington Post*); a professor Goodman, a thirty-something white woman (Ellen Goodman, columnist for the *Boston Globe*); and a young white male professor named Nelson (Avi Nelson, commentator for TV station TNCVB, Boston). All were hired at approximately the same time. All three meet the university's tenure standards with regard to scholarship and teaching but, we learn, professor Nelson is slightly better than Goodman, and Goodman is slightly better than Raspberry, as a classroom teacher.

The scenario sketched above is the context for the hour-long discussion of the ongoing controversy surrounding affirmative action, one of the most contentious and divisive subjects in American life over the past 30 years. Indeed, few constitutional questions in recent years have stirred so much debate, and the controversy shows no signs of abating. In addition to Stewart, Bork, Raspberry, Hufstedler, Goodman, Nelson, and Shanker, the seminarians include *New York Times* columnist (and lawyer), Anthony Lewis; Jim Lehrer, associate editor, the McNeil-Lehrer News Hour; Eleanor Holmes Norton, law school professor and former EEOC chairperson; Irving Kristol, editor, *The Public Interest,* and a leading conservative theorist; William Reynolds, assistant Attorney General, Civil Rights Division of the Justice Department; Joseph Califano, attorney and former Secretary of HEW; Charles Rangel, Democrat, member of the House of Representatives, and others. Naturally, these participants were not chosen at random, but were selected in order to rehearse the views of those who champion affirmative action as a remedy for past discrimination (especially against black Americans), and the arguments of those who view affirmative action as nothing short of affirmative discrimination.

In making the case for affirmative action, proponents (all of whom are predictable), are heard to argue that race-based preference is absolutely essential if equality for minorities is to be achieved. This is especially so when present inequalities are seen as a direct consequence of long-standing past inequalities. The most powerful impulse behind affirmative action, argue proponents, is compensation for historical abuse. Additionally, so-called traditional criteria (SAT, I.Q., and LSAT scores, and others) that are used to admit, judge, and promote individuals are culturally biased against minorities. Equally important, affirmative action programs represent a significant symbolic denunciation of racism; such programs will produce a group of "role models" thereby demonstrating to black youngsters that there is hope for their own future. Moreover, insist proponents of race-based remediation, sociocultural diversity in the workplace, in the professions, indeed throughout the society, should mirror the diversity characteristic of the society as a whole. Lastly, proponents argue that American institutions, even institutions of higher learning, have never been the meritocracies they proclaim to be. Military veterans, sons and daughters of wealthy alumni, athletes, and Alaskans have attended prestigious universities despite undistinguished test scores. As for the equal protection clause of the Fourteenth Amendment, this constitutional guarantee is not offended by group-based preference since blacks were enslaved, segregated, and discriminated against as a group, and therefore it is only fair that they now be assisted on the basis of their group membership.

In countering these justifications in support of preferential treatment (again predictably, given the opposition's well-known identification and association with conservative organizations, and articulation of conservative philosophy) opponents make the following responses. There is no such thing, insist opponents, as good or "benign" discrimination, and the discrimination cure for discrimination will create much fresh evil of its own. Second, statistical disparities in income, education, and the work force are not inevitably—or even primarily—the result of race discrimination. Moreover, note opponents, the civil rights community (officers, bureaucrats, community leaders, activists) has a vested interest in affirmative action programs and policies (as conservative black professor Thomas Sowell has observed, many in the civil rights establishment are modern-day equivalents of those missionaries of old who came to do good, and stayed to do well!). Additionally, compensatory justice based on group identification subordinates the individual to the group and tends to be overinclusive and underinclusive in scope. More importantly, though the point is not raised in the pro-

gram, by encouraging the use of history as therapy ("Feel Good History," as it has been called), compensatory justice means, inevitably, the corruption of history as history. Put to such use, history becomes the "parade of horribles" used to demonstrate how whites have systematically victimized blacks, or else the search for truth degenerates to the level of fantastic fantasy we have come to know as the Afrocentric Myth (everything can be traced back to Africa; see especially "The AfroCentric Myth" by Mary Lefkowitz in the *New Republic,* February 10, 1992, pp. 29–36). Historical abuse aside, government-supported remedial action, detractors argue, should be based on specific findings of discrimination, never on generalized historical assertions about conditions somewhere, at some time, in the American past. Also, argue opponents, affirmative action programs all too often foster a dependent attitude which demands government largesse as an entitlement; such an attitude denies the importance of achievement based on the acquisition of relevant qualifications, and inevitably exacerbates racial tensions by encouraging a white backlash. Equally important, affirmative action programs adversely affect blacks' self-image, and simultaneously perpetuate a pervasive attitude among whites that blacks cannot make it on their own.

Finally, detractors offer the following ammunition in their attack on affirmative action. Unfortunately, but effectively, preferences reinforce the white paternalist stereotype that proclaims that blacks and other minorities are in need of special advantages. And for those who view affirmative action as little more than reverse discrimination, distributing preferences based on race has the paradoxical effect of perpetuating thinking in racial terms, a consequence sure to perpetuate racial separation. Opponents also insist that in a democracy *ends,* no matter how worthy, can never justify using an unfair, immoral, or illegal *means,* and affirmative action is decidedly the wrong means (morally, pragmatically, and constitutionally) to achieve the admittedly desirable social end of racial equality. The function of government, insist opponents, is to enhance, not redistribute, opportunity based on race, gender, or some other "accident of birth" over which individuals have no control. The only guarantor of equality of opportunity possible in an equalitarian society, we are told, is merit. "In a society in which men and women expect to succeed by hard work and to better themselves by making themselves better, it is no trivial moral wrong to proceed systematically to defeat this expectation. . . ." (Alexander Bickel, a professor at the University of Chicago, cited in *From Brown to Bakke* [Oxford Univ. Pr., 1976], p. 265.) Granted that minority professors, physicians, and lawyers are few, the "proportionate society" is neither wise nor workable and it certainly is not the function of government to bring about "statistical parity" by supporting or encouraging race-based preferences. Lastly, note opponents, affirmative action is an administrative nightmare: implementing preferences requires Solomonic wisdom in deciding imponderables like who should be compensated, in what form, how much, and for how long.

Needless to say, any attempt to deal with a subject as complex and contentious as affirmative action or affirmative discrimination in a 60-minute format will be both incomplete and often analytically thin. But this is an observation, not a criticism. A number of critical comments are, however, warranted.

First, it should be noted that the nature of the debate over affirmative action has changed substantially in the ten years since the program was produced (1982). In the 30 years since affirmative action policies have been in place, the black middle class has tripled, and in 1992 it accounts for one-third of the black population. The video could not present the views of the new black conservatives who were not present in 1982. These individuals would have been opposed to affirmative action on the grounds that it both homogenized the whole black population and gave rise to the idea that all blacks needed it while overlooking a substantial number of blacks who were already middle-class. As a result, many black professionals—some of whom themselves benefited from affirmative action programs (Clarence Thomas, Thomas Sowell, Stephen Carter, William Raspberry, the so-called Black Conservatives)—are now convinced that such programs have outlived their usefulness. In his *Reflections of an Affirmative Action Baby* (Basic Books, 1991), Stephen Carter, a middle-class, Ivy League law school graduate, Supreme Court law clerk, and the first black to receive tenure at the Yale Law School, chronicles the ambivalence and frustration of being the beneficiary (or, as he observes, the "suspected beneficiary") of affirmative action.

A second criticism of the telecast, one articulated by many of the black neo-conservatives, is the implied belief it offers that there is indeed a "black view" of the world. The notion that race is a proxy for viewpoint or outlook, confuses race with culture. The implication, to quote professor Carter, is "that black people who gain positions of authority or influence are vested with a special responsibility to articulate the presumed views of other people who are black—in effect to think and act and speak in a particular way—the black way—and that there is something peculiar about black people who insist on

doing anything else." In Derrick Bell's (a black professor at Harvard Law School who recently resigned over an affirmative action issue) unfortunate phrase, "the ends of diversity are not served by people who look black and think white."

The predictable positions of those chosen to participate in the seminar unintentionally, but nonetheless effectively, reinforce the expectation that race, gender, and ethnicity results, inevitably, in a sort of collective "Group Think." (William Raspberry is seen here defending affirmative action, apparently out of conviction; however, in the intervening decade since the program was produced, his views, judging by his columns written for the *Washington Post*, have changed substantially if not completely.)

The silent message communicated by the program is that only white males can overcome race, gender, and ethnic provincialism enabling them to be philosophically and programmatically eclectic in their social commentary and analysis. The positions of women and minorities, by contrast, are largely predetermined by their gender and their race. As the composition of the classroom (teachers and those taught) becomes increasingly diverse, the subject, only adumbrated in the program, will likely generate healthy classroom discussion.

Instructors should find the following titles helpful in preparing to use this program in the classroom.

Stephen L. Carter. *Reflections of an Affirmative Action Baby.* Basic Books, 1991.

Nathan Glazer. *Affirmative Discrimination: Ethnic Inequality and Public Policy.* Harper, 1975.

Kent Greenwalt. *Discrimination and Reverse Discrimination.* Knopf, 1983.

Kermit Hall, et al. *American Legal History: Cases and Materials.* Oxford, 1991.

Michael Kammen. *A Machine that Would Go of Itself: The Constitution in American Culture.* Vintage, 1986.

Richard Polenberg. *One Nation Divisible: Class, Race, and Ethnicity in the United States Since 1938.* Penguin, 1980.

"Race on Campus." A special issue of the *New Republic.* February 18, 1991.

Gerald N. Rosenberg. *The Hollow Hope: Can Courts Bring About Social Change?* Chicago, 1991.

Ralph A. Rossum. *Reverse Discrimination: The Constitutional Debate.* Dekker, 1980.

Arthur M. Schlesinger Jr. *The Disuniting of America: Reflections on a Multicultural Society.* Whittle Direct Books, 1991.

Jacobus tenBroek. *Equal Under Law* (originally published as *The Antislavery Origins of the Fourteenth Amendment*). Collier, 1951, 1965.

J. Harvie Wilkinson III. *From Brown to Bakke: The Supreme Court and School Integration, 1954–1978.* Oxford, 1979.

George A. Levesque, Department of Africana Studies

USETHCLA

Title:	**America and Lewis Hine**
Producer:	WNET, New York City
Directors:	Nina Rosenblum and Daniel V. Allentuck
Distributor:	Cinema Guild
Release Date:	1984
Technical:	56 min. / color / English
Purchase Price:	$850
Rental:	$125
Presentation:	Documentary, with interviews, period footage, and period stills

Content: This film ecumenically deals in a non-partisan way with the white ethnic heritage of the American Northeast and South. It makes few efforts to advocate a stiff political position or portray a chosen ethnic group—a task already done incomparably well by films like *Hester Street*—but it calmly and beautifully gives a sensitive grasp through images, both visual and verbal, of immigrant and poor white society in the early decades of the 20th century.

Critical Comments: As a film in a university diversity program, *America and Lewis Hine* offers students a vital and convincing connection among themselves, their families' pasts, and the diverse roots of American culture and society. In so doing, it accomplishes directly much of what the diversity agenda seeks to do—in this case, helping to understand that in an odd sense, we're all immigrants and minorities in this society.

How does this modest film so unpretentiously accomplish this task? Through a biography—do we use the term *biopic?*—of Lewis Hine, one of the most important "social problems" photographers of the

20th century. His photos have the black-and-white hyperrealism of a Mapplethorpe without the potentially lurid (depending on the inclinations of the observer) implications. The lens is not an "objectif" observer for Hine, distancing itself from its subject through a process of hard, technological framing. Instead, it is a humanizing device. The faces in Hine's photos—and, oh, what faces!—bespeak the common humanness of all Americans in much the same way as the famous *Family of Man* exhibit of the 1950s did for the peoples of the world. One can sense the estranged wonderment and quiet enthusiasm in the eyes of the 15-year-old immigrant Jewish girl, or the sense of wistful promise in the eyes of the Calabrian peasant as he arrives at Ellis Island. These subjects are real, they are us. The man with a huge wrench tightening the nuts on a massive end cap is not only a wonderfully poetic image, he is our past, our roots.

Plot? Perhaps this film has one, perhaps it has a narrative line, such as it is, provided by the life course of the biographical subject. But in an unassuming way—of which Hine himself would have undoubtedly yet modestly approved—the subject of the film is not Hine, but the people in his photos. As he would wish, the photographer almost becomes invisible.

The "almost" is significant, however. For those who wish to understand the life of the artist working for social change, this film offers quite a bit. Hine was born of a downwardly mobile petit bourgeois family in Oshkosh, Wisconsin, worked in the local wood products industry for a while, then migrated to Chicago. While there he studied briefly at the University of Chicago and then migrated to New York City, where he got a job teaching at the Ethical Culture School. Though the film doesn't say, it was probably there and in the streets of lower Manhattan that Hine developed his fervor for reform. His supervisor at the school had Hine learn photography, and the rest was, as they say, history.

Hine photographed immigrants starting in 1904, and later moved onto workers (his photos of metal workers and bridge builders are indelibly printed in the minds of millions of Americans), Pittsburgh, and child laborers. As a participant in the Pittsburgh survey (one of the first social scientific investigations of urban conditions), Hine began to understand that the camera was a particularly astute device for documenting social injustice. It was in photographing child laborers in the South, however, that Hine began to use the lens as a weapon in the battle for social reform. Who could withstand the facial expressions of bedraggled preteens astride massive cotton spinners? The emaciated boot blacks?

Nonetheless, Hine was not a revolutionary, and this film's political analysis reflects accurately his own brand of middle class reformism. The photos were intended to shock the right-thinking middle and professional classes, showing them the human devastation behind their more comfortable lives. He seems never to have attacked the class which directly profited from the exploitation of children. Similarly, he seems to have been caught up in the patriotic fervor of American participation in World War I—the soundtrack plays "Over There"—and merely documents the conditions without really giving a sense of the grisly mass murder of that conflict. A similar shallowness infects the film's discussion of political economy.

But one doesn't view this sort of film for its incisive politics or economic analysis. One looks into this film for its images—and they are all so well-reproduced, both movies and stills—and one sees diversity in backgrounds, in appearances on the surface. But one also sees the common humanity behind the different faces. If there is an America beneath the thin and breathless patriotism of yellow ribbons and desert conquests, it is in the faces of Lewis Hine's people. They live in the images, and they are us. In their honesty, dignity, and innocence they are what we should all wish to be.

Robert L. Frost, Department of History

USETHCOM

Title:	## American Tongues
Producers:	Louis Alvarez and Andrew Kolker
Directors:	Louis Alvarez and Andrew Kolker
Distributor:	Center for New American Media
Release Date:	c1987
Technical:	56 min. / color / English (40-min. high school version available)
Purchase Price:	$285
Rental:	$85 per screening
Presentation:	Documentary with interviews, narration, and inserted text
Study Guide:	12p. booklet, "American Tongues, An Instructional Guide"

Content: This video presents interviews and recordings of real-life scenarios that exemplify regional, social, and ethnic differences in American speech, as well as various attitudes towards such differences. It presents three major topics: the nature and causes of dialect differences in American English; attitudes towards dialects in American society; and the uses of both standard and vernacular forms of speech.

Classroom Use: *American Tongues* is well-suited for use in different contexts: educational institutions from grade school to the university, as well as in civic groups, community gatherings, and other public meetings, regardless of the social and educational background of the viewers. It is suitable for use in courses on American English, dialectology, American studies, sociology, or intergroup communication. The instructional guide provides a summary of the principal concepts, along with an excellent set of questions that can be used to stimulate and orient post-viewing discussion about the major topics of the video.

Critical Comments: *American Tongues* is structured so as to build on the natural curiosity of Americans about differences in speech in the United States. It can serve to educate viewers about the nature of dialect differences and their causes, to stimulate their observation of language usage, and to help them question the nature and underlying causes of attitudes about language variation. The organization of the material allows for interruption of the video in order to direct attention and discussion towards the topics centered around the various inserted texts.

The video begins with a brief narration by a woman from the South describing the fun she has in getting people to try to identify the place represented by her "accent." Attention is drawn to some major differences in pronunciation through recordings of "Mary had a little lamb," as recited by speakers representing various parts of the country. Background music provides some of the lyrics of "You say either and I say either . . ." and the narrator asks, "Who do you think has a funny accent? . . ." The narration also points out the following: "When someone expresses an opinion about how someone talks, he may be making a judgment about more than their speech. . . . Since your speech is so much a part of what you are, when someone is criticizing the way you talk, you might feel that they're criticizing you. . . . When people put down the way others speak, they sometimes forget that everyone speaks with an accent. . . . What sounds funny or odd to the ears of one person is music to the ears of another. . . ."

The first inserted text states: "An accent or dialect means the words we use and how we pronounce them. It doesn't mean slang, which includes words or expressions that are passing fads. And it doesn't mean jargon, which is the vocabulary of a special group—you can have an accent and still speak computerese. . . .'' The point is made that how many dialects or accents one identifies depends on how you want to "cut the pie," since differences in speech are numerous and relative. Examples of regional speech are given. Of special interest is some recorded conversation from Tangier Island, Virginia. Although many viewers will find that form of local speech particularly striking and difficult to understand, an older inhabitant of the community states that they are beginning to speak like everyone else! A brief discussion of some of the major settlement patterns of English colonizers serves to illustrate the historical basis of some of the current differences in regional speech, with distinctions becoming less evident as one goes from east to west. Folklorist Cratist Williams comments on how our ways of speaking relate to how we live our lives, providing examples from the Kentucky Appalachians to Texas.

The second inserted text states: "In different parts of the country, foreign languages have left their mark. For example, German has influenced the speech of Pennsylvania Dutch, African languages shaped the Gullah dialect of South Carolina, and French and English are intermingled by the Cajuns of Louisiana." Some colorful examples are provided of both ethnic- and geographic-based differences in speech. Examples of differences in regional vocabulary are given: "cabinet" in Rhode Island (a milkshake); "gumband" in Pittsburgh (rubber band); "antigogglin" in the South and West (skewed or crooked); "snickelfritz" in Pennsylvania, from German (rowdy child); "pau hana" in Honolulu, from Hawaiian (work is finished); "jambalaya" in Louisiana, from French (a spicy rice dish); and others. Sociolinguist Walt Wolfram comments on the process by which children acquire local speech. The topic of dialect alternation according to social context is introduced.

The third inserted text states: "There is no such thing as one standard English accent that's better than all others, but there is a type of English favored by actors and radio and TV announcers. It may lack something in personality, but everyone can understand it." As an example of relatively neutral speech, a brief interview is shown with a woman who provided the voice for directory assistance for much of the country. The goal of her recordings was a kind of "generic speech"—one that did not sound as if it were from anywhere in particular. Several examples are provided to illustrate attitudes towards differences in speech, varying from extremely negative to positive.

The fourth inserted text states: "There is a long-standing tradition in America of regional and ethnic humor. From Will Rogers to the Borscht Belt, performers have used familiar, non-standard accents to get laughs." This serves both to introduce examples of dialect-based humor from the entertainment world and to extend the topic of attitudes towards local dialects to consideration of the possible social, professional, and psychological consequences of using certain forms of regional speech.

The fifth inserted text serves to introduce the topic of socially based differences in speech: "The accents of the upper crust can be just as noticeable as blue-collar speech, particularly in the Eastern United States. One such dialect is that of the Boston Brahmins, whose British-sounding speech is becoming a thing of the past." A conversation between two elderly gentlemen of the elitist Boston Brahmins is followed by examples from North End working class speech and Black English. The point is clearly made that language differences which are stigmatized in some contexts can be used to advantage under certain common conditions.

The final part of the video speaks out against the notion that television is making everyone speak the same way. Senior linguist Fred Cassidy, who is the principal editor of the *Dictionary of American Regional English,* points out that minor differences are not likely to change, as long as they don't prevent communication; he asks, rhetorically, "Why should we all sound alike?"

In summary, this video can contribute to promoting an understanding of the nature and causes of differences in the ways Americans speak, and knowledge of the nature and implications of attitudes towards dialect differences. The topics have a broad appeal because of their intrinsic interest to many, and the subject matter is presented in an attractive, well-structured fashion. The excellent exemplification of differences in American English and of attitudes towards them, is combined with clear, simple commentary and helpful inserted texts.

Brian F. Head, Department of Hispanic, Italian, and Portuguese Studies

USETHECO

Title:	**Asianization of America**
Series:	Currents Series, Films for Humanities
Director:	Michael Rosenblum
Distributor:	Films for the Humanities and Sciences
Release Date:	1986
Technical:	26 min. / color / English
Purchase Price:	$149
Rental:	$75
Presentation:	Actions, images, and ''talking heads,'' both Asian and Caucasian

Content: This video deals with ''Asianization'' in two senses: the growing number of Asian immigrants to the United States and the increasing influence of Asian enterprises on the American market. It briefly reviews the negative stereotypes and the hostility which Americans have had and have shown toward Asian immigrants in the past, as well as our propensity toward ''Japan-bashing'' today.

The video proposes that instead of such negativity Americans should adopt a more favorable image of Asians, recognizing the emphasis given in Asian cultures to harmony, cooperation, and hard work.

Critical Comments: In this video the word Asian seems to mean Chinese, Japanese, and possibly Korean. Little distinction is made between these groups, and therefore the video requires additional work on the part of the instructor. I would suggest using it to start discussion of the alternating positive and negative stereotypes of Asians. Discussion could also focus on how both historically and today we interweave the international relationship between the United States and Asian nations with domestic relations between Asian immigrants, Asian-Americans, and other Americans.

Walter P. Zenner,
Department of Anthropology

USRACPOL

Title:	# The Autobiography of Miss Jane Pittman
Producers:	Robert W. Christiansen and Rick Rosenberg
Director:	Daniel Petrie
Distributor:	Prism Entertainment
Release Date:	1974
Technical:	106 min. / color / English
Purchase Price:	see local video store
Rental:	see local video store
Presentation:	Videorecording of the CBS television dramatization of Ernest J. Gaines's novel of the same title published in 1971. Starring Cicely Tyson and Richard Dysart
Awards:	Nine Emmy Awards, including Best Direction, Best Teleplay, and Best Actress for Cicely Tyson in her portrayal of Miss Jane Pittman

Content: This video tells about the life of a black woman from her childhood as a slave in the pre-Civil War South to her personal involvement, at the age of 110, in the civil rights movement. Also depicted are white slave owners, white plantation owners, klansmen, law enforcers, "understanding and benevolent" bosses, and others who, in one way or another, hindered the achievement of freedom by black Americans. Ernest J. Gaines, the author of *The Autobiography of Miss Jane Pittman*, is a black novelist and short story writer. He was born in Louisiana where his novel is set. His aunt, Augusteen Jefferson, is said to be the inspiration for Miss Jane Pittman.

Context: The fictional story of Jane Pittman takes place within the larger context of the struggle for civil rights by blacks, from the emancipation until 1962. Looming in the background are the larger events of American history which affected achievement for blacks, such as Reconstruction, the wars the United States engaged in during the last hundred years, and the Great Depression.

Synopsis: In Louisiana in the summer of 1962, Miss Jane Pittman is being interviewed by a young white journalist from the North on the occasion of her 110th birthday. She recounts events from her childhood as "Ticey" the slave, and then as a newly "freed" individual who had to face the vindictiveness of Southerners and threats to her life. Her story includes her struggles as a sharecropper and as a

"privileged" house servant, and her life as the wife of a black cowboy and the adoptive parent of a child whose mother had been killed by whites. The death of her husband, who needed to prove his manhood in a white world, the murder of her adopted son, who lost his life by proselytizing for the education of blacks, and the assassination of a young civil rights worker, all gave Miss Jane the resolve to defy the Louisiana authorities. At the close of the film, we see her walk up courageously to the courthouse in order to drink out of the "for whites only" water fountain. She thereby becomes the symbol of black resistance to white oppression.

Some other books which would prove helpful in the presentation of the film are: *A Black Woman's Civil War Memoirs* by Susie King Taylor (Weiner Publications; 1988 [reprint of 1902 edition]) and *Eyes on the Prize* by Juan Williams (Viking, 1987).

Classroom Use: Aside from its values as drama, this video can aid the study of black feminism, the role of black women in American history, and the civil rights movement. It can be related to contemporary United States experience to examine how civil rights laws are enforced and applied. Examples can be taken from the film to show how the subjugation of blacks was directly related to the economic well-being of white men and women. This correlation can be extended to the present to encompass other categories of people who suffer from economic discrimination. The many political, social, and cultural contributions by black women can also be studied with the help of this film.

Critical Comments: Although the film speaks through the fictional character of Miss Jane Pittman, it has an authenticity because it is situated within familiar historical events. We are drawn into the life of its central character as she witnesses acts of oppression and personal victories over political and social obstacles in the struggle for autonomy. The viewer becomes particularly aware of the personal heroism needed by African Americans to survive abject conditions and to fight the established white power structure in order to gain even a modicum of respect.

The film was made some 20 years ago and there is a sense at times that it is somewhat dated. For example, there is a lack of focus on the particular problems that African-American women had to contend with, such as forcible separation from their children and sexual abuse. In addition, the film contains a romanticism which at times tends to skim over the events. Furthermore, noticeably absent from the film is the disenchantment that has since become more evident as political victories for blacks have not been commensurate with economic and social realities. Nevertheless, the film is carefully researched and gives an accurate picture of the degradation and humiliation of servitude and of the great suffering that each victory cost. *The Autobiography of Miss Jane Pittman* offers a valuable aid for teaching about the struggle for civil liberties and for dramatizing the horrors of slavery, beatings, lynchings, hard labor, and indentured servitude. It gives a bird's eye view of the historical 100-year ''freedom march'' of black Americans.

Cicely Tyson's portrayal of Miss Jane Pittman magnificently projects the pains and gains experienced by her character in a heartless white world. In addition, Tyson is said to be the first dark-skinned African-American actress to play leading roles in American films. She is also recognized as having successfully defied the stereotype of the ''mammy'' image in her portrayal of the strong black woman.

Regina W. Betts, Department of Theatre

USETHGEN

Title:	**Back Inside Herself**
Producer:	Saundra Sharp
Director:	Saundra Sharp
Distributor:	Women Make Movies
Release Date:	1984
Technical:	5 min. / b&w / English
Purchase Price:	$125
Rental Price:	$30
Presentation:	Dramatization of poem ''Back Inside Herself,'' by Saundra Sharp, put to film by the author
Awards:	First Place, 1984 Black American Cinema Society; First Place, 1984 San Francisco Poetry Film Festival

Content: This short film is a poetic rendering of a black woman's search for identity and her internal voyage toward self-liberation. At first, the character of Herself is seen as bearing all of the burdens that the world of whites and the world of men have assigned her: the exoticism, the sexuality, the servitude. Shackled by high heels, covered with a wig, disfigured by makeup, this African-American woman is only what others call her. Herself's liberation and self-discovery comes when she is willing to take risks by throwing off her imprisoning trappings and the symbols of her enslavement: the heels, the cosmetics, the straightened hair. When she moves away from these ''spirit killers'' to liberate herself, she finds her black womanhood, the African woman within her, the center of her being, free of all the demeaning disguises that hatred has imposed on her.

Classroom Use: The film would be useful to Africana studies, sociology, African-American studies, women's studies, theater, film studies, and in courses that deal with racism, sexism, and classism. It can also serve well in human diversity courses. In order to realize fully its implications, the video needs to be complemented with discussions regarding the significance of the humiliating masks of survival that the black woman has had to wear. Additionally, the following subjects would need to be addressed: black pride in African ancestry; racial self-presentation versus misrepresentation; self-awareness and search for identity;

and the implication of what it means to be a black woman in the United States today.

Despite its brevity, I found *Back Inside Herself* helpful in my classes in theater and drama when used in conjunction with Ntozake Shange's play *For Colored Girls Who Have Considered Suicide/When the Rainbow Is Enuf,* which poetically evokes many aspects of black womanhood's experience. Other useful texts include: Toni Morrison, *The Bluest Eye* (Washington Square Pr., 1970); Terry McMillan, *Disappearing Acts* (Viking, 1989); Wanda Coleman, *Heavy Daughter Blues: Poems and Stories* (Black Sparrow Pr., 1987); and Gloria Huall et al., *All the Women Are White, All the Blacks Are Men, But Some of Us Are Brave* (Feminist Pr., 1982).

Critical Comments: *Back Inside Herself* is a little gem of a film. Its poetic minimalism is Haiku-like; its images few but eloquent. But the work's terseness is also its limitation for most classroom use since it does not fully explore the issues of racism, stereotyped representations, and quests for self-identity. It necessitates that the viewer already be sensitive to and knowledgeable of the particular plight of the African-American woman.

Other works by Saundra Sharp include the films *Life Is a Saxophone* and *Picking Tribes;* the play *The Sistuhs;* and a book of poetry, *Typing in the Dark.*

Regina W. Betts, Department of Theatre

GLRELCUL

Title:	# Bahia: Africa in the Americas
Producer:	Broadcast Video Productions
Directors:	Geovanni Brewer and Michael Brewer
Distributor:	Univ. of California, Berkeley, Extension Media Center
Release Date:	1988
Technical:	58 min. / color / English
Purchase Price:	$395
Rental:	$40
Presentation:	Documentary with extensive commentary
Study Guide:	6 pages; includes selected bibliography of works in English

Content: The video describes the origin, evolution, nature, and influence of the candomblé religion, which it views as the basis of contemporary Afro-Brazilian culture. While this religion has spread throughout Brazil, the film focuses on the place where it was first implanted: the northeastern state of Bahia, referred to as "the capital of African culture in the Americas."

The correlative material found in the study guide is useful not only because of the detailed information it provides on candomblé, but because of its notes to instructors and lists of ideas for pre-screening and post-screening discussions in the classroom. The suggestions are particularly useful in courses in African-American studies, although they are also relevant to other areas.

Classroom Use: Courses on cultural anthropology, African-American studies, Brazil, Latin-American studies, and comparative religion would benefit from this video.

Critical Comments: The opening scenes of the video are of the state's principal city and capital, Salvador, commonly called by the same name as the state itself. Signs of African presence are evident in many features of everyday life: food, dress, music, and dance, and, above all, in the widely practiced candomblé religion.

Bahia: Africa in the Americas offers special interest to American students since questions relating to the nature and extent of African influence in Brazil

invite comparison with corresponding ones in reference to the United States. After all, both Brazil and the United States, which are approximately the same size and were officially discovered by explorers from southern Europe less than ten years apart, are both complex, industrialized societies with large minority groups. As the two countries of the New World to make the greatest use of forced labor by Africans during a period that ended little more than a century ago, they played similar roles in the African slave trade during the colonial period. Yet the influence of African culture has evidently been much greater in Brazil than in the United States. A closer look at the history of Africans in Brazil might suggest perspectives that could lead to a better understanding of correlative questions in the United States.

African influence in Brazil became established through processes different from those that took place in the United States. Not only did the enslavement of blacks begin much earlier in Brazil, dating from the mid-16th century, but also legal slave trade lasted more than forty years longer there. It was in the final half-century of slave trade that the source of the distinctive cultural influence from Africa was implanted in Brazil, through the massive importation of people from the current West African countries of Nigeria and Benin, where prolonged wars among the Yoruba kingdoms facilitated slave trade through the frequent practice of selling the people defeated in battle. The influx of large numbers of these slaves caused Yoruba culture to be superimposed on the slaves of other origins in Brazil and to become the dominant African cultural influence there.

The video presents ideas of some of the leading specialists on candomblé. Professor Vivaldo da Costa Lima of the Federal University of Bahia comments on the highly organized nature of the religion, stressing its complex hierarchy, with worship centered on the Orishas, created by a higher god, Olorun (or Olodumare), maker of the world and of all life. Renowned French sociologist Pierre Verger, adopted son of Bahia and pioneer in the study of the religious continuum between Africa and Brazil, describes the Orishas as forces of nature, and explains how they evolved from some 400 in Yorubaland to fewer than 20 in Bahia.

In Yoruba religion, the Orishas are responsible for specific elements of nature such as oceans and rivers, the forest, thunder and lightning, and for things from the earth which people use such as iron and medicinal plants, as well as for features of human life including communication, love, peace, and justice. Since the Orishas are viewed as responsible for all life, their worshippers try to understand them and to do their will. The Orishas have their favorite foods and beverages, each is represented by certain symbols and colors, and each has a particular temperament. Because the Orishas have human-like features and are identified with the ever-present forces of nature, candomblé worshippers feel very close to their gods.

The film shows several scenes from candomblé ceremonies. It describes religious concepts and practices common among Afro-Brazilians, and it explains how the religion of Yoruba was adapted to form part of its new cultural and social setting. It also accounts for not only the survival but also the continued expansion of candomblé in context with Catholicism, showing how the Afro-Brazilian religion has become a spiritual feature of many aspects of daily life.

In addition to its wealth of visual material, the film is enhanced by a highly informative text, including several commentaries by anthropologist Sheila Walker. To viewers fascinated solely or primarily by the images shown, the commentaries may appear disruptive or occasionally seem lengthy and dense, but they are necessary for explaining such complex matters as possession by the spirits and the problem of the contrasting interpretations of the combining of different forms of belief and coexistence in describing the relationship between Afro-Brazilian candomblé and the Catholic church. The film does not provide a remote, merely historical account; it gives due attention to ongoing dynamics in the practice and spread of the religion of Yoruba origin.

Brian F. Head, Department of Hispanic, Italian, and Portuguese Studies

USETHPOL

Title:	## The Ballad of Gregorio Cortéz
Producer:	Montesuma Esparza and Michael Hausman
Director:	Robert M. Young
Distributor:	Media Basics
Release Date:	1983
Technical:	99 min. / color / mostly English, with some Spanish (no subtitles)
Purchase Price:	$14.95
Rental:	n/a
Presentation:	Dramatization based on a study by Americo Paredes; video recording of a feature film

Content: Taking place on the Texas-Mexico frontier, the film presents a dramatization of the life of Gregorio Cortéz, beginning with a 1901 incident in which he killed a sheriff who was attempting to arrest him, then fled to the border eluding a 600-man posse, was captured due to betrayal by another Mexican, and was tried and convicted. The film is based on a study by Americo Paredes, *With a Pistol in His Hand, a Border Ballad and Its Hero* (Austin: University of Texas Pr., 1958).

Classroom Use: This video is recommended for use in courses on criminal justice, American studies, Mexico, immigration studies, Latin-American studies, Chicano studies, cultural anthropology, and folklore.

Critical Comments: As the title of the film suggests, the focus is not so much on Gregorio Cortéz the man, but rather on the events which gave rise to popular ballads about Gregorio Cortéz the folk hero. He was viewed by Anglo-Texans as a ''greaser'' horse thief and vicious killer; to Mexican-Texans he became a rebel hero. In fact, for ten days over a distance of more than 400 miles, he eluded Texas Rangers and posses numbering in the hundreds that used tracking by dogs and Indians, communication by telephone and telegraph, and transportation by fresh horses and railroad in the pursuit of a single fugitive relying only on his horsemanship and wits. Instead of a vicious killer, Gregorio Cortéz is shown as a desperate, frightened common man who killed to defend himself, and who ran when he could not hide. Yet the greatest manhunt in Texas history

could not run him down, the search ended only when the exhausted fugitive was betrayed by a fellow Mexican who was eager to collect the $1,000 reward offered by the government.

Before any images, the video presents the following text: ''At the turn of the century, more than fifty years after Texas had, through war, won its independence from Mexico, two cultures—the Anglo and the Mexican—lived side by side in a state of tension and fear. From a true story of that era come different accounts of the same event.''

An inserted text at the end of the film completes the story: ''Four months later [following the initial trial, represented in the film] the conviction of Gregorio Cortéz was reversed. However, he was brought to trial six more times. He was acquitted of killing Sheriff Morris and Henry Schnabel. But he was convicted of killing Sheriff Glover, and was sentenced to life imprisonment. He was also convicted of stealing the horse on which he fled. In 1913, Gregorio Cortéz was pardoned by the governor of Texas and released. He had spent 12 years in prison. He died a few years later. 'El corrido de Gregorio Cortéz' is still sung today along the border.''

The two central events in the life of Gregorio Cortéz on which the accusations of murder were based are represented in the film as follows:

Two men, Sheriff Morris and a cowhand named Boone, go to Cortéz's home to find out if he recently traded a horse. When they arrive, Cortéz is there with his brother and his wife and children. Since Cortéz does not speak English and the sheriff does not speak ''Mexican,'' Boone serves as interpreter.

But Boone's knowledge of Spanish is quite poor, and it is difficult for the sheriff and Cortéz to communicate with each other. A major misunderstanding takes place when Cortéz denies having traded a horse (caballo), admitting only to having traded a mare (yegua). Boone does not understand the distinction, and he fails to communicate to the sheriff everything that Cortéz has said. Suspecting that Cortéz is lying, the sheriff places him under arrest. Cortéz objects, for he sees no reason for the arrest. When his brother steps between Cortéz and his accuser, the sheriff fires his gun, inflicting a mortal wound on the brother. Cortéz returns fire, killing the sheriff.

A new sheriff, Glover, is sworn in. He goes with a posse to look for Cortéz at the home of another Mexican, where, it turns out, Cortéz has taken his brother. The sheriff and his posse have been drinking, and they arrive at night when visibility is poor. Amid confusion, shooting breaks out and, on opposite sides of the house, two more people are killed: Sheriff Glover and a man named Schnabel. Cortéz will later be tried for the deaths of both, in addition to that of Sheriff Morris.

Following the two incidents described above, Cortéz flees for the Mexican border followed by a large posse headed by a captain in the Texas Rangers.

This film is structured around several contrasts. At a time when both the social order and the legal system in practice were at the threshold of profound and permanent change, the film shows contrasting attitudes—and occasional conflicts—among the Anglo-Texans, between those wanting to do "justice" with their own hands, and those seeking to follow due process. Even more crucial, however, are the contrasts between different perceptions and interpretations of the events surrounding the shootings, in which simple misunderstanding, originating from differences in language, resulted in killings. Ultimately, the film depicts forces in the formation of contrasting myths. For example, the reporter accompanying the posse invents a "Cortéz gang" for his stories, because he listens to what some members of the posse imagine, instead of simply reporting what has actually been seen.

At several points in the dramatization there is singing in the background of "corridos" (ballads) in which the feats of the folk hero are preserved for future generations of Mexicans and Chicanos. One of the inserted texts at the beginning of the film mentions that folk ballads about Gregorio Cortéz are still sung "along the [Mexican] border"; in fact, they have spread to many other parts of the Spanish-speaking Americas.

Brian F. Head, Department of Hispanic, Italian, and Portuguese Studies

USIMMETH

Title: **Becoming American: The Odyssey of a Refugee Family**

Producers: Ken Levine and Ivory Waterworth Levine, Iris Film and Video

Distributor: New Day Films

Release Date: 1983

Technical: 58 min. / color / English

Purchase Price: $425

Rental: $65

Presentation: Documentary, interview, and narration

Study Guide: Available and quite good

Content: The film traces the journey of a single Hmong (a Laotian hill tribe or ethnic group) family from Laos to a United Nations refugee camp in Thailand in 1974, to Seattle, Washington in 1980. The family is composed of a young man, his wife, and baby son, and his brother's widow and her five children. The eldest of the children is 13. The complex family structure is used to provide information about Hmong traditions and the deceased brother provides the link to the Central Intelligence Agency (CIA) war. The strong cultural and family values of the Hmong people in the face of hundreds of years of adversity are emphasized.

More Hmong culture is seen as the family prepares to leave Laos and goes through the ritual of having the Shaman prepare the spirits for travel. During a three-week period, after 20 hours on a bus, some medical exams, and 24 hours on a plane, the family arrives in Oakland, California—nine people with everything they own in five suitcases. We follow them to their new apartment in Seattle and watch their process of learning to "become American." The vividness of the details, like using the stove and the shower, and the overwhelming importance of literacy to success in U.S. society is very clear. The film ends with a summary of where the Hmong people live in the United States and shows their sense of community as they help each other adjust.

Editor's note: This video also illustrates the challenge that people of an oral culture face in becoming functional in a literate society such as the United States.

Critical Comments: *Becoming American* is an excellent film about the resettlement of the Hmong people in the United States. The footage is about equally divided between Southeast Asia and the United States, so the many contrasts between the two cultures are very vivid. While focusing on only one group, the Hmong, the film is broad in perspective. It explains much of the history of the Hmong and their interrelationships with other groups, the background of the CIA and the United States in the secret war in Laos, and compares the experiences of the Hmong to those of European immigrants to this country.

The section on the relationship between the United States/CIA and the Hmong in fighting the war in Laos is particularly well-done. The length of their involvement with the United States, their casualty rate ten times that of U.S. soldiers, and the continued persecution of the Hmong are well-presented and serve to validate their claim to refugee status and their connection to the United States. The film also uses the experiences of the family to talk about the U.S. federal and state programs to help resettle refugees and to show the responses of native-born Americans to the newcomers. The magnitude of what needs to be learned and the small amount of resources available are made extremely clear.

This film is an excellent device for talking about assimilation, Asian-Americans, refugees, forced migration, American responses to newcomers, and U.S. foreign and domestic policies. It requires very little set up on the part of the instructor, though some of the key concepts and historical facts could be discussed briefly to set the stage. The story moves along quickly and is very effective in getting the viewer to identify with the refugees without preaching at them.

Nancy A. Denton, Department of Sociology

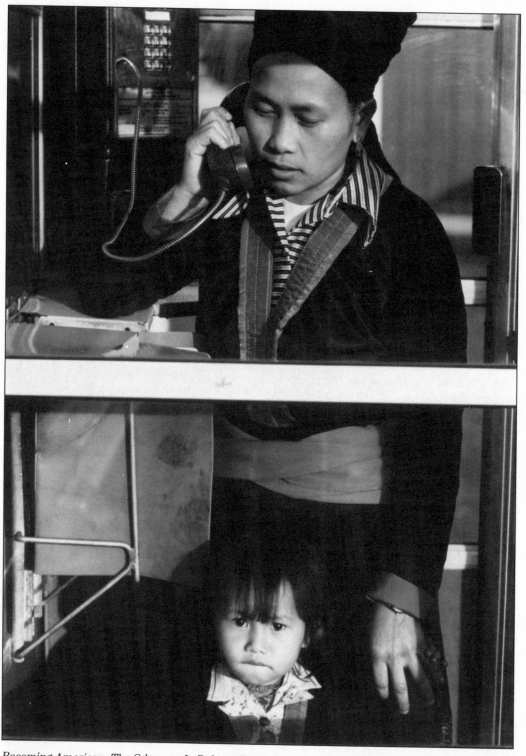

Becoming American: The Odyssey of a Refugee Family portrays a Hmong family's saga of resettlement, from war-ravaged Laos to a refugee camp in Thailand to Seattle, Washington. Above, "Mang Vang makes her first telephone call." (Courtesy New Day Films)

USGENSTE

Title:	**Before Stonewall: The Making of a Gay and Lesbian Community**
Producers:	Robert Rosenberg, John Scagliotti, Greta Schiller
Director:	John Scagliotti
Distributor:	Cinema Guild
Release Date:	1984
Technical:	87 min. / color / English
Purchase Price:	$695
Rental:	$125
Presentation:	Historical documentary using interviews, photographs, and film footage
Award:	Emmy Award for Best Historical Program

Content: *Before Stonewall* charts the changes in homosexuality in the United States from the early 20th century through the 1960s. This is one of the few films ever made tracing changes in the lives of homosexuals and in the very meaning of homosexuality.

Classroom Use: I have used this film in a number of classes. Its historical point of view provides a sympathetic understanding of this minority group and a sense of its changing place in American society. Students have generally appreciated the film as a way to introduce the topic.

Critical Comments: This film shows how the meaning and role of homosexuality changed in the course of the 20th century. In the early years of this century, individuals whose desires were for members of the same sex often did not call themselves homosexuals. They may have been married or lived as single persons. They may have engaged in homosexual relations and behavior. But they didn't necessarily define themselves as homosexual. From roughly the 1930s through the 1950s, such individuals began to be described as homosexuals. Their same-sex desires became a basis of identity and gradually community affiliation. The film shows how the beginning of the rise of gay and lesbian institutions in the 1940s and 50s was met with resistance and repression. After World War II, the government mounted a campaign to purge homosexuals from the state and society. The crusade against communists extended to homosexuals and the lives of many Americans were ruined.

Resistance by homosexuals to the oppression of the state and the medical-scientific establishment was symbolized by the Stonewall revolt in 1969. Stonewall was a bar in New York City frequented by lesbians and gay men. Like many such places it was subject to repeated police raids and its gay customers to police harassment and arrest. In June 1969, a police raid was met with resistance. The gays and lesbians in Stonewall fought back and sparked several days of rioting. From this revolt was spawned a gay liberation movement. Stonewall has come to symbolize pride and dignity for lesbians and gay men.

The film takes the point of view that lesbians and gay men are now a minority akin to African Americans. Like ethnic minorities, lesbians and gay men are subject to a range of discrimination, harasssment, and oppression. They are, in many localities, denied civil rights; they are stereotyped in public representations; they suffer from a stigmatized identity and social marginality; and they are subject to harassment and violence. Yet, *Before Stonewall* makes it clear that lesbians and gay men should not be treated simply as victims. They have responded to social oppression by creating their own social and cultural institutions with affirmative identities and life-styles. They have evolved political organizations and strategies to fight discrimination and oppression. Like other minorities, they have acquired a certain social legitimacy. This is a film that takes the perspective of a self-affirming homosexual. It assumes the legitimacy of homosexuality; it assumes the illegitimacy of homophobia. It probes the reasons why so many Americans are troubled by homosexuality. Through the numerous interviews with homosexuals, it gives a voice to lesbians and gay men who want their stories heard.

As the numerous awards won by this film indicate, it is exceptionally well-done and forceful. Although it clearly represents an advocacy standpoint, it is done with humor and subtlety. One of its chief merits is that it equally includes lesbians and gay men and that it often gives voice to people of color as well as working class gay people.

I have two reservations about the film. First, its beginning segment on homosexuals in the early years of this century does not adequately contextualize the discussion. It highlights gender inversion as critical to homosexuality in these years but does not sketch out the context and meaning of this phenomenon. The result is that it may unintentionally reinforce certain stereotypes of homosexuals. Second, it does not cover the making of the gay community in the 1970s, which is a serious shortcoming. Unfortunately, no other documentary presently available fills this gap. Notwithstanding these two limits, it remains a very useful pedagogical tool.

Steven Seidman,
Department of Sociology

USETHEXP

Title:	**Beyond Tradition: Contemporary Indian Art and Its Evolution**
Producer:	David M. Strang
Distributor:	Jacka Photography
Release Date:	1989
Purchase Price:	$29.95
Rental:	n/a
Technical:	45 min. / color / English
Presentation:	Documentary of Native-American art with a focus upon the Southwest United States; written by Lois and Jerry Jacka

Content: Indian art collectors Jerry and Lois Jacka appear at the beginning of this video, which documents their collection of Native-American art and shows the roots of contemporary native works. The video is based upon a book of the same name. Most of the art shown is an extension of the traditional crafts of Indian people: pottery, stone carving, weaving, etc. Some painting is also included, but it is not the specific focus. The Jackas live in the Southwest, so their collection is drawn mainly from tribes living in that area. The point is made early on that this geographical area is the cradle of Native-American art and that new developments or trends generally proceed from this region. Jerry Jacka narrates for brief stretches, and then Indian music accompanies the display of art objects within each category.

Classroom Use: *Beyond Tradition* can be used most effectively in an anthropology class or in a class that focuses upon American or contemporary art. Part of the video's value is its straightforward demonstration of dominant-culture power and implicit values tempered by good intentions. In any class this video would be an appropriate way of challenging and deconstructing those assumptions and it could be especially useful in cultural diversity classes.

Critical Comments: The unfortunate drawback to the use of this video is that the prominence of white collectors of Indian art objects may be objectionable from a native standpoint. Certainly native craft tradition is maintained by many Indian artists as a way to reaffirm their cultural heritage. Although the market for Indian works in the United States has benefited Native-American people economically, it has just as often served to restrict and confine artists' developments in non-traditional directions. One of the ways in which Native Americans are stereotyped is through being frozen in the past. This video might be construed as an attempt to do just that. The contemporary innovations discussed are mainly continuations in the production of collectable objects rather than reactions to existence in post-modern America.

Another objection that might be raised about the film is the geographical limitation of its presentation. The Southwest has, of course, been important in the development of Indian art, but innovation is not confined to that area of the country and the claims at the beginning of the video may be slightly inflated. In calling the video ''contemporary,'' Jerry Jacka has laid himself open to criticism regarding what is left out. For instance, the Hopi have a strong tradition of photography that is certainly beyond tradition, but never mentioned in the film.

Jeanne Laiacona, Department of Art

USETHREL

Title:	**The Biggest Jewish City in the World**
Series:	Destination America
Producer:	Peter Tiffin for a British Thames Television series
Director:	Peter Tiffin
Distributor:	Media Guild
Release Date:	1976
Technical:	53 min. in two segments / color with b&w / English
Purchase Price:	$445
Rental:	n/a
Presentation:	Documentary using archival footage, photographic stills, interviews, and live footage of present-day scenes

Content: *The Biggest Jewish City in the World* presents an overview of the Jewish immigrant experience in America, concentrating on Jews from eastern Europe who came to the United States between 1880 and 1920 and settled in New York City. The first segment of the film discusses the violent persecution and economic insecurity Jews left behind in eastern Europe and details the poverty and hardship they found in America. Themes include harsh working conditions in the garment industry, tenement life, involvement in the labor movement (particularly the important roles played by women), the quest for education, the cultural and nurturing richness of the Yiddish press and theater, religious transformations, intergenerational tensions, and the changing faces of anti-Semitism.

The second segment of the film deals with the contemporary, often upwardly mobile lives of the children and grandchildren of immigrants, stressing Jewish emphases on education, philanthropy, and social concerns. Also discussed are the emotional ties many American Jews feel towards Israel, and the insecurity about its safety that even the most successful American Jews feel.

Classroom Use: This film has obvious uses in Judaic studies courses which touch on the Jewish experience in America, but I think its appeal is much broader. It could be used with valuable effect in sociology, anthropology, women's studies, literature and history courses (among others) that deal with the history or literature of immigration, urban studies, the study of American ethnic groups, labor history, economic mobility, women's experiences, or contemporary American religions.

Critical Comments: This is a historically accurate and multi-faceted film which is sensitive to gender, class, and diversity concerns. It makes excellent and effective use of both documentary sources and interviews. Those whose voices are heard include elderly Jews, both men and women, recounting their experiences as immigrants; well-known interpreters of this experience such as Irving Howe and Sam Levenson; and children and grandchildren of immigrants. Although the film is devoted to the Jewish experience, many of its themes of struggle, the importance of family, and the process of acculturation are universal, making it applicable to any American audience. Indeed, the film was intended for general, non-Jewish viewers, and succeeds admirably in providing a first-rate introduction to the American Jewish experience for the novice to the subject.

If there is any limitation to the film, it is the implication that all American Jews have made the transition from poverty to prosperity, which is not the case. It also does not address issues of religious, intellectual, and ethnic diversity within the contemporary American Jewish community.

Judith Baskin, Department of Judaic Studies

USETHRAC

Title:	**Birthwrite: Growing Up Hispanic**
Producers:	Jesús T. Treviño, KAET-TV, Phoenix, with the Hispanic Research Center, Arizona State University
Director:	Luis R. Torres
Distributor:	Cinema Guild
Release Date:	1989
Technical:	60 min. / color / English
Purchase Price:	$295
Rental:	$90
Presentation:	Documentary, with dramatization and readings

Content: This documentary, made for public television, includes interviews with Latino writers born or raised in the United States of Mexican and Puerto Rican parents, along with dramatizations of major scenes from selected works by these authors. The interviews provide moving insights into the different worlds these writers experienced in their childhoods as they faced with their families and communities the hardships and rejection of being part of a minority group. The included dramatizations illustrate different aspects of the particular experience of growing up or being a Latino in U.S. society.

Among the major issues introduced are racism and discrimination, women's subordination, migration, urban life, poverty and hardship, and the conflicts between different cultural worlds and generations. The documentary is very poignant in its underscoring of these issues as well as in emphasizing the similarities and differences in the historical and cultural experiences of the various Latino groups in the United States.

Among the writers interviewed are the Mexicans Rolando Hinojosa, Lorna Dee Cervantes, and Alejandro Morales; and Puerto Ricans Nicholasa Mohr, Judith Ortiz Cofer, Tato Laviera, and Edward Rivera. Poets Cervantes, Laviera, and Cofer also provide moving and dramatic readings of their own works.

Classroom Use: This documentary is an excellent complement to courses in minority literatures, minority groups, and Latino cultures, or any other course in which selected fiction or poetry works by these writers are discussed.

Edna Acosta-Belen, Department of Latin American and Caribbean Studies

GLRACPOL

Title:	**Black and White in Color**
Producer:	Arthur Cohn
Director:	Jean-Jacques Annand
Distributor:	Baker & Taylor
Release Date:	c1987
Technical:	88 min. / color / French with English subtitles
Purchase Price:	$39.98
Rental:	n/a
Presentation:	Dramatization (historical fiction)
Award:	1976 Academy Award, Best Foreign Language Film

Content: This video portrays what can happen when black Africans find themselves caught up in the conflict among white Europeans. French, Germans, and the indigenous people of French West Africa are portrayed in the colonial sociocultural context at the outbreak of World War I. When the film opens, the whites (the Germans and the French) are friendly with one another. When word of the war arrives, they are suddenly mortal enemies. Then each side conscripts blacks to do its fighting—and dying.

The French officer has no white soldiers and no field experience. He allows merchants and missionaries to "recruit" and "train" a small, slipshod platoon. The recruiting is done by trickery. The black men don't know what they are getting roped into;

their training is rushed and inefficient. The result is a tragic joke. The Frenchmen—borne on litters by their "soldiers"—choose a comfortable spot from which to observe the battle (not too close). It looks like they're on a Sunday picnic. The confrontation is brief: their men are routed and an African is killed. The picnic is over.

A young geographer who has felt all along that the indigenous people should be treated like human beings, persuades the commander to let him lead a campaign. He explains that, although he has no field experience, he has studied military history. The officer, realizing that he has been a fool, consents. The new commander trains a small but viable fighting force, again comprised of blacks who are taught to sing patriotically of France: ". . . and for her a

Frenchman must die.'' He nevertheless initiates racial reform. His black aide conducts himself with dignity and expects common courtesy, as does the young commander's black lover. She is the subject of gossip among the other Frenchmen, who consider the relationship scandalous.

There is another battle. This one is long and grueling, identical in every way to its European counterparts, right down to the trenches, mud, disease, and casualties. In the midst of it all, the Africans undergo a cultural assimilation. The German commander calls across the lines: ''Come over to our side . . . We have food, blankets, and medicine. . . . Germany is good to us!'' A ''French'' African replies: ''Go to hell!'' Such loyalty is portrayed as futile.

An English regiment arrives, led by an Indian commander. He informs them that the war is over, and that England now has control of the area. The French are incensed until they realize that this will not really change the situation. ''It just means,'' one of them reasons, ''that the blacks who were German are English now!'' The assumption appears to be: ''We are French, not English. Our blacks are our possessions, so they remain French, not English.''

There is a celebration of the cessation of hostilities, attended by blacks and whites alike. We see the Africans behaving in a dignified and reasonable manner. We see the Europeans drinking, joking, and slapping each other on the back as if their friendship had never been interrupted. An African turns to his friend, commenting, ''Whites! really!''

Classroom Use: This video is appropriate for anthropology, colonial history, and sociology classes at any level, francophone culture study, and French classes at the 300 and 400 levels (with students who should be able to ignore the subtitles, more or less).

Critical Comments: Unlike many other popular films to come out over the years, this one portrays the indigenous people as reasonable and intelligent, and the colonials as foolish and irresponsible (which they often were).

The cinematographer's point would be all the more well-taken by a viewer who was aware of the era's racial biases, the fact that colonialization included exploitation as a matter of course, and that all of this was regarded as perfectly normal in the European mind. Despite its wartime setting, the film's main theme is prejudice engendered by ethonocentrism. The Europeans consider it proper that the blacks should fight their battles—and die—for them. This is an excellent topic for discussion in any classroom.

Michael Taran Doyle, Department
of French Studies

GLETHGEN

Title:	**Blood Wedding (Bodas de Sangre)**
Producer:	Emiliano Piedra
Director:	Carlos Saura
Distributor:	Media Home Entertainment
Release Date:	1986
Purchase Price:	$59.95
Rental:	n/a
Technical:	71 min. / color / Spanish with English subtitles
Presentation:	Videorecording of 1981 film; part documentary which includes the preparation for a rehearsal/performance of the flamenco ballet adaptation of Federico Garcia Lorca's 1933 play, *Blood Wedding*

Content: Federico Garcia Lorca, the noted surrealist poet and playwright, often interwove myth and reality as he dramatized the events and described the men and women of rural Spain. Lorca's *Blood Wedding* is about love and honor, passion and revenge, the place of women and the duty of men. It is also about the aridity and fertility of the Spanish land and the peasants who populate it. *Blood Wedding* concerns a young bride who runs away on her wedding night with her married lover. Urged by his mother to avenge his honor, the bridegroom pursues the lovers. The two men engage in a knife duel, during which they both die. At the end, the surviving women, the bride, the mother, and the wife, mourn their losses.

Classroom Use: *Blood Wedding* is valuable for the study of Spanish drama and dance. Taken in conjunction with Lorca's play, the video may also be useful in courses dealing with gender relations and the concept of machismo, and with the influence of the Catholic church on Spanish culture. The film is valuable for its aesthetic qualities, but it needs to be enhanced with additional study aids in order for it to serve human diversity course requirements and to permit adequate comparisons between Spanish and contemporary United States experiences, perhaps in regards to Latinos. The play on which the ballet is based is in a volume entitled *Three Tragedies of Federico Garcia Lorca* (New Directions, 1956). Also helpful to the understanding of the concept of machismo is the videorecording, *A Man When He Is a Man* (re-

viewed on p. 130) and the study, *La Chicana: The Mexican-American Woman,* by Alfredo Mirande and Evangelina Enriquez (University of Chicago Pr., 1979).

Critical Comments: This beautifully directed film captures the nuances of Antonio Gades's choreography. As interpreted by Antonio Gades, the former director and leading dancer of the National Ballet of Spain, *Blood Wedding* becomes a ballet in which elements of desire, jealousy, and retaliation are emphasized. Lorca's poetic tragedy is masterfully interpreted by the flamenco dancers. The austerity of the costumes and the stylized movements and gestures counterpoint the sensuality and the overwhelming inner passions of the protagonists.

In addition, the vocal interpretations of three of Lorca's poems set to music add moods of hope, longing, regret, and loss to the dance. The production is riveting—the dancing is beautiful and the feelings are wonderfully rendered—but it resembles Lorca's play only in outline. Regrettably missing are Lorca's interweaving of tradition and desire; the lyricism of his poetry; the magic realism of his settings; the strong influence of the Catholic church; and the presence of supernatural elements. Also lacking is the emphasis on the character of Lorca's women; imprisoned by tradition, respected but at the service of their men. They are driven by duty and honor to serve their husbands and fathers.

Regina W. Betts, Department of Theatre

GLCULPOL

Title:	**Brazil: Heart of South America**
Producer:	Somona Video Productions
Directors:	Michael and Suzi Heuman
Distributor:	International Video Network
Release Date:	1988
Technical:	55 min. / color / English
Purchase Price:	$24.95
Rental:	available for preview only
Presentation:	Documentary in travelogue style

Content: This video provides a basic introduction to contemporary Brazil, including people of different social, ethnic, and geographic groups. The presentation attempts to integrate information on size, natural resources, demography and ethnic diversity, flora and fauna, geography and climate, folklore, and other features of the country and its people, through the perspectives of social, cultural, and economic history.

Classroom Use: Recommended for beginning-level courses on Latin-American studies and Brazil.

Critical Comments: The opening sequence of scenes and accompanying text provide an exuberant overview of the country as a vast land of contrasts, with a wide variety of scenery and a territory which covers half of South America, bordering all other countries in the continent except two. Reference is made to Brazil's economic growth, which has made it the eighth leading power of the world in terms of gross national product. The five major regions are identified and briefly characterized with selected views. After mentioning some of Brazil's material resources, the film refers to the people as the country's "greatest natural resource," in what it describes as a "dynamic cultural melting pot." Brief views of ethnic and religious diversity are presented, along with a historical sketch of colonial times.

The film then presents scenes and information on the major regions of the country, with attention to the respective historical, cultural, and economic contexts. The scenes are well-filmed and the selec-

tion is good, coupled with simple, generally accurate (though sometimes scant) descriptions, they provide sufficient substance to convey not only a clear notion of major features of each region, but also a representative overview of sociocultural and geographic diversity throughout the country.

The Northeast is presented first, in accordance with the early development of Brazil as a colony. Emphasis is on the city of Salvador, capital of the state of Bahia and first capital of the country, and on the special features of the cultural and economic history of the region, due largely to the influence of peoples brought from Africa.

Noting the expansion of colonial Brazil due to the discovery of gold in the state of Minas Gerais, the video introduces the Southeast. First it shows the city of Ouro Preto (known as Vila Rica when it was capital of Brazil's 18th-century gold rush) and the region's architectural and sculptural attractions of the baroque period. Then it presents modern Rio de Janeiro through various scenic views and correlative information.

The section on the South presents scenes and information emphasizing cattle raising, the influence of European immigrants, and the region's natural wonders, including the strange rock formations, chasms, and world-famous Iguacu on the border of Argentina and Paraguay, with its "275 separate falls, each higher than Niagara."

The North is described in terms of the vast forests of the Amazon, with their enormous variety of plants, birds, and animals, and the region's economic history and potential. Due attention is given to the major cities, Manaus and Belem, as well as to special features of life along the Amazon River.

At this point, the video returns to the Northeast, where it shows parts of coastal Ceara, including the capital city, Fortaleza. There are scenes of the production of various types of folk art typical of the region, which economic changes are making increasingly scarce. The effects of relentless droughts, which have taken place for several years, are described. Hardships suffered during the repeated droughts have forced many peasants to migrate southward in search of better living conditions.

The problems caused by the droughts of the Northeast provide a point of departure for return to the Southeast, where the video next introduces São Paulo, Brazil's industrial capital, which has attracted many migrants from the Northeast. It describes the industrial and economic growth of the city and the surrounding urban satellites. Zoological attractions found in "the third largest city in the world" are shown, along with contrasting features of the manifestation of great wealth and of the results of extreme poverty. The commentary links poverty and unemployment to the stifling of economic growth by the country's large international debt. This section also provides scenes and information on "the world's largest Japanese population outside Japan" and on Santos, "Brazil's busiest port."

In its final section, the video turns to the West Central region, showing Brasilia, the country's capital since 1960, which is said to "provide a vision of the future," with its ultramodern architecture and innovative city planning. In closing, the video stresses Brazil's "promising future," attributing to former President Juscelino Kubitschek the notion that Brazil is "a land with the natural and human resources to eventually become one of the world's great nations." Unfortunately, this section fails to show other parts of the West Central region, commonly considered the country's last frontier. In general, the scenes and descriptions presented in the various sections described above follow a well-planned sequence; they are usually linked in meaningful ways, although once or twice only superficially. In general, this video is artfully filmed, skillfully edited, and enhanced by clear, accurate text. But, for this reviewer's taste, the text is too often marred by an elementary error (e.g., "This is . . . a country so large that while it's winter at one end, it's summer at the other."), a maladroit metaphor (e.g., the use of "glittering tropical tiara" to refer to the country as a whole, after labeling each of the five regions a "gem"), a gross generalization that is either questionable or meaningless (e.g., "Brazilians are an optimistic . . . people."), or a specious superlative. Such flaws notwithstanding, there can be little doubt that most general viewers will find the video not only aesthetically appealing but also interesting and informative; naive neophytes to Brazilian studies may even be "turned on" by the apparent enthusiasm of the script.

However, in view of Brazil's profound economic, social and political problems as the country enters the 1990s, well-informed viewers should be skeptical of the video's generally optimistic bias, in keeping with the century-old cliche that Brazil is "the country of the future." Fortunately, the overall tone is at least tempered by one or two well-founded caveats. Cautious students may also be weary of the seemingly endless concatenations of superlatives used in many of the available audio-visual materials dealing with Brazil. The present video certainly has an ample dose of such statements—although perhaps not more than do others.

Brian F. Head, Department of Hispanic, Italian, and Portuguese Studies

USETHCLA

Title:	**The Bronx: A Cry for Help**
Producer:	Brent Owens Productions
Distributor:	Filmakers Library
Release Date:	1990
Technical:	59 min. / color, b&w / English
Purchase Price:	$495
Rental:	$85
Presentation:	Documentary
Awards:	American Film and Video Festival, 1989; Berlin Film Festival, 1989; Santa Fe Film Expo, 1990

Content: This film describes the South Bronx between 1976 and 1988, focusing on the living and working conditions of ordinary people. Coverage is representative of the racial, ethnic, gender, age, and class composition of the area, concentrating on Latin-, African- and Euro-American people. Particular attention is given to the majority Hispanic population of the area, most notably to Puerto Rican Americans, and to the special problems of the large numbers of very poor people in the area. Issues discussed are relevant to economics, sociology, political science, anthropology, geography, city planning, public administration, social welfare, labor studies, gender studies, Latin-American studies, and Africana studies. There is a brief discussion of the history of the South Bronx (using old photographs to show its former elegance), but the film concentrates on the 1970s and early 1980s. The key book to accompany this film is by Jill Jonnes, *We're Still Here: The Rise, Fall, and Resurrection of the South Bronx* (Boston: Atlantic Monthly Pr., 1986).

Classroom Use: This is a good film to use in a wide range of undergraduate and graduate courses. It is particularly suited to undergraduate courses with a public policy focus, and to courses examining poverty, inequality, immigration, and segregation.

Critical Comments: The film provides a graphic and realistic view of urban poverty in metropolitan America, and a well-balanced analysis of one of the most notorious urban slum areas in the country. The film has a shocking and sobering effect, reminding us of the magnitude of inner-city poverty, the suffering of millions of poor Americans, and the immense difficulties of solving inner-city problems in a system where other concerns take priority. The strong point of Brent Owens's film is that it concentrates on the mundane realities of poverty rather than on spectacular or sensationalized aspects. The film devotes most of its attention to the day-to-day problems of the poor: landlords who won't fix or repair anything, high rents, poor services, obstructive bureaucracies, rats, vandalism, muggings, arson, and drugs. It shows how poor people so often "get the runaround:" referred from one ineffectual agency to another until they become exhausted or run out of subway tokens; visited by politicians who make false promises or absurd recommendations; or provided with "token solutions" that clearly won't work.

The Bronx: A Cry for Help describes the virtual collapse of the South Bronx between 1950 and 1980, shifting from a fairly poor, orderly, and law-abiding tract of the city, to one of America's most notorious centers of abandonment, arson, and violent crime. This collapse is paralleled by a massive demographic shift—the "flight" of Euro-Americans, mainly of Jewish, German, Italian, and Irish origins, and the arrival of large numbers of Puerto Ricans and African Americans. The underlying problems, of course, are how to explain the neighborhood collapse and the dramatic demographic change from whites to minorities, and how to determine whether there is any cause-and-effect relationship between neighborhood collapse and demographic change.

The film alludes to many potential explanations: the destruction caused by expressway construction and urban renewal programs; neighborhood redlining by banks and city planners, allotting the South Bronx the role of ghetto and future industrial park; the massive prejudice against minorities and the application of "tipping point" theories (the idea that, when a percentage of minority residents reaches a certain point, it promotes flight from the neighborhood); some sort of "landlord conspiracy" in real estate, to gouge the poor, commit or provoke arson, and then reap the fruits of fire insurance; the negligence of public officials, cutting services and support systems so as to cut overall expenditures while continuing to favor richer neighborhoods; and the social devastation wreaked by the invasion of drugs and associated violent crime. Clearly there is no single or simple answer, and the film provides food for thought without reaching any premature conclusions. Owens's film includes interviews with a broad range of community leaders and former officials who are genuinely concerned for the South Bronx, as well as numerous highly memorable quotes:

> The situation in the South Bronx is one of the tragedies of modern urban warfare, the warriors being those who are in charge, and the victims being those who are the poor;

> The poor people, the blacks and the Puerto Ricans, have been written off by the City of New York;

> We can't claim to be the greatest country on earth and have a neighborhood like the South Bronx.

Through its choices of interviewees and statements, the film helps the student see different perspectives on the same issue. For instance, the discussion on tenement abandonment and arson includes a tenement landlord, a former district attorney, a fireman, and various tenants and housing activists.

As a film related to issues of diversity, *The Bronx: A Cry for Help* helps the student to interrelate issues of race, ethnicity, and gender with issues of class and poverty. Ideally, more students will become interested in inner-city poverty issues and in the search for ways to overcome the most serious problems faced by the nation's minorities. This film provides considerable stimulus to such concerns, some pointers about the role of local initiatives and community action, and a clear indication that improvements in the nation's inner cities will require policy changes and new investments by the federal government.

Ray Bromley, Department of Geography & Planning

GLPOLCUL

Title:	# Canada: True North—A Song for Québec
Producer:	National Film Board of Canada and WTVS/Detroit in association with the Global Television Network
Director:	Dorothy Todd Henaut
Distributor:	Encyclopaedia Britannica Educational Corp.
Release Date:	1988
Technical:	59 min./ color/ English with some French dialog with subtitles
Purchase Price:	$195
Rental:	varies (available from Penn State)
Presentation:	Documentary with narration, archival footage, and interviews

Content: *Canada: True North—A Song for Québec* opens in Montreal with a brief introduction by journalist Robert MacNeil, who was born and raised in that city. MacNeil readily admits that, like most English-speaking Québecers growing up in the second-largest French-speaking city in the world, he chose to ignore the language and culture of the French-speaking majority. The remainder of the film documents the history of the Québec separatist movement as experienced by singer Pauline Julien and poet Gerald Godin, two of the movement's key players and one of Québec's most famous couples. Pauline and Gerald met in 1962 when he was a journalist and struggling poet, and she was one of Québec's most popular singers. Both knew first-hand the frustrations and limitations of being French-speaking Québecers and both chose to express their pride in being French through their art.

Classroom Use: This film is appropriate for viewing in French-language courses as well as in courses dealing with cultural and linguistic diversity.

Critical Comments: English dominance over the French in Québec began a little over 200 years ago when Québec City, which had been settled by the French in 1534, was captured by the English under the command of General James Wolfe. As a result of that defeat, French-speaking Québecers became second-class citizens in their own land and spent the next two centuries fighting for the right to speak their language and enjoy their rich culture.

Following World War II, nationalist feelings on the part of French-speaking Canadians living in Québec began to grow. Forced conscription during the war, which required that Québecois be sent to Europe to defend England, surely added to the resentment French Canadians already felt toward their English oppressors. It was not until the late 1950s, however, with the death of prime minister Maurice Duplessis —who, although French, had continuously played into the hands of the English—that French-speaking Québecers demanded to, once again, be "masters in their own house." This could only happen, many believed, if Québec seceded from the rest of Canada and became an independent nation.

In 1960, the desire for self-rule proved to be the catalyst which brought about what was to become known as the "Quiet Revolution." However, it was still two decades before, under the leadership of prime minister René Lévesque, the people of Québec were given the opportunity to decide, by referendum, whether to become a sovereign nation or to remain a Canadian province. Those 20 years, while exhilarating ones for French-speaking Canadians, were also violent ones, as the terrorist group known as the FLQ (Québec Liberation Front) used kidnappings, murder, and bombings to draw attention to the separatists' cause.

Although past and recent referenda have gone down to defeat, those wishing to see the French language and culture survive and thrive in Québec have realized some gains. Language laws requiring that commercial signs be written in French only have been passed and are strictly enforced. As for the separatist movement, many believe that the dream really died in 1987 with the sudden death of René Lévesque. Those who still support it insist that the secession movement has not been abandoned but that it has simply been "put on the back burner," where it will simmer for a while before coming to a boil again at some future time.

Canada: True North—A Song for Québec provides an accurate, condensed history of English dominance over the French province of Québec in matters of government, business, industry, and language. The film cleverly presents the history of the sepa-

ratist movement through the recollections of Pauline Julien and Gerald Godin as they watch, and give their reactions to, archival film footage of the movement. This technique adds a human touch to the documentary, making it more interesting and allowing viewers to feel as though they have been invited into the Godin's home to listen as they reminisce about what was for them, and many others, the most exciting, albeit disappointing, period in Québec's history.

Christine Pearce, Department of French Studies

USIMMRAC

Title:	**Carved in Silence**
Producer:	Felicia Lowe, Asian Women United
Director:	Felicia Lowe
Distributor:	National Asian-American Telecommunications Association (NAATA)/CrossCurrent Media
Release Date:	1987
Technical:	45 min. / color / English, Chinese dubbed in English
Purchase Price:	$375
Rental:	$65
Presentation:	The film uses recreated scenes, some documentary footage, and interviews with those who were processed at the immigration center called Angel Island

Content: The subject matter of the film, the story of Angel Island, California, the "Ellis Island of the West," has been discussed in several sources, including Him Mark Lai, Genny Lim, and Judy Yung's *Island: Poetry and History of Chinese Immigrants on Angel Island 1910–1940* (San Francisco, HOC-DOI publication, 1980). All the authors of that book were consultants for this project. The film focuses on Chinese Americans. Though other immigrants were processed at Angel Island, they were not subjected to the same type of scrutiny as Chinese immigrants. Unlike Ellis Island, where the immigrants were processed in a day or two, immigrants from China, facing the Chinese Exclusion Laws, were put through a grueling interrogation and physical examination

which could last from two weeks to two years. The Chinese entering the United States via Angel Island were typically sons of those who had immigrated before the exclusion laws were passed in 1882, or were fathers who were here sponsoring their sons, or were husbands who returned to China to bring back their wives. After the San Francisco earthquake of 1906, when the birth records of many residents were destroyed, some Chinese fraudulently sought to claim U.S. citizenship by birth. Angel Island and its intensive schedule of interrogation was set up to check such perceived misuse of the citizenship rights of entry. Consequently the immigration station became more like a functional prison. The officials asked questions to verify the true identity of the immigrant. Many of the immigrants, intimidated by the environment and the officials, gave erroneous responses and were deported back to China. This included many who were legitimate immigrants.

For the women, after a month-long journey and seasickness, the first encounter in America was an order to appear naked for a physical examination by a white doctor. This was often traumatic and shocking. It was followed by a period of confinement to make sure that no one had contagious diseases. Husbands and wives, even those traveling together on the trip, were separated in men's barracks and women's barracks and not allowed to communicate. And one by one, separately, the immigration inspectors interrogated the passengers. If the information the inspectors had did not match the responses in every minute detail, the immigrant was ''failed'' and deported. Many, out of sheer fright and confusion, gave wrong answers or forgot details. The processes of interrogation and appeal, pending deportation, took many months during which the person was kept on the island. The title of the film, *Carved in Silence,* refers to the poems the detainees at Angel Island carved on the walls of the rooms, as they waited months and sometimes years within sight of San Francisco, unable to disembark.

Classroom Use: A very well-made film, *Carved in Silence* is suitable for use at all levels of instruction. Some of the early history of Chinese immigration is covered, so that students do not need much prior preparation. The film is obviously useful in American history courses, in courses on race and ethnicity, and in a range of diversity courses. The interviews are nicely organized so that the sadness and frustration of those who went through the experience are conveyed directly to the viewer. The film would also be useful for a discussion of civil rights.

Critical Comments: The film is quite fast-paced and the recreations and reenactments give it a dramatic intensity that documentaries alone don't have. The purpose of the film is to point to the racism and discriminatory practices experienced by some ethnic groups, and the sympathies of the film-maker are obvious. But I think this does not detract from the film; rather, it makes it a much more personal story.

Sucheta Mazumdar, Department of History

GLRELCUL

Title:	## Christians, Jews and Muslims in Medieval Spain
Series:	The Birth of the Middle Ages, Films for the Humanities
Producer:	Rafael Cortés, with cooperation of the Spanish Ministry of Culture
Distributor:	Films for the Humanities
Release Date:	1989
Technical:	52 min. / color / English
Purchase Price:	$159
Rental:	$75 per single day
Presentation:	Documentary consisting of contemporary color film footage of various Spanish locales with narration in English by Robert Lancaster; some dramatizations of medieval scenes; footage without narration accompanied by various examples of medieval Iberian music

Content: This film traces the history of Christian, Jewish, and Muslim life in the Iberian peninsula from late Roman times through the Muslim Conquest of 711 to the Christian Reconquest of Spain which was completed in 1491. The major thematic emphasis is on the unique coexistence and fruitful symbiotic relationships of Muslims, Jews, and Christians under Muslim rule, and to some extent under restored Christian rule. The film stresses the fact that Spanish culture is an amalgam of influences from all three of these traditions. The film centers particularly on the city of Toledo as its example of cultural interchange, but highlights other Spanish locations as well. Particular attention is put on Jewish and Christian history in Spain; less attention is paid to the Muslim experience.

Classroom Use: This film would be valuable in courses in medieval culture and history, and Hispanic and Judaic studies, if the students are well-prepared before the film is shown.

Critical Comments: The film assumes a great deal of knowledge, mentioning without explanation the Visigoths, the Merovingians, Charlemagne, Cordova, Cluniac monasteries, Moses Maimonides, and Mozarabs, among many others. It is very useful in providing visual images of the art, architecture, and symbols of the various cultures of medieval Spain, but less reliable as an unsupported source of history. This may be because of the film's public relations nature: it is very anxious to stress the peaceful coexistence of Christianity, Islam, and Judaism in medieval Spain. What it does not make clear is that this coexistence was mostly under Muslim rule. The general intolerance of the Spanish Roman Catholic church and Spanish crown towards non-believers, which ultimately led to the disappearence of Muslims and the 1492 expulsion of all Jews, is not discussed at all, nor is the role of the Inquisition. In fact, the film's historical approach throughout is superficial and anecdotal, the tone resolutely upbeat.

Christians, Jews and Muslims in Medieval Spain is rather slow-moving. Moreover, its narrative is disjointed and out of chronological order; detailed discussion of the Visigoths (seventh and eighth centuries) comes at the end of the film, after discussions of the Muslims (eighth to twelfth centuries), and such Jewish thinkers as Moses Maimonides (d. 1204). This film's visual and musical images bring an immediacy to the Spanish Middle Ages, but it is not an introduction for the uninitiated. It would be most useful as a review and enrichment of material already taught.

Judith Baskin, Department of Judaic Studies

USPOLRAC

Title:	**The Civil War: Episode One—The Cause, 1861**
Series:	The Civil War
Producers:	Ken and Ric Burns, for Florentine Films and WETA/TV, Washington, D.C.
Distributor:	PBS Video
Release Date:	1989
Technical:	99 min. / color, b&w / English
Purchase Price:	$79.95
Rental:	n/a
Presentation:	Documentary series produced for television (9 episodes, more than 11 hours total viewing time); narrated by David McCullough
Study Guide:	An educational resource package including teacher's guide, Civil War map, timeline, etc., available from PBS Video
Awards:	A landmark series, widely praised

Content: The *Civil War* series by award-winning documentary filmmaker Ken Burns, was five years in the making. The nine episodes vividly present the entire sweep of the war: "from the battlefields to the homefronts, from politicians and generals to the enlisted men and their families, from the causes of the war and the opening guns at Fort Sumter, to the stillness at Appomattox and Lincoln's assassination and beyond." It is a remarkable, indeed, unprecedented portrait of the most terrible war in American history. The greatest virtue of this series is that it successfully refocuses attention on slavery as the taproot of sectional discord and civil war. Seen from this perspective, the Civil War emerges as something very much more than battles, generals, troop movements, and politicians—the traditional "stuff" of Civil War documentaries.

Episode One—The Cause, 1861 is about the role of blacks as agitators (Douglass, etc.), soldiers, and contraband, and about women, some of whom spent the entire war at the front. Also unprecedented is the focus on the lowly foot soldiers who left diaries and letters of their experiences, and on the impact of the war on family life and hometowns, from Vermont to Florida. Most importantly, the series demonstrates how the war transformed America. The most dramatic example of the political and social change wrought by the war was the transformation of slaves into free laborers and "equal" citizens. Complementing the wealth of archival photographs—some seen here for the very first time—the beautiful cinematography, and the original period music, is a narrative which reflects the input of some of the country's principal Civil War specialists, a narrative read by the likes of Jeremy Irons, Julie Harris, Morgan Freeman, and Shelby Foote, the principal on-camera commentator.

Critical Comments: It was called the war between the North and the South, between the blue and the grey, but it was much more. The opening episode of this series is particularly effective in demonstrating just what the war was about: what began as a bitter dispute over union and states' rights ended as a struggle over the meaning of freedom in America. Indeed, as David McCullough reminds us, there was never a moment in the nation's history when slavery was not a sleeping serpent; it lay coiled up under the table during the deliberations at the Constitutional Convention, and owing to the invention of the cotton gin, it was more than half awake thereafter.

On the all-important question of the impact of slavery on the slave family, the documentary takes a sensible middle-of-the-road position. We learn that a slave entered the world in a one-room, dirt-floored shack, drafty in winter, reeking in summer; that slave cabins spread pneumonia, typhus, cholera, lockjaw, and tuberculosis; that a child who survived to be sent to the fields at 12 was likely to have worms, rotten teeth, dysentery, and malaria; and that fewer than four in a hundred would live to be 60. And yet, slaves confronted the system whenever possible: they resisted enslavement and, more importantly, they struggled to hold their families together under the worst of conditions. In decisive ways, however, they could not control those conditions, and this lack of control crippled many thousands of men and women and did have heartrending consequences for the relations, roles, and identities of all.

The opening episode is also especially good in defining what might be described as the American National Character. As historian Shelby Foote notes, ''Any understanding of this nation has to be based on an understanding of the Civil War. It defined us. If you are going to understand the American character in the 20th century, then you need to learn about this enormous catastrophe of the middle of the 19th century.'' The impact of the Civil War on the country is revealed in statistics: three million Americans fought in the war; 600,000 Americans, two percent of the population, died; American homes became army headquarters; American churches and schoolhouses sheltered the dying; large foraging armies swept over American farms and burned American towns; Americans slaughtered one another wholesale in their cornfields and peach orchards. In two days of fighting at Shiloh, more Americans died than in all previous American wars combined!

Finally, the opening episode introduces the cast of characters—Lincoln, Grant, Lee, Douglass, Clara Barton, Jefferson Davis, et al.—and offers little-known information about them. The crusade to abolish slavery, the abolitionist movement, is seen here for what it was, a powerful catalyst for bringing on the war, and a movement which broadened the war aims to include emancipation and equality in addition to the goal to preserve the union.

Background reading on topics dealt with in this opening episode can be found in:

Dudley Taylor Cornish. *The Sable Arm: Negro Troops in the Union Army, 1861–1865.* Norton, 1966.

Merton L. Dillon. *The Abolitionists: Growth of a Dissenting Minority.* Northern Illinois University Pr., 1974.

Elizabeth Fox-Genovese. *Within the Plantation Household: Black and White Women of the Old South.* University of North Carolina Pr., 1988.

William W. Freehling. *Prelude to Civil War.* Harper & Row, 1966.

—— *The Road to Disunion: Secessionist at Bay, 1776–1854.* Oxford University Pr., 1990.

William S. McFeely. *Frederick Douglass.* Norton, 1991.

Stephen B. Oates. *Abraham Lincoln: The Man behind the Myth.* Harper & Row, 1984.

Stephen Sears. *The Landscape Turned Red: The Battle of Antietam.* Ticknor & Fields, 1984.

Geoffrey C. Ward. *The Civil War: An Illustrated History.* Knopf, 1990.

George A. Levesque, Department of Africana Studies

GLETHCUL

Title:	**A Clash of Cultures**
Series:	The Africans: The Triple Heritage (program 8 of 9), part of the Annenberg/CPB Collection
Producer:	Peter Bates, for the British Broadcasting Co. and WETA, Washington, D.C.
Director:	Charles Hobson
Distributor:	Intellimation
Release Date:	1986
Technical:	60 min. / color / English / close-captioned
Purchase Price:	$29.95 (each cassette)
Rental:	No rental; can preview up to 21 days
Presentation:	Documentary, written and narrated by Ali A. Mazrui
Study Guide:	Available for purchase separately is the book *The Africans: A Reader* by Ali A. Mazrui ($14.95); a study guide is available for $8.95.

Content: This video explores African cultural adaptation to outside forces, primarily European colonialism and Moslem encroachment. The narrator, Ali A. Mazrui, who grew up in Mombasa, takes viewers on a wide-ranging tour of various African locations where the indigenous population has adapted and manipulated colonial influences in order to create its own unique and composite cultural identity.

Mazrui tells the viewer that Africa is in the throes of ''cultural compromise and confusion'' as a result of the ways in which indigenous practices have been affected by foreign ways of living and thinking. There are many fascinating examples to illustrate this point: Ethiopians who practice Judaism and long to immigrate to Israel, contemporary university students in Nigeria who take courses in traditional divination, and middle-class women in the Ivory Coast who buy elaborate white wedding gowns from Europe and incorporate them into non-Christian ceremonies. With little transition the video moves rapidly from one African culture to another—11 different countries in all—noting the distinctive characteristics of each while simultaneously suggesting that there is a Pan-African sensibility that has been affected drastically by foreign intervention. Using various examples from particular cultures, the video

makes the point that enormous differences in world views sometimes have created conflict between African and European or Moslem ways of life. Some of the major issues include cultural adaptation in religious practices, styles of architecture, health care, language, dress codes, and community rituals.

Classroom Use: This video might be of use in the classroom if it were introduced or followed with contextual and historical information about colonization in Africa. It could be used in courses in Africana studies, anthropology, and sociology as a way of introducing students to the notion of cultural diversity and some of the ways in which cultural practices may be transmitted, annihilated, and adapted.

Critical Comments: One of the problems with the video is its attempt to make sweeping generalizations about all African societies, without sufficient attention to the specific histories and circumstances distinctive to particular groups and geographic areas. Although I found *The Africans: A Clash of Cultures* useful in providing a basic introduction to some of the complexities of African culture and history, I would have preferred a more sophisticated analysis of the impact of colonization on indigenous societies. On the one hand, Mazrui disputes the notion that African cultures have been displaced or destroyed by foreign encroachment, arguing instead that the melding of traditional African customs and European or Moslem practices has created rich and fascinating new composites that are still meaningful for African peoples. In other moments, Mazrui comments that because of foreign encroachment ''we Africans seem to have lost our way.'' He notes that colonialism and exploitation have resulted in a confusion of values and a dramatic rise in mental illness among Africans. However, there is little critique of capitalism and colonialism as systemic forces that have radically altered African societies.

In a section that focuses on gender roles and the effects of westernization, there is some mention of the ways in which the white, Euro-American beauty standard has affected some African women's self-perceptions. Unfortunately, the video is completely structured from a male point of view. Never do we hear women's own voices or views of their situations. Toward the end, the video concludes on a stronger note, critiquing Euro-American influence on African dress and languages and arguing that, while the appropriation and incorporation of colonial influences do not necessarily lead to the destruction of existing societies, indigenous practices should be the foundation for African cultures. However, this message is confusing when so much of the video makes political dynamics and international intervention invisible by failing to mention or critique them.

Although it ends on a stronger note than it begins, this video may or may not help American students see Africa as anything more than a far and exotic site where the people are ''other'' or are very removed from life as we know it. There is little sense of connectedness between the policies and histories of first world nations and the current situation in Africa, nor do I believe that American students who watch the video will come away with the idea that colonial powers are in any way responsible for, or involved in, what has happened to Africans.

Linda Pershing, Department of Women's Studies

USAGESOC

Title:	**Coming of Age**
Producers:	Josh Hanig and Dennis Hicks
Director:	Josh Hanig
Distributor:	New Day Films
Release Date:	1983
Technical:	60 min. / color / English
Purchase Price:	$570
Rental:	$65
Presentation:	Scenes from consciousness-raising sessions and spontaneous interpersonal encounters that reveal the tensions between young men and women and varying racial or ethnic groups
Awards:	Blue Ribbon, American Film and Video Festival; Special Jury Prize, U.S. Film Festival; First Prize, Big Muddy Film Festival

Content: Using selected footage of group sessions, conversations, and public speakers, this video explores American teenagers who are grappling with issues of race, gender, and class differences. A group of 180 young people and 25 adult counselors gather for one week at a summer camp in the mountains outside of Los Angeles. The teenagers, male and female, come from a wide range of racial and ethnic backgrounds and economic circumstances—"from gang members to student body presidents"—to confront personal conflicts that are created by racial tensions, sexuality, and social differences. Viewers are informed that all participants in the camp agreed to be filmed, with the explicit understanding that the cameras would be turned off if anyone made such a request. In small and larger group sessions that focus on increasing levels of awareness and personal interaction, teenagers express their most intimate feelings about race, class, family, and sexuality. The video captures revealing moments between young people of different backgrounds as well as candid—and sometimes explosive—confrontations between males and females, heterosexuals and gay men. The conclusion includes interviews with several participants one year later as they reflect back upon their experiences at the camp and the effects it had on their lives and subsequent relationships with others. *Coming of Age*

was directed by Josh Hanig, who also directed and produced *Men's Lives* (see p. 131).

Classroom Use: *Coming of Age* may be appropriate for classroom viewing at the undergraduate level, providing it is properly introduced (see comments below). It would be of use in addressing diversity issues with regard to race, gender, and homophobia. It might be used in courses in American culture, sociology, women's studies, racial relations in the United States, or psychology.

Critical Comments: The video addresses some important issues, including the prejudices that young people inherit from their parents and society, men's fears of intimacy with other men, male prejudices against women, and the strained relationships between not only whites and African Americans, but also between African Americans and Hispanics, whites and Asians, Asians and African Americans, and heterosexual and gay men (unfortunately, lesbians are never mentioned in the video). It can be a useful tool for helping students get in touch with the emotions concerning racial and gender differences, and it fosters the recognition that racism, sexism, and homophobia are not simply abstract issues, but that they affect personal, everyday interactions.

The one-hour documentary *Coming of Age* captures the interactions of 180 young people gathered (with 25 counselors) for a one-week summer camp outside Los Angeles. Greatly varying backgrounds result in tense confrontations over sexuality, race, class, and religion. (Courtesy New Day Films)

However, the video is based on the assumption that a therapeutic, psychological model is sufficient for dealing with prejudice and injustice. There is not much focus on the societal or systemic nature of racism or sexism, and the video lacks the in-depth analysis that moves bigotry and misogyny from the private to the public realms. There is some attention, for example, to the experiences of women who are tired of being devalued and physically abused, but there is no analysis or commentary about why this occurs so frequently in American society. In addition, the video is somewhat dated. The hairstyles and dress of teenagers living in the 1960s and 1970s may distance some contemporary students from the message of the film. In places such as a lengthy segment in which a young man cries during a group session about men abusing women, the video seems strained and overdramatized, and this may alienate some viewers.

Linda Pershing, Department of Women's Studies

USGENSOC

Title:	**Common Threads: Stories from the Quilt**
Producers:	Bill Couturie, Robert Epstein, Jeffrey Friedman, for Telling Pictures/Couturie Co.
Directors:	Robert Epstein, Jeffrey Friedman
Distributor:	Direct Cinema
Release Date:	1989
Technical:	79 min. / color / English / close-captioned
Purchase Price:	$45
Rental:	n/a
Presentation:	A documentary featuring interviews, voice-over narration by Dustin Hoffman, and scenes from the NAMES Project events
Award:	Academy Award for Best Feature Documentary, 1989

Content: *Common Threads* is a video about AIDS and the lives it has affected. It is emotionally charged and intended to reveal the human element behind the cold statistics of the AIDS epidemic. Through interviews with loved ones, and sometimes with the victims themselves, it tells the stories of five males from different walks of life—including an Olympic athlete, an 11-year-old child, and a married man who struggled with drug addiction—who contracted and eventually died of AIDS. They are interviewed by the filmmakers with great sensitivity and described by loved ones as they battle this debilitating and misunderstood disease. Toward the end of the video the viewer learns that these five people are now commemorated in panels of an ever-growing quilt that would cover over 14 acres if displayed at one time—the NAMES Project AIDS Memorial Quilt. The video, narrated by Dustin Hoffman, tells of their lives and deaths, the support they found, the enormous obstacles they faced, and the thoughts and feelings of the loved ones they left behind who made quilt panels to honor them.

There is a splendid companion volume with plenty of color photographs of quilt panels: *The Quilt: Stories from the NAMES Project* by Cindy Ruskin (New York: Pocket Books, 1988).

Classroom Use: *Common Threads* is appropriate for classroom viewing at the university level, both undergraduate and graduate. I have used this video with great success in courses on diversity in the visual arts, gender, and the study of folklore. It could easily be incorporated into courses about gender roles, American culture, social movements, and gay culture.

Critical Comments: The video encourages viewers to think about the AIDS epidemic in terms of the tragic loss of individual human life while cel-

ebrating the enormous creativity and resilience of the human spirit. The goals of the video are to educate the viewer and to advocate the need to find a cure for AIDS. There is an attempt to demonstrate that this disease is affecting a wide range of people—gay and straight, black and white, adults and children (although it pays little attention to the spread of the epidemic among women, see comments below). It decries the ways in which governmental leaders and bureaucrats have been slow to recognize the enormous proportions of the disease as it spreads at an alarming rate throughout the American population. However, *Common Threads* manages all of this without seeming dogmatic or cynical, largely because of the warmth and humor of its five subjects, and the beauty and meaning of the quilt. The video offers a fascinating study of how art forms, which are conventionally seen as domestic and privatized, are often used for public, social, and political purposes.

One of the few shortcomings of the video is that it doesn't adequately address AIDS among women, and the only African-American AIDS victim it depicts is a former drug addict, which only fuels already-existing stereotypes. I suggest that these problems be addressed directly in introducing and discussing the video.

Linda Pershing, Department of Women's Studies

GLRACECO

Title:	## Contact: The Yanomami Indians of Brazil
Producer:	Geoffrey O'Connor, Realis Pictures
Distributor:	Filmakers Library
Release Date:	1991
Technical:	28 min. / color / English
Purchase Price:	$295
Rental:	$55
Presentation:	Documentary
Awards:	Gold Award, Houston International Film Festival, 1990; American Film and Video Festival, 1990

Content: This short film informs the viewer about the lives of others far removed from the Western world. The Yanomami Indians are one of several indigenous groups still inhabiting the South-American rainforest; many other groups have been exterminated. The film portrays the interactions between the indigenous groups and non-Indians, specifically gold miners who are flocking to Amazonia for its buried riches in the 20th century.

Critical Comments: The video paints a clear picture of the causes and consequences of intercultural contact of the type characteristic of North America in the 16th through 19th centuries. The Indians receive some material goods in exchange for their land, livelihood, and lives: soap, metal tools, plastic buckets, and guns, to name a few. They also have malaria, respiratory diseases, infectious diseases, cultural disintegration, and genocide.

The overall similarity between the decimation and relocation of the Yanomami of Brazil and the same fate of the Cherokee of northern Georgia in the 19th century is staggering. From the discovery of gold to the forced removal of the native populations, the script runs true. The justifications espoused by the miners and their representatives are as shallow as they are provocative. The Indians, we are assured, love the miners, welcome them to their lands, and cannot live without the benefits of the civilization provided. We see sick children, denuded forests, and dispirited populations as evidence for this "love" of mining. In a particularly moving scene, we are told by a storekeeper how grateful the Indians are for the presence of the miners and their goods. This scene follows one that clearly depicts the Indians' fear and depression at being reduced to begging for rice from this same storekeeper.

In the face of decimation from introduced diseases, the Indians respond with heightened shamanistic curing rituals—designed to rid the patients of the source of the illness—and visits to the overwhelmed missionary nursing station, where medicines are taken to remove the symptoms of the illness. This depiction illustrates well the mixture of traditional and western medicine so commonly observed in traditional societies under attack from new pathogens.

Finally, a Yanomami spokesman offers us a sadly prophetic view of his tribe's fate: if the destruction of the forests continues, it will not simply be the death of the Yanomami, but of all humans in all places. Such global concerns from an isolated Yanomami are reasons for pause.

Richard G. Wilkinson, Department of Anthropology

USGENCLA

Title:	**Crystal Lee Jordan**
Producer:	KERA TV, Dallas
Distributor:	Indiana University Audio Visual Center
Release Date:	1974
Technical:	16 min. / color / English / 16mm only
Purchase Price:	$240
Rental:	$12.15
Presentation:	Documentary with narration

Content: *Crystal Lee Jordan* is the story of a textile worker's struggles to organize J. P. Stevens employees into a union in Roanoke, North Carolina, and to secure company recognition of the group. The film *Norma Rae* was based on this woman.

Critical Comments: *Crystal Lee Jordan* is a poignant portrayal of the struggles of a white union organizer at the J. P. Stevens textile factory in Roanoke, North Carolina, who conducted a door-to-door campaign to solicit the support of coworkers. While the viewer witnesses the creation of the union through Jordan's eyes, hers is the story of the many women and men who participated. J. P. Stevens was a powerful economic force with which to be reckoned. It owned the bank and other business enterprises in the town, so there were far-reaching implications for the involvement of these people in union activities. Jordan's activism challenged notions of race and gender in the South during the 1960s and 1970s.

The film depicts the tactics the company used to discredit Jordan and other women. Company officials drew upon their community's conservative views of a woman's place to attack the women's characters and other aspects of their personal lives.

Through their involvement in the organizing activities, the women learned that it would also be necessary to change their relationships with their families. Many of their husbands assumed the chores of cooking, cleaning, and childcare that previously had been defined as woman's work. Children also were drawn into the movement.

The women also defied traditional race relations through their interracial organizing activities. Black and white workers realized that they were being exploited and refused to yield to racial bigotry. They created, in essence, a benevolent organization that fought for better working conditions. Their efforts were successful and they affiliated with the Textile Workers Union of America.

This film, like most that highlight an individual's accomplishments, creates an image of a person who is larger than life. It would have been useful to know more about the supporting cast of workers who were always present with Jordan. Beyond this the film gives the viewer a rare glimpse of women laborers' attempts to address their exploitation; simultaneously, these activities are personalized through the experiences of Jordan.

Lillian S. Williams, Department of Women's Studies

USRACETH

Title:	**Do the Right Thing**
Producer:	Spike Lee, for Forty Acres
Director:	Spike Lee
Distributor:	MCA Home Video
Release Date:	1989
Technical:	120 min. / color / English / close-captioned
Purchase Price:	$89.95
Rental:	n/a
Presentation:	Dramatization, originally produced as a motion picture
Award:	Orson Welles Film Award, 1990

Content: Set in Brooklyn, New York, in the 1980s, this film provides an African-American perspective on race relations in the post-civil rights movement era. It raises the following question: Has the dismantling of the legal foundations of racial segregation been accompanied by the erosion of racism? Spike Lee, its producer and director, is unambiguous: racial and ethnic tensions pervade the United States. The film explores racism's form in the current era and asks: Can race relations in the United States be changed through peaceful legislative means or does it require a recourse to violence? This is a powerful, compelling portrait of the black experience in America.

Classroom Use: I have used this film a number of times in undergraduate classes and students have found it moving and compelling. It has always led to fruitful class discussions. People of color have appreciated it because it represents an African-American perspective.

Critical Comments: The story revolves around events that occur in a pizza store owned by an Italian-American family (a father and his two sons) in a predominantly black neighborhood. The interaction between the black customers and Sal—the owner of the pizza store—and his two sons is the dramatic center of the film. For example, Mookie (played by Spike Lee) is a young black man who works for Sal. He is portrayed as lacking any loyalty to Sal, largely unmo-

tivated, and carefree bordering on being irresponsible in his approach to work. Does he represent, as his sister implies in the film, the lazy black man who shirks responsibilities to get by with as little as possible? Is this a statement about the failure of the black man or community? Or do his carefree work attitudes reflect his resistance, even hostility, to working in a dead-end job for whites who profit from exploiting the black community? Does the fact that the only businesses shown in this community are either owned by Italian-Americans or Koreans make a statement about racism in America or about the failure of the black culture?

The power of the film lies in the fact that its characters dramatize race relations in complex, ambiguous ways. People aren't presented as simply racist or not; everyone is shown as holding racist attitudes. Yet, even the most racist people in the film are depicted as ambiguous. For example, Sal's older son repeatedly makes racist statements. Yet he also admits that he idolizes several black musicians, athletes, and actors. Sal is often seen as someone who genuinely cares about his black customers and their community. Yet he fails to understand even the most basic elements of black culture and ultimately acts out his racism by responding in an inappropriately violent way to the challenges of a young black man. Similarly, Mookie is portrayed, at one level, as someone who is not racist. Yet it is Mookie who ultimately turns against Sal and sparks a race riot.

Indeed, one of the themes of the film is that racial tensions are endemic and their potentially explosive violence can easily be tapped. And it is not simply black-white tension that is volatile; the film shows that racism is pervasive. Whites hold racist attitudes towards blacks who in turn exhibit racist feelings towards Asians; Asians hate Jews while Hispanics appear in tension with all the above groups. Between the races there is little understanding and little meaningful communication. At times, the film suggests that each ethnic or racial group has evolved its own culture and created almost separate islands that allow little communication between them. It's clear, for example, that Sal and his sons have no understanding of the black community they've worked in for two decades. Similarly, there is little understanding of Sal's Italian-American cultural values by his black customers. Violence is an ever-present possibility even though no one wants it. It comes as no surprise that the final scene of the film is one of violence. A fight breaks out between Sal and one of the young black men. Police are called and two white policemen end up killing the young man. This is not, we are led to believe, an intentional act, but an almost unconscious expression of racism.

Blacks in the film are presented as complex persons with integrity and dignity. Stereotypes are avoided. A sense of a black culture with its unique dress, language, and lifestyle codes is presented in interesting ways. Yet Spike Lee does not avoid raising controversial issues about black life. For example, Mookie is repeatedly taken to task by his sister for not holding down a job and for not living up to his full responsibilities to his girlfriend and child. What is the message? Is it that black men are irresponsible or that racism has victimized them by denying them good jobs or by robbing them of their self-pride and motivation?

The film does have some flaws. Chief among them is the fact that women do not play a central role. To the extent that women appear—and they do so largely in peripheral roles—they function in fairly stereotypical ways (e.g., in domestic roles as strong figures angry towards black men). Also, while Spike Lee aims to present black life with a certain pride and integrity, it comes across as somewhat sterile or purified. Everyone seems dressed so fashionably well; the streets seem uncharacteristically clean for New York City; not one person smokes, uses drugs, or drinks. There's an upbeat, almost sustained cheerful feel to the characters that seems unconvincing.

The message of the film is ambiguous. The final scene suggests that racism is firmly entrenched in the United States. The white policemen killing the young black man suggests that whites have all the power and privileges today, as in the past. Yet, the film is not simply a story of racism destroying America. There are hopeful moments. Many characters are depicted as beyond racism; scenes of racial harmony and possibilities for mutual understanding and respect are presented; blacks are not presented as victims; progress has clearly been made. The viewer is left to make up his or her own mind about where we go from here.

Steven Seidman, Department of Sociology

GLGENECO

Title:	**The Double Day**
Producer:	Jane Stubbs, for International Women's Film Project
Director:	Helena Solberg-Ladd
Distributor:	Cinema Guild
Release Date:	1975
Technical:	53 min. / color / dialog in Spanish, narration in English
Purchase Price:	$595
Rental:	$85
Presentation:	Documentary with interviews and recordings of women speaking in a consciousness-raising session; footage shot in Argentina, Bolivia, Mexico, and Venezuela

Content: The film depicts the situation of working women in Latin America. It emphasizes the strategies poor women have undertaken as new capitalist relations developed. It shows the frustration of Bolivian Indian women who need to find jobs but who are discriminated against in the factories for being Indian. It describes the exploitation of Bolivian miners, both men and women, and emphasizes the fact that women are not employed in the mines and are left with no source of income if and when their husbands or sons die in the mines. The tendency of these women to establish strong solidarity networks, to organize, and strike although their situation is nearly hopeless is also discussed.

The film spends quite some time talking to and commenting on the large percentage of women in Latin America who make a living as servants or "domestics." Many of these women would prefer to work in factories instead and be treated with some dignity by their bosses but are unable to do so. In one case we see a factory that only employs men, supposedly because of the skill required to perform those jobs, according to the employer interviewed, who adds that women are preferred for certain tasks that require "patience."

Editor's note: Although the reviewer judged this video, on balance, unsuited to the particular diversity courses at the University at Albany, I have included it in the guide as worthy of consideration for use elsewhere, depending on local needs, audience background, and options. Three such videos appear in the guide.

Classroom Use: The film would be appropriate for courses on work, Latin America, or gender and class in Latin America; however, I do not think the film provides much information or interesting graphic stimulus. It may still incite class discussions, although I cannot recommend it strongly. The film is of average artistic quality and the sound is good so that the overlapping of both languages does not interfere with the comprehension.

Critical Comments: In addition to its design limitations, some of the content is dated. Women in many Latin-American countries are now asked to take jobs traditionally taken by men, especially where migration for men is more common due to the limited jobs and low pay in their own countries. Where new labor-intensive industries have opened up, usually motivated by the search for cheaper labor, women are being employed. Gender biases, discrimination, and poverty do continue, but the film is rather slow and often repetitive on these issues. Several interviews do not represent the wide range of situations in which women are found. The film describes some of the problems women face in their need for cash and work, but all sectors (rural, manufacturing, clerical) are not well-represented. There are other films about women in Latin America which focus on individual countries and socioeconomic sectors that may serve the purpose of class discussion more efficiently than this particular video.

Liliana Goldin, Department of Anthropology

USIMMLAW

Title:	**El Mojado (The Wetback)**
Producer:	J. J. Meeker
Director:	Danny Lyon
Distributor:	Facets Video, Facets Multimedia Center
Release Date:	1974
Technical:	14 min. / color / dialogs in English and Spanish, with subtitles for most
Purchase Price:	$49.95
Rental:	$10 for members of Facets Video Club
Presentation:	Documentary

Content: The video focuses on the contemporary issue of Mexican workers who migrate illegally to the United States through the Mexican-Texas border country. The camera follows Eduardo from Ciudad Juarez to Albuquerque in his search to provide for his family. The video also includes interviews with other undocumented workers and members of the U.S. Border Patrol.

Classroom Use: This video is suitable for use in courses on contemporary Mexico, Latinos/Hispanics in the United States, immigration studies, and American studies.

Critical Comments: As the title comes on the screen, the background shows a poster used for identifying and classifying different kinds of shoe soles, which is hanging on the wall of a border patrol office. The first shots are of a Mexican migrant walking through the country near the border. We hear an immigration policeman talking about his work. He tells of illegal migrants hiding in trees or in people's homes. He speaks of hunting for them and says, "This is the most interesting part of the job. We really like it because it's just like a hunter, only you're stalking a human being, and that really makes it a lot more fun." The interview with this official is interspersed with brief scenes of workers from Mexico.

A conversation between several migrants who walked from Mexico to Texas is shown. They discuss distances, checkpoints, their personal experiences. One of them states that it took him seven days to walk to San Antonio, having crossed the border at Palomas. He says that after some 80 kilometers (50 miles), one can slow down "because that's where they really check every day." Another describes his experience in a rather rambling narrative style: "We walked in the mountains. There was a gringo there looking for treasure. If we helped him, he'd give us a ride to Albuquerque. He told us to sleep in a cave and build a fire to keep the animals away. He said to burn a trunk, and in the morning he would bring us food. Then the patrol came. They said, 'Hello, got a lot of work?' 'We did, but now you're going to take us.' They asked, 'You have papers?' 'No, we don't.' 'Who do you work for?' 'Some man from here.' 'Is he around?' 'I think so.' 'Let's go,' they said and took us to Hatch. One of the other men asks, 'Can you keep the photographs they're taking here?' 'No.' 'I don't like these things.' " When one of the men stands up to leave, the members of the group introduce themselves and say goodbye to each other.

The next scenes show migrants being picked up by the police, their documents being checked, and the men being questioned at the border patrol station. An immigration policeman asks such questions as: "Where were you born? What is your father's name? When were you born? How old are you? How many times have you been arrested in Mexico? Why? How much did you pay as a fine? How many times have you been picked up by the immigration police? When was the last time? How much money do you have?"

Although the questions are simple, the captives seem to have difficulty in answering or even understanding some of them. Views of the interrogation of various captured migrant workers are interspersed with shots of other Mexicans being picked up. The next scene is of one of the same men back in Mexico. He is building a house with crude concrete blocks, which he makes himself. He stops to rest and eat, entering a shack with a woodstove. While he eats, he listens to a broadcast in Spanish from a radio station in the United States. At the close of the broadcast, the ''Star Spangled Banner'' is played.

In the final sequence, we see the same Mexican man as above, walking back through the border country. An American immigration policeman talks by radio to another one who is patrolling the border by airplane. The latter does not think it will be possible to catch someone who has just been seen going into the mountains. The camera returns to the migrant worker shown before and continues to depict his journey back into the United States. Carrying a plastic bottle for water and a few belongings, he walks slowly along, both in the heat of day and at night. Here the video ends, in the same manner in which it began: with a scene of a migrant worker illegally entering the United States along the border between Texas and Mexico.

This film clearly conveys the notion that the illegal immigration of the Mexican worker is a continuous cycle, with secret entry, capture, and deportation followed by another illegal entry which reinitiates the cycle. In view of their living conditions in Mexico, the migrant workers, shown as poorly educated and socially marginal, have strong motivation for attempting to migrate, and, because the system of control at the border sometimes fails, they have hope that someday they will succeed. Until that day comes, they keep trying. Once in the United States, they at least have a chance to earn a few dollars through manual labor, until they are caught and deported by the immigration officials. Then they may try to enter again.

Brian F. Head, Department of Hispanic, Italian, and Portuguese Studies

USIMMECO

Title:	**El Norte**
Producer:	Anna Thomas
Director:	Gregory Nava
Distributor:	CBS/Fox Video
Release Date:	1984
Technical:	141 min. / color / Spanish and Kekchi with English subtitles; some English
Purchase Price:	$45.95
Rental:	n/a
Presentation:	Dramatization; originally a motion picture

Content: This film dramatizes the experience of Guatemalan migrants as they make their way to the United States. The film portrays the present-day experience of two young Guatemalan peasants, a brother and a sister, who leave their country when their father is assassinated by the military and their mother is interned. It illustrates the social, economic, and political forces which often lead Central-Americans to leave their country, enter illegally into Mexico, and then form part of the low-wage labor force in the United States.

Classroom Use: This film certainly falls within the subject matter deemed appropriate for the human diversity rubric. It provides a comparative international perspective on the issue of migration to the United States. It highlights differences between northern and southern cultures, but also retains the heterogeneity that exists among different Latin-American societies. The tone of the dramatization provides a collective balance highlighting negative and positive aspects of the migrant's societies of origin and destination. Faculty should consider integrating *El Norte* into social science courses, particularly those that treat the growth of ethnic minorities in the United States or compare the migratory experiences of different groups in a historical perspective. Other topics covered in the film include indigenous perceptions of other cultures, political authoritarianism in Latin America, systems of land tenure, economic impact of labor migration on receiving areas, low-wage labor markets, and the impact of migration on family structure.

Critical Comments: *El Norte* received critical acclaim when it was first shown in the United States. Its portrayal of Central-American migrants to the United States clashed with the often uninformed debates concerning the impact of Latin-American migration to the north. In a quite subtle but very effective manner, it points to the economic and political conditions that foment migration in the country of origin. Issues such as land tenure, political authoritarianism, and food insufficiency form the backdrop for the motivations of potential migrants. In addition, portrayals of living conditions in the United States, generally exaggerated by the media as well as by return migrants, serve as an attraction to the naive and unsuspecting migrant. The role of intermediary countries, such as Mexico in the case of *El Norte*, provides an often-overlooked aspect of international migration. The description of the low-wage labor market in the United States, and the instability of employment in this sector, is another interesting aspect of this film.

Carlos E. Santiago, Department of Latin American and Caribbean Studies

USIMMLAW

Title:	**El Otro Lado (The Other Side)**
Producer:	Danny Lyon
Distributor:	Facets Video, Facets Multimedia Center
Release Date:	1978
Technical:	60 min. / color / Spanish with subtitles in English, some English
Purchase Price:	$59.95
Rental:	$10 for members of Facets Video Club
Presentation:	Documentary

Content: This film depicts illegal migrant workers in Maricopa County, Arizona, in actual life and uses their real names. It is a compelling, true-to-life documentary. There is little dramatization nor is the film structured around any special sequence of events. It merely documents the routine activities of Mexican workers for whom periodic illegal migration to "el otro lado" is a way of life.

Classroom Use: Recommended for courses dealing with immigration, Latin-American studies, Mexico, and international relations.

Critical Comments: In the opening scene, a peasant farmer in central Mexico is shown tilling the soil. Two men are shown drinking; they laugh at a dog jumping up at a donkey. Old peasants and small children are carrying firewood along a dirt road. An inserted text provides the setting for the next scene: "Deep in Mexico two brothers sit in a plaza discussing a broken fuel pump. In a few days they will leave to work. With their father and some friends, they will ride a bus 1,300 miles north and enter the United States by walking through the desert. They call America 'el otro lado,' the other side."

In a plaza where there is an old cathedral, two young men are shown talking about problems with a vehicle. Much of their dialog lacks subtitles, but even without knowing what is being said in Spanish, it is apparent that they are having a routine, banal conversation. The men are Reginaldo and Francisco Garay. A small band of percussion and wind instruments plays lively Mexican music in the background. An inserted text describes the setting: "The Garay family live on an ejido, communal land distributed by the government. One man has accused another of planting trees on land not allotted to him."

The group of common people are assembled to discuss the matter. They have the tired, worn faces of those who have endured continuing hardship. They discuss when to plant the maguay tree, and compare this year's yield with that of last year. Views of everyday life are shown: children gathering fruit, men making cement blocks, women removing the grain from ears of corn.

The camera turns to a group of young men who are talking about their experiences as migrant workers in the United States. "This year I'm going to Texas." "Texas is full of *cabrones.* There is no state worse than Texas." "Last year I was caught four times." "Oh, then you're a regular client." [Laughter.]

The camera shows a young girl cooking in the street on an open fire. A storm is gathering. Soon heavy rainfall begins; it interrupts the street vendors. Most of the men go inside where they are shown drinking and playing pool. Partly sheltered, the band continues to play on the sidewalk. People protect themselves from the rain as best they can; some wrap sheets of plastic around their bodies. Inside, the singer of a band intones, "I was just a little boy when my father died. . . ." A young man flirts with a girl in the street as the rain subsides.

The next scene shows a bus heading north. It reaches the border of the United States. The camera provides a panoramic view of the mountains near the border; a barbed wire fence runs along the boundary. Several men are shown walking across the barren border country. Some are wrapped in blankets; most are carrying common plastic jugs for water, with few or no other belongings. The same group of men is shown around an open fire eating tortillas, canned sardines, and cold meat. In the

group are the two brothers, Reginaldo and Francisco Garay, and their father, D. Bernabe Garay. The latter jokes, "Like Christ, this is my last supper." The others laugh. One says, "With this meat, we can feast two days." The men discuss their plans, where they will work, and people who are against the migrants. One of them observes that if "La Migra" (the U.S. Immigration Service) does not catch them, they will be lucky. Another says that what he fears most is the airplane which patrols the border country.

The next scenes are from orchards in Maricopa County, Arizona. The men are shown walking along a road, then playing cards, talking and eating, and listening to radio broadcasts in Spanish. They sleep on the ground, wrapped in blankets. Their conversation is banal, often in a joking tone. (Almost all of it is without subtitles.) The men are shown entering orange groves, setting up long ladders, and picking the fruit, tree by tree. One of them sings about the problem of immigrating: "La Migra deports us but we come back again. The problem of the mojado could be easily solved. . . ." The solution proposed in his song is to marry an American, get a green card (for permanent residence), then be divorced. After the men fill their sacks with fruit, they empty them into bins, calling out their respective numbers in order to receive credit for the fruit they pick. A foreman keeps count; the workers watch him closely to make sure he gives them proper credit. They compare the yield of different trees.

In the evening, the men play cards, listen to music, and talk. They tell stories about their problems with the immigration officials. One of them notes that when the officials can't catch the "mojados," they destroy their belongings. They say that "La Migra" sometimes catches a few of the illegal migrant workers, but never very many. On Sundays, when the men are not working, they wash their clothing and take baths in a large channel used for irrigating the orchard. There is much talking and singing of sad, romantic Mexican songs on such occasions. Following a scene of the migrants during a day when they are not at work, a new scene shows them returning to the groves. Many of them are wrapped in blankets as they walk along the road. Some stop to burn brush in order to get warm. One man tells of sending money to Mexico by telegram. As the men arrive at the groves, they set up their ladders and resume their labor. The following inserted text comes on the screen: "Garza, the majordomo, records a number for each bag a worker picks. The men are suspicious that they might not be properly credited. Following a strike, pay has risen from 30 cents to 50 cents a sack of oranges."

The men watch a lift unloading the bins they have filled with fruit. More picking and loading of the bins is shown. While most of the men are young, some of them appear to be too old and tired to be climbing the ladders, picking the fruit, and carrying the heavy sacks. The camera shows bright sunshine coming through the trees. The lively Mexican music heard before, in the scenes at the plaza back in Mexico, returns to the soundtrack, as the film ends and the lists of participants and credits begin: ''The desert walk was reenacted by the following undocumented workers: Bernabe Garay, Francisco Garay, Reginaldo Garay. . . .''

Brian F. Head, Department of Hispanic, Italian, and Portuguese Studies

USRACSTE

Title:	**Ethnic Notions: Black People in White Minds**
Producer:	Marlon Riggs for KQED TV, San Francisco
Director:	Marlon Riggs
Distributor:	California Newsreel
Release Date:	1986
Technical:	56 min. / color, b&w / English
Purchase Price:	$295
Rental:	$75
Presentation:	Documentary on the iconography of American race relations narrated by Esther Rolle
Awards:	Peabody Award; 1989 National Emmy; Red Ribbon, American Film and Video Festival
Study Guide:	Free; also, 80-page program book, $10

Content: The focus of this video is on what historian George Fredrickson, who is featured in the documentary, has called the ''Black Image in the White Mind,'' and on what historian Leon Litwack has called ''the pornography of American race relations.'' It takes viewers on a voyage through American history, from the 1820s to the 1960s, for the purpose of illustrating how pervasive, long-standing, and pernicious anti-black stereotypes have been, and how they functioned to fuel American racism, and help white society justify slavery, segregation, economic exploitation, and lynching.

The video presents caricatures and stereotypes of black-Americans in film, fiction, television, advertisements, cartoons, greeting cards, popular songs, folklore, and household artifacts. Illustrative materials have been drawn from various archives, including the Archives for the Performing Arts in San Francisco, the National Archives, the Harvard Theater Collection, the National Museum of American History, the Library of Congress, and the Bancroft Library at The University of California/Berkeley. The video also presents informed commentary from scholars, many of them specialists in African-American history and literature from Berkeley and other Bay-area colleges and universities. Some dramatization is included (e.g., choreographer Leni Sloan on the career of Bert Williams).

The key questions addressed by this documentary are: how did the images and caricatures of black Americans (''loyal Toms,'' ''carefree Sambos,'' ''faithful mammies,'' ''coons'' and ''savage brutes'') shape the enduring and profoundly negative attitudes white Americans have of black people and black culture? To what extent have the old stereotypes persisted and have new stereotypes been created? And how will future generations judge contemporary American culture on its depiction of blacks and black-American culture?

Critical Comments: The racial caricatures paraded before viewers in this documentary were so pervasive that they came to be seen as a genuine reflection of reality; these were the images that decorated our homes, that amused us, and made us laugh. The images worked their way, insidiously, into the mainstream of American life. "Contained in these cultural images," observes Esther Rolle, "is the history of our national conscience, a conscience striving to reconcile the paradox of racism in a nation founded on human equality, a conscience coping with this profound contradiction through caricature."

From a historical perspective, this documentary has many strengths and a few glaring weaknesses. On the positive side, *Ethnic Notions* situates each stereotype historically, thereby demonstrating convincingly how white America's changing need to justify racism accounted for the prevailing stereotypes in any given period. The most portentous and contentious issue in the nation's history before the Civil War was slavery. Not surprisingly, the four decades before the war were fertile for the creation of some of the most enduring racial stereotypes. The happy Sambo became one of the classic portrayals of black men during the slavery era: carefree, irresponsible, reveling in the easy pleasures of food, dance, and song, his life was one of childlike contentment. Sambo was a necessary and convincing caricature because he mirrored the prevailing belief that slavery was good for the slave since it drew on his *natural* inferiority (blacks were enslaved because they were inferior, not inferior because they were enslaved) and willingness to serve.

The same was true for the black mammy who was portrayed as the antithesis of the ideal of white womanhood: fat, ugly, pitch black, asexual, and independent. Her inferiority was manifest when compared to the cult of true womanhood which depicted (white) women as beautiful, fragile, and dependent. Even the fugitives who managed to escape slavery, the so-called free blacks, who could be found in southern as well as northern cities, were seen in caricature as proof that blacks were naturally inferior and could not benefit from freedom. Zip Coon, a dandy and buffoon, mocked the notion of racial equality and conveniently served those who insisted that slavery was the natural lot of black people.

The emancipation period, the second largest historical era dealt with in the documentary, also illustrates in a compelling way the connection between national/sectional developments and stereotypical imagery. Slavery apologists had long defended slavery by arguing that the institution was a "positive good" because it kept the lid on the presumed natural negative Negro personality: Africans were bestial and savage, and the regimen and control of enslavement prevented blacks from reverting to their original condition. Now, in the post-slavery period, the fear was widespread that blacks were reverting to their original condition. Ergo, the most influential theory advanced by Negrophobes at the turn of the century was the idea known as retrogression theory.

Politicians, writers, and other imagemakers (notably the popular press) argued that blacks were regressing to their original bestial, savage, and licentious condition. The image of the oversexed Negro male was deeply rooted in the white racist imagination. But the image came to the fore in a new and spectacular way in the late 19th century and the early decades of the 20th century. The message was clear: It was absolutely essential that a program of racial segregation and ostracism be established and legitimized. And, as C. Vann Woodward (emeritus Sterling Professor of American 20th-century History at Yale) has shown, race-based exclusion extended to churches and schools, to housing and jobs, to eating and drinking establishments, and eventually extended to almost all forms of public transportation, to sports and recreations, to hospitals, orphanages, prisons and asylums, and ultimately to funeral homes, morgues, and cemeteries.

This was the highest stage of white supremacy ever seen in western culture. In the post-World War II period, especially since the 1960s, America made rapid and significant strides in dismantling the vast system of legal and defacto segregation that had been in place for more than a century. The consensus of those interviewed here seems to be that much time has passed, but very little has changed: past experience reveals that it is (apparently) easier to desegregate bodies than it is to desegregate souls; that we should not pretend that in three decades (1960–1990) we have escaped the grip of a historical legacy of racism that spans three centuries. America may have formally repudiated racism, but it remains imprisoned by the past which continues to influence and mould the present.

While the documentary does situate each stereotype historically, at times it gives the impression that the imagemakers (moviemakers, writers, cartoonists, et al.) caused the efforts to separate and otherwise deny black Americans full participation in American life. Conversely, it would be inaccurate to see the stereotypes merely as the consequences of larger historical forces. My own feeling is that the racist thoughts and images depicted, and the exploitation they justify, generated each other. *Ethnic Notions* is unclear on this important point, and teachers using the documentary might want to raise this point in class discussion.

The second reservation I have about *Ethnic Notions* is that it truncates American history by ignoring the colonization and colonial/revolutionary periods and the powerful anti-black images they fashioned. The parade of bigotry highlighted in *Ethnic Notions* is only 150 years long; but in reality it is 300 years old. The purpose of the documentary is to show us the origins of American racism. These are to be found not in 19th-century America, but in the cultural baggage transplanted English settlers brought with them to the New World. As Winthrop D. Jordan (professor of American History at the University of Mississippi) has shown, slavery could not have caused negative black perceptions, because the concept of blackness was loaded with intense negative meaning long before the English migration to America. In short, the ethnocentric impulse to find blackness repulsive was itself a major explanation for the enslavement of Africans. Rather than seeing Sambo as a creation enabling whites to perpetuate the slavery system, the English conviction that Africans were the original Sambos—barbaric, un-Christian, and libidinous—goes a long way toward explaining the institutionalization of slavery in British North America.

In like fashion, by beginning its search for stereotypes in the 19th century, *Ethnic Notions* bypasses the crucial revolutionary era and the making of the Constitution when the paradox of inequality existing in a society founded on human equality was especially self-evident. The failure, and the reasons behind the failure, to resolve what has been aptly described as the central paradox in all American history—the existence of slavery in an otherwise egalitarian society—helps explain the reemergence of numerous anti-black stereotypes in both the antebellum era when slavery faced its severest challenge, and in the post-slavery period when anti-black stereotypes justified the need to keep Negroes separate and unequal.

These caveats notwithstanding, *Ethnic Notions* succeeds admirably in challenging students to think about and appreciate the devastating impact race-based exploitation has had, and continues to have, on American life. If truth leads to understanding, and understanding to a measure of acceptance, then this documentary is a superb teaching aid to help get this important point across.

The following titles complement and in some instances supplement themes dealt with in *Ethnic Notions*:

John W. Cell. *The Highest Stage of White Supremacy.* Cambridge University Pr., 1982.

Jannette L. Dates and William Barlow. *Split Image: African Americans in the Mass Media.* Howard University Pr., 1990.

George M. Fredrickson. *The Black Image in the White Mind . . . 1817–1914.* Harper & Row, 1971.

Winthrop D. Jordan. *White over Black: American Attitudes toward the Negro, 1550–1812.* University of North Carolina Pr., 1968.

Lawrence W. Levine. *Black Culture and Black Consciousness.* Oxford University Pr., 1977.

Rayford W. Logan. *The Betrayal of the Negro, from Rutherford B. Hayes to Woodrow Wilson.* Collier, 1954.

Robert Toll. *Blacking-Up: The Minstrel Show in Nineteenth-Century America.* Oxford University Pr., 1974.

William L. Van Deburg. *Slavery and Race in American Popular Culture.* University of Wisconsin Pr., 1984.

C. Vann Woodward. *The Strange Career of Jim Crow.* Oxford University Pr., 1955.

George A. Levesque, Department of Africana Studies

USETHCUL

Title:	**The Exiles**
Producer:	Richard Kaplan
Distributor:	Filmakers Library
Release Date:	1990
Technical:	116 min., 2 pts. (63 min./53 min.) / color, b&w / English
Purchase Price:	$495
Rental:	$100 for one week
Presentation:	Documentary, with interviews and archival footage
Awards:	1990 Edinburgh International Film Festival; 1990 Berlin International Film Festival; 1989 Montreal International Film Festival
Study Guide:	A comprehensive viewer's guide is available.

Content: *The Exiles* describes the escape of refugees from Nazi Germany before and during World War II and the impact they have had on life in the United States. It begins with a brief but effective account of the rise of Nazism in Germany and how this forced a number of political opponents to emigrate before the start of the war. The workings of U.S. immigration policy and the efforts of the Emergency Rescue Committee are analyzed, and the exodus is placed in a broad context of the holocaust and the working of American society.

In the second part of the film, the impact that this tide of refugees had on intellectual and cultural life in the United States is explored. Through interviews with many of the more celebrated refugees—such as Erich Leinsdorf, Billy Wilder, Hannah Gray, Bruno Bettelheim, and Edward Teller—the contribution they made in fields as diverse as psychoanalysis and nuclear physics is explained.

Classroom Use: *The Exiles* is suitable for classroom use at the high school and college level. It is so comprehensive in its coverage that it does not require a great deal of introduction. If there is a bias or limitation in its approach, it is in its congratulatory tone for the successes these exiles have subsequently had.

The Exiles' wealth of historical detail makes it a bit difficult to use for teaching diversity in the classroom. Certainly Part I would be an effective addition to a history course on the Holocaust. Part II could contribute to discussions of how diversity enriches the arts and sciences and the life of a society. The video certainly draws on the experience of specific groups to illustrate the dynamics of diversity.

Critical Comments: The celebrated exiles interviewed here did, of course, make noteworthy contributions to American life. However, the implications of this are not considered in relation to the exclusion of the great mass of holocaust victims during World War II. It is appropriate to consider the benefits received from giving haven to these refugees. But U.S. immigration policy was exclusionary; refugees were viewed as a burden not an asset, and this film—while speaking eloquently to this problem indirectly—does not make the direct link which needs to be made. The assumption that flows from this, that American society benefited from and was hospitable to victims of Nazi persecution, needs to be qualified.

Donald S. Birn, Department of History

USPOLRAC

Title:	**Eyes on the Prize, Part II: America at the Racial Crossroads—1965–1985**
Producer:	Sheila C. Bernard, et al., for Blackside, Inc.
Distributor:	PBS Video
Release Date:	1990
Technical:	8 episodes, 60 min. each / color, b&w historical footage
Purchase Price:	$59.95 per episode, $395 series
Rental:	n/a
Presentation:	Documentary with interviews and narration
Study Guide:	Available separately at Blackside, Inc. (486 Shawmut Ave., Boston, MA 02118), Eyes on the Prize: America at the Racial Crossroads, 1965–1985: A Viewer's Guide to the Series

Content: This series details the major events of the civil rights/black rights movement from 1965 through 1985 and highlights the role of various individuals and organizations. Among the organizations highlighted are the Southern Christian Leadership Conference, Congress on Racial Equality, Student Non-violent Coordinating Committee, the Black Panther Party, and the Nation of Islam. Individuals featured include Malcolm X, Dr. Martin Luther King, Jr., Floyd McKissick, Stokely Carmichael, Carl Stokes, Bobby Seale, Huey Newton, H. Rap Brown, Fred Hampton, and Muhammad Ali.

Episode Synopses:

The Time Has Come (1964–1966) describes the rise and transformation of Malcolm X and his wide-ranging influence on blacks. It introduces viewers to the early 1960s African-American community outside the southern-based freedom movement, and demonstrates the movement's struggle to develop new goals and create new strategies in the post-Voting Rights Act era. It examines the context of the call for "Black Power."

Two Societies (1965–1968) explores the southern civil rights movement's first attempt to organize in the North. It presents the frustration and desire for change felt by black residents of northern cities, and looks at the 1967 uprising in Detroit.

Power! (1966–1968) explores the political path to power for Carl Stokes, the nation's first black mayor of a major city, Cleveland. It describes the founding of the Black Panther Party in Oakland, California, and examines the education experiment in New York's Ocean Hill-Brownsville section and the power and fragility of coalitions.

Ain't Gonna Shuffle No More (1964–1972) illustrates the pervasiveness of the black consciousness movement throughout the country in the mid-1960s and early 1970s. It chronicles heavyweight champion Muhammad Ali's challenge to America to accept him as a minister of Islam who refuses to fight in Vietnam. It describes the student movement at Howard University for black studies, and explores the "coming of age" of black politicians and political activists through a description of the National Black Political Convention at Gary, Indiana.

A Nation of Law? (1968–1971) examines the government's response to dissent from the Black Panther Party in Chicago and rebelling inmates at the Attica (N.Y.) Correctional Facility. It chronicles the FBI's covert program to disrupt and neutralize selected black organizations, and explores the call for "law and order" as a campaign issue and as government policy. It documents the activities of an FBI informant in infiltrating the Black Panther Party.

The Keys to the Kingdom (1974–1980) describes Boston's black community's efforts to achieve high-quality education for its children and the eventual desegregation of Boston public schools following the 1974 court order. It assesses the success of affirmative action under Atlanta's first black mayor, and examines

A twenty-year panorama of modern civil rights/black rights history unfolds in *Eyes on the Prize: America at the Racial Crossroads—1965–1985*. Malcolm X, Dr. Martin Luther King, Stokely Carmichael, and H. Rap Brown are among the many individuals featured in the eight-episode series. Above, the Selma to Montgomery march, 1965. (Courtesy PBS Video)

the effects of the controversial Supreme Court ruling in the Bakke case.

Back to the Movement (1979–1980) contrasts the situations of black communities in Miami and Chicago in the early 1980s and explores the themes of power and powerlessness. It describes the grassroots organizing efforts leading up to Harold Washington's election as mayor of Chicago and the continuing coalitions that evolve from the campaign. It also offers highlights of the entire 14-part television series *Eyes on the Prize*.

Classroom Use: This series is appropriate for undergraduate and graduate students studying history, political science, government, sociology, communication and social movements, or African-American stud-

ies. It provides an excellent historical overview and analysis of the civil/black rights movement.

Critical Comments: This series candidly portrays the efforts of blacks to gain equality in the United States, as well as attempts by the opposition to thwart their efforts.

Some underlying theoretical assumptions are: The aim of this movement was to have the United States more fully realize its principles of freedom and democracy; in the process, many flaws in the implementation of these principles were illuminated. Nevertheless, significant gains were made by the civil/black rights movements.

Salome Raheim, Department of Communication

GLRELCUL

Title:	**The Five Pillars of Islam**
Series:	The World of Islam
Producer:	Michele Arnaud, RM Productions
Director:	Michele Arnaud
Distributor:	Films for the Humanities
Release Date:	1988
Technical:	30 min. / color / English
Purchase Price:	$149
Rental:	$75/day
Presentation:	Documentary consisting of contemporary color film footage and narration by Ian Holm; there are some older film clips; originally a French-language film (1983) entitled *The Pilgrims of Mecca;* English version written by Michael Bakewell

Content: *The Five Pillars of Islam* explains the major religious principles of Islam to a general audience. These five principles (the declaration of faith, daily prayer, fasting, giving of alms, and pilgrimage to Mecca) are discussed both generally and in detail. In addition, the film details the historical origins of Islam in Arabia, including the life and message of Muhammad, the formation of the *Koran,* Islam's remarkably successful military and religious conquests, and the continuing spread of Islam in the present day. Other themes of concern include the uniformity of Muslim practice across geographic boundaries, the egalitarian nature of Islam (at least as far as males are concerned), the role of the mosque in communal life, and various understandings of the concept of jihad, usually translated as "holy war."

Classroom Use: This is an excellent introduction to Islam as a religious tradition which would certainly enhance classroom lectures on this or related topics. It has obvious uses in a wide variety of courses that touch on Islam, or issues connected with the Middle East, whether in religious studies, history, political science, economics, or ethnic and area studies.

Critical Comments: The film is very well-illustrated with scenes of Muslim life throughout the Islamic world, and the pilgrimage scenes in Mecca are particularly effective. The film is traditional in format (narrator and footage), and rather slow in pace, but clear and instructive throughout. It is not interested in nor sensitive to gender, class, and diversity concerns, beyond stressing how egalitarian a religion Islam aims to be.

Judith Baskin, Department of Judaic Studies

USETHREL

Title:	**Flight of the Dove**
Producer:	Nancy da Silveira
Director:	Nancy da Silveira
Distributor:	University of California-Berkeley Media Center
Release Date:	1989
Technical:	60 min. / color / English, some Portuguese subtitled in English
Purchase Price:	$195
Rental:	Varies (available from the Media Center at the University of California–Berkeley)
Presentation:	Documentary, with interview material
Awards:	Royal Anthropological Institute (U.K.) Film Festival, Society for Visual Anthropology, and American Anthropological Association

Content: One of the first documentaries ever to deal with the culture and experiences of Portuguese-Americans, *Flight of the Dove* examines the effects of celebrations of the Holy Spirit Festival on a Portuguese-American family in a dairy-farming community in the Chino Valley of southern California.

The film traces the evolution of the festival from its origins centuries ago to the present forms in which it is celebrated in Portuguese-American communities in California. The film reveals that some of the changes in the festival have helped to bridge the gap between immigrants and their children, and to reinforce the sense of identity of the participants as both Portuguese and American.

Classroom Use: This video is recommended for use in courses on biculturalism, immigrants in the United States, Portuguese studies, cultural anthropology, religion, sociology, folklore, and American studies.

A special introduction should be provided on the background of Portuguese immigrant communities in the United States and on Portuguese religious festivals, especially the Holy Spirit Festival. Although there is no study guide to the video, a very useful publication can be recommended: *Festas Acoreanas: Portuguese Religious Celebrations in the Azores and California,* (Oakland Museum History Department, 1981).

Critical Comments: Focusing on the effects of the Holy Spirit Festival on the members of a single Portuguese-American family, this sensitive, tasteful, and insightful video portrays a form of accommodating contrasts and of resolving conflicts due to cultural differences that is not often presented in materials dealing with immigrant communities in the United States: the maintenance of traditional customs and the values they embody, coupled with the development of new practices through successful adaptation to the new social and cultural surroundings.

In the opening scenes of the video, various members of a family in the Portuguese-American community of Chino describe what their ethnic background means to them. The mother clearly states that she feels Portuguese, since she was born in the Azores and that was the only place she knew during the first 15 years of her life; but she also says that she loves the United States. Her husband strongly states that he feels American, pointing out that his children were born in the United States and that this is where his life is; but he also says that he can feel either American or "totally Portuguese," depending on the circumstances. Their older daughter shows that she has pride in her Portuguese origin; but, even while getting dressed in special clothing to participate in the community's traditional Portuguese festival, her younger sister explicitly rejects the feelings of identification with Portuguese ethnicity which other members of the family are trying to instill in her. The ambivalent feelings manifested within the family, both between different members and by the same person, illustrate well the conflict between the traditional cultural values of the ethnic group of origin and the customs and values of the immigrants' new social environment.

The first Portuguese immigrants to California from the Azores arrived in the mid-1800s; more recent Azorean immigrants and their descendants have settled in the dairy region of the Chino Valley, where the community shown in the video is located. Several other similar immigrant communities have been established in the same region. The video states that one of the first civic acts such communities undertook was the establishment of a Holy Spirit Society for the purpose of promoting the important annual religious festival. According to the video, it is the Holy Spirit Festival, more than anything else, that has kept Portuguese-Americans together.

According to legend, the Holy Spirit Festival dates back to 1325 when Queen Isabel prayed for relief from the famine and strife which plagued Portugal at the time. After the relief came, a feast for all of the people was held, at which the good Queen won the hearts of her countrymen forever by placing her crown on the head of a poor child and saying, "In the eyes of God, we are all equal." The occasion is commemorated annually in many Portuguese communities in the United States and in former Portuguese colonies, although it is no longer celebrated on the mainland of Portugal. (Research has shown that the festival is actually older than the legend claims.)

The Portuguese communities in the Chino Valley are unique in that they hold two separate Holy Spirit Festivals: a traditional one brought from the Azores and another which has evolved in the United States, more in accordance with customs and values in this country. The video describes both.

The traditional version of the festival is basically a religious, family occasion. Portuguese-American families prepare for the events by erecting decorative altars in their homes. The principal symbol of the festival is a crown surmounted by a sphere with a dove on top; the components represent respectively the government, the world, and the Holy Spirit.

For seven Sundays the members of the community go to different homes of relatives and friends, where they gather at the altars to worship the Holy Spirit. The principal woman to appear in the video points out that being with all of the other members of the family on the occasion of the festival brings back the feeling of being together with the family in the original home, back in the Azores. Thus, the festival is important for both religious and family values. Although the ritual visits do not have the same meaning for the youngest daughter that they have for her mother, she nevertheless participates and is

exposed to the traditional religious and cultural values that are so important to the Portuguese.

On the eighth Sunday, which is Trinity Sunday, there is a procession to carry the crown to the local church, where there is symbolic crowning of children from the community, recalling the crowning of the poor child by Portugal's Queen Isabel centuries ago. As in the Azores, those who sponsor the festival select the children to be crowned, traditionally called "the innocents." Although this ritual may have little. meaning for those born in the United States, the following feast is a popular event celebrated by all. Traditional Azorean foods are served, and there is typical Portuguese folk music and dancing. An amusing part of the feast is a competition of improvised humorous songs in Portuguese among the dairy farmers who provide support for the event. The contest is similar to one traditionally held between the festival sponsors back in the Azores. To those more closely linked to Azorean culture and traditions, the festival helps recall the past and to strengthen ties with their ethnic origin and with others of similar background.

Much more recently an Americanized version of the festival has evolved; it is a more elaborate celebration, incorporating aspects of life in the United States. In this version, the focus is not on the children to be crowned, but on the selection of new junior and senior queens each year. The principal symbol is not shown on altars in the home, but on the cape and crown of each queen. While there is no competition to become queen, since selection is made by the festival's committee, there is strong feeling of rivalry both between the new queen and her predecessor and between concurrent queens of different communities, each of whom wishes to outshine the other.

The newer, Americanized version of the Holy Spirit Festival is the one which takes place in the Portuguese-American communities throughout California. In it the march to the church by the festival's participants is not called a "procession" as in the traditional, religious version, it is called a "parade." At the church the new queens are crowned rather than the children. After the coronation at the church there is a large party; it is a modern social gathering with American music and dancing, in sharp contrast to the traditional feast of the original, more religious version of the festival. Finally, while visits also occur in the new version, they take place after the coronation and are between the concurrent queens who go to each other's communities for parades on successive weekends. To outsiders, these visits surely depict ethnic unity among the Portuguese-Americans. Moreover, the practice of holding a more social, less religious festival reveals that the Portuguese-Americans have adapted themselves to their new cultural environment, while maintaining a sense of continuity with the customs and values of the traditional culture of origin.

Although the new version of the festival is very popular among members of the younger generation in the community, older members have reservations about the costly, less religious, American-style festivals that are held nowadays in Portuguese-American communities in California. This is demonstrated by a simple anecdote about trying to get into Heaven: ". . . I reached the gates of heaven. When it was my turn, I spoke to Saint Peter. He did not remember me. Confidently, I said, 'I'm Freitas. I organized the festival of Our Lady, the festival of the Holy Spirit, of the Christ Child and of Saint Anthony. I helped build the church, and I was the friend of several priests.' Saint Peter looked at me and said, 'Tony, you're from California. Look here, my son. This thing about putting on festivals to look good in the eyes of the public doesn't carry much weight around here'."

On the other hand, the video also quotes various members of the community, including some representing different generations in the same family, who express the opinion that the newer version of the festival has positive effects, even through its competitive nature. The overall thesis is that both versions of the Holy Spirit Festival fulfill important functions in the lives of the members of the Portuguese-American communities where they are celebrated.

Brian F. Head, Department of Hispanic, Italian, and Portuguese Studies

GLETHSOC

Title:	**Foster Child**
Producer:	Jerry D. Krepakevich, for the National Film Board of Canada
Director:	Gil Cardinal
Distributor:	National Film Board of Canada
Release Date:	1987
Technical:	45 min. / color / English / 16mm only
Purchase Price:	$300
Rental:	$70
Presentation:	Autobiographical documentary

Content: As an autobiographical documentary, *Foster Child* records the filmmaker's rediscovery of cultural roots. As a toddler, Gil Cardinal, a Meti, was taken in by a white middle-class family. This comes out in initial conversations with his white family in the beginning of the film. He is now 35 years old and gathering as much information as he can about the circumstances of his early childhood and agency placement. After speaking to his family, Gil goes to Social Services and attempts to read his file, but he is denied access. He may only have access to the records through an appointed social worker who interprets the text for him. He finds that she selectively withholds facts or statements from him when she feels they will cause him distress.

Two examples of her reticence involve the alcoholism and arrest of his natural mother and a recommendation against adoption because of his Meti background. Gil has previously learned of his mother's death through an obituary notice. Through the help of the guilty social worker, the publication of information in Native newsletters, and contact of relatives, Gil begins to meet his family. He goes to see an uncle who did not even know of his existence.

There he is given a picture of his mother for the first time. He meets a World War II veteran who is probably his father, and listens to him deny the fact. In a continuation of bad luck, Gil finds that he has two brothers: one has just died, and the other will not see him. Nevertheless, he journeys to the north country to meet with his widowed sister-in-law who tells him of his brother's life and art, more about his mother, and offers him support and consolation. In the process of discovery, Gil finds peace within himself and reluctant acceptance of his life situation. He marks his mother's anonymous grave with a handsome headstone and attends the weddings of two nieces, one from each of his families, native and white. There is a sense at the end that he cannot help but constantly wonder how things might have been different.

Classroom Use: This video is of interest to classes of sociology and psychology, as well as cultural diversity courses dealing with Native-Americans. Problems like alcoholism and its consequences for native people are poignantly presented. Women's studies courses will find a sensitive treatment of the plight of a poor, single, minority woman in contemporary society.

Critical Comments: *Foster Child* is a good example of the kind of autobiographical documentary that seems to appeal to Native-American filmmakers. In this type of presentation, the filmmaker records his or her own rediscovery of cultural roots. Another well-known example is Arlene Bowman's *Navajo Talking Picture,* which deals with her return to the reservation to make a film about her grandmother, who is unenthusiastic and even uncooperative about the project. The film focuses upon Bowman's relationship with her grandmother and the collision of cultural differences that the film provokes. In *Foster Child,* Gil Cardinal has recorded his own emotional journey through bureaucratic red tape and severed family ties to a discovery of his native roots.

It is important to remember, for cultural-diversity purposes, that this is a Canadian film, but the issues are also immediately applicable to the United States. Gil is Meti, a kind of half-breed (Scottish and Indian), and the Meti people also live in the northern United States. The term *Meti* has become a popular one for designating a half-breed of any sort. It appears in the writings of Gerald Vizenor (Chippewa) and Joseph Bruchac (Abenaki).

The practice of placing Indian children in foster homes is similar to their placement in boarding schools in that both actions separated children from their families and cultural heritages. American and Canadian governments advocated this kind of separation and assimilation. There seem to be more films in Canada dealing with social issues and problems regarding natives than there are in the states, presenting a possible discussion topic for class.

Jeanne Laiacona, Department of Art

USRACECO

Title:	**Freedom Bags**
Producers:	Stanley Nelson and Elizabeth Clark-Lewis, Abena Productions
Distributor:	Filmakers Library
Release Date:	c1990
Technical:	32 min. / color, b&w / English
Purchase Price:	$295
Rental:	$55
Presentation:	Documentary interview, archival footage, narration

Content: Beginning with the idea that freedom equalled a train ticket to the North, this film documents, through the eyes of women, the great migration of African Americans from the South to the North in the early part of this century. The women, like their male counterparts, were in search of better wages and working conditions, but because of their sex, nearly 80 percent were only able to find work as domestic servants. This employment subjected them to sexual harassment. As one woman remarked, "men never choose the ugly, only the good-looking and young" as servants. Their job choices were limited by the fact that in no southern state was school attendance mandatory for blacks, the ratio of spending on white versus black children's education was 12 to 1, and factory jobs were reserved for whites.

The film is basically a series of interviews with these women who are now quite old. They describe their reasons for starting out as a search for a better living and talk about traveling on the segregated trains, where they had to bring their own food. The cities they went to included New York, Chicago, Detroit, Washington, and Philadelphia. Since the trains went through Washington's Union Station, many were afforded their first memories of urban life in that station and the densely packed houses around it. One woman recounts that when she found her first job, she just stayed right there—from 1918 to 1980. Salaries were five to eight dollars per week, and there were no teenage labor laws. They lived in the basements of the houses; they couldn't stay upstairs with the white people. Emancipation had freed them only from physical bondage.

Offensive cartoons of the era are shown (some of the same ones as in the film *Ethnic Notions*, dis-cussed on p. 76) and the attitudes of both whites and blacks are discussed in relation to the stereotypical images of Aunt Jemima and Mammy and the reductionist idea that all blacks need to be happy is "rhythm." The women's discussion of their sexual harassment implies that they accepted it as a matter of fact given their limited job opportunities, their lack of freedom to unionize, and the fact that the labor laws of 1935 mandating social security, disability, and old age insurance did not cover domestic workers. The women describe the attitudes of whites as "dumb"—blacks were allowed to care for their children but the whites wouldn't sit next to them and they fed them leftovers. Their honesty was always in question and frequently money was left lying about the house as a "test."

During the Works Progress Administration of the Depression years (1930s), the federal government taught household training because good household help was hard to find. Courses emphasized efficiency in the kitchen and argued that it would leave housewives "more time to keep themselves young and beautiful." By the 1930s, most domestic workers did not live in at their jobs. They were able to meet each other on buses and escape some of the loneliness of their earlier lives, plus have social groups and the freedom to go places with each other—Thursday nights were their main recreation night. The film ends by emphasizing the large role of these and other black migrants in creating today's cities.

Classroom Use: While some parts of the film duplicate material in *Ethnic Notions* and *Roots of Racism*, those are the effective parts and the duplications are a small percentage of the total. Thus, there is no problem in showing the films to the same class, only in showing them too close together. I recommend it highly.

Critical Comments: This film is extremely well-done and combines the issues of work, feminism, migration, race, and sexual harassment into a good historical package. It requires little set-up on the part of the instructor. The music in the film is particularly effective, including songs like "Darkies Never Dream," "Sadie's Servant Room Blues," and "Working Woman Blues" by artists like Bessie

Smith, Duke Ellington, and Huddie Ludbetter. Using women as the migrants and storytellers is very effective as many think of the great historical movements like the black migration as being the work of men. The film also provides a link to the special degradation women suffered under slavery because of their sex and their beauty, as reported in books like *Narrative of a Slave Girl,* and demonstrates that this treatment did not end with emancipation.

Nancy A. Denton, Department of Sociology

GLCULEXP

Title: # Frida Kahlo (1910–1954)

Producers: Eila Hershon, Roberta Guerro, and Wibke Von Bonin, for RM Arts Production (Munich, Germany)

Distributor: Home Vision; also Facets Video

Release Date: 1983

Technical: 62 min. / color, b&w stills / English

Purchase Price: $39.95

Rental: $10 for members of Facets Video Club

Presentation: Documentary, narrated throughout by Sada Thompson

Content: This film depicts the life and art of one of Mexico's most renowned painters, Frida Kahlo. The film centers on the many personal and political influences upon Kahlo's art: among them, Mexican folk culture and the rural Mexican landscape, the illnesses and accidents that plagued her throughout life, Communism, Catholicism, the surrealist painters, and, of course, her marriages and infidelities to Mexico's legendary muralist, Diego Rivera. The script is culled verbatim from Hayden Herrera's critically acclaimed biography *Frida* (New York: Harper and Row, 1983), and also relies much on Kahlo's own journals penned during the final ten years of her life.

Tracing the development of an individual artist is not the only goal of the film. It also shows how Frida's body of art, including 70 self-portraits, calls attention to her nation's attempt to find itself in a mix of many legacies: pre-Columbian and European, agricultural

and technological. The film liberates Kahlo from typical depictions of her as "the genius's adoring wife," and shows how she in turn inspired Diego's art, challenged critics of Mexico's "primitive" cultures, and emerged as a legend among women of her time.

Classroom Use: This film will be most applicable in diversity courses that include discussion of Latina culture, visual arts, racial or ethnic self-determination, and such gender-related issues as clothing as a form of self-presentation. Courses that focus on the themes of intergenerational and intercultural relationships will also benefit from a screening of this film, in that much of Kahlo's art explores her Mexican-German ancestry, her connections to parents and siblings, her relationship to her beloved Mexico's so-called "savage" past, and her place as a woman in the continuum of death and life.

Frida Kahlo (1910–1954), the mesmerizing life story of the Mexican painter, can be used to stimulate discussion of ethnic and gender-related issues as well as symbolism in the visual arts. (Courtesy Films Incorporated)

Critical Comments: Kahlo's life is a mesmerizing one and the film skillfully relies upon this and her art to enchant viewers. Her story is told so clearly and exhaustively that it requires no special introduction to college-level viewers. Some viewers might benefit from prior discussion or background reading about political and artistic figures who are mentioned as influences upon Kahlo's work. Chief of these are Leon Trotsky, André Breton, and Rivera himself. However, I do not think it absolutely necessary to do so, as the film itself supplies sufficient background of all of these figures, and even provides extensive discussion of lesser-known inspirations for Kahlo, such as Juan Guadaloupe Posada, a popular Mexican printmaker, cartoonist, and satirist.

To underscore Kahlo's extensive artistic roots in Mexican popular culture, the film tells her story by panning from object to object in her home, now preserved as a national museum in Mexico City. Three religious objects from Mexican culture are connected in particular to her art: (1) the Judas figures: paper-maché effigies exploded in commemoration of Christ's betrayal; (2) the sugar skulls: candy sold during festivals in honor of the dead; and (3) retablos: tin paintings offered to the saints in gratitude as gifts for miracles performed.

Viewers might use this technique as a catalyst to discuss symbols of the female and the generative in Kahlo's art—water, blood, and flora, for example—or to discuss other cultural symbols and signs that appear in literature, music, and visual arts.

Barbara McCaskill, Department of English,
now at the University of Georgia, Athens

USCULETH

Title:	**Gefilte Fish**
Producer:	Karen Silverstein
Director:	Karen Silverstein
Distributor:	Ergo Media, Inc.
Release Date:	1984
Technical:	15 min. / color / English
Purchase Price:	$29.95
Rental:	No rental by Ergo
Presentation:	Documentary with interviews

Content: *Gefilte Fish* is ostensibly about the different ways three women representing three generations in one Jewish family, prepare gefilte fish (mixed fish croquettes), a traditional holiday dish, and how they feel about what they are doing. In fact, through discussion of food preparation, the film raises questions about the consequences of social and technological change for women's traditional roles in a rapidly changing world. The elderly grandmother describes how she used to buy a live fish to ensure freshness, then spend hours chopping in a wooden bowl with a metal chopping knife inherited from her mother-in-law. Her daughter-in-law is shown purchasing three types of fish from a fishmarket, chopping the fish, and mixing in the other ingredients in an electric food processor. The granddaughter, a young woman in her twenties, prefers to purchase the already-made gefilte fish in a jar, maintaining that it tastes just as good and doesn't require a day and a half of work which her lifestyle would not accommodate.

Classroom Use: *Gefilte Fish* would be valuable for a wide range of courses dealing with social change, gender roles, and the consequences of technology, whether from the point of view of social history, sociology, anthropology, ethnic studies, or women's studies.

Critical Comments: *Gefilte Fish* is a humorous and moving vignette on social change and the wish to hold on to tradition, but not at any cost. Its concerns with women and their connections to each other and to their larger community are universal, making this film suitable for any audience sympathetic to gender and diversity concerns. It raises numerous issues

about female roles in traditional societies where women function primarily as nurturers and culture bearers, and prompts reflection on what is lost and what is salvaged as societal pressures and new opportunities lead women to other avenues of identity and achievement. The film also centers attention on food and food preparation as a focus of cultural affiliation, raising universal questions about personal identity and group definition in a pluralistic society.

Judith Baskin, Department of Judaic Studies

USETHSTE

Title:	**Geronimo and the Apache Resistance**
Series:	The American Experience, PBS
Producer:	Neil Godwin, for Peace River Film, Inc.
Director:	Neil Godwin
Distributor:	PBS Video
Release Date:	1988
Technical:	60 min. / color, b&w stills / English / close-captioned
Purchase Price:	$59.95
Rental:	n/a
Presentation:	Television documentary narrated by David McCullough with interviews, photographs, memoirs, and historical documents from the Smithsonian Institution and other sources
Awards:	Blue Ribbon, American Film and Video Festival; Ciné Golden Eagle 1988

Content: The videotape tells of the rebellion by Geronimo and other Chiricahua Apaches against the inroads made by whites into Native-American culture and land. The film removes Geronimo as an object of mythic fabrication, reveals his 20-year battle against the overwhelming force of the U.S. Government, and his subsequent 27-year detainment as a prisoner of war. According to the film, the past for the Apaches is a closed chapter and the dead are not to be spoken of. However, much of the information given in *Geronimo and the Apache Resistance* was

gathered from the renegades' descendants, who for the first time break the silence in order to reveal the reality behind the myth. Geronimo is shown as being not the murderous and pillaging savage made popular in whites' perceptions. Instead, it is disclosed that he was a shaman (a medicine man) and an advisor to Naiche, the hereditary chief of the Chiricahua Apaches.

The Chiricahuas were a warrior nomadic people whose home was what is now known as Arizona. Before the expansion of the American West, the Apaches had to resist the Mexican inroads into their territory. Geronimo's wife, children, and mother were killed during one of the raids from the south. Believing the land sacred and not anyone's to give away, the Apaches also rebelled against the United States' incursions after Mexico ceded the Southwest. The video chronicles the resistance by the native people, the cruelty and betrayal by the whites who were moved by the idea of a Manifest Destiny. Geronimo was never conquered, but time and again he gave himself up when he believed the promises that the lot of his people would improve; and time and again he escaped when the treaties were broken. The Chiricahua Apaches were seen as a threat to the white settlers and were moved numerous times in boxcars by the U.S. Government. They were held for 27 years as prisoners of war in alien environments, variously in Florida, Alabama, and Oklahoma.

Classroom Use: *Geronimo and the Apache Resistance* should be used in American history courses and Native-American studies. Studied together with *INDIANS* by Arthur Kopit, it can be used in a course on theater. The video fulfills diversity course requirements as it debunks the preconceived notions of Native-American knavery and savagery versus the white man's bravery and moral superiority instilled in students by cultural icons such as the cowboys-and-Indians movies. The video can also be used to show the Native-American people's reverence for their land juxtaposed against such desecrations as the Mount Rushmore Monument, and can illustrate the clash of differing cultures and the effects of dominance.

The following works can also be studied in conjunction with this video: *Bury My Heart at Wounded Knee,* by Dee Brown (Holt, 1971); *God Is Red,* by Vine Deloria (Grosset, 1973); and *The Vanishing Race and Other Illusions,* by Christopher Lyman (Smithsonian Institution Pr., 1982).

Critical Comments: This video gives an authentic voice to an area of American history shrouded in myth. The testimony by the Chiricahuas' direct descendants unveils the true stature of Geronimo and the causes of his people's rebellion. It shows very clearly their attachment to their land in the Southwest and their reluctance to give up their ancestral ground. This still existing affinity to the land is emphasized in the moving declarations by the Chiricahuas' descendants who were able to return to the region. The video also shows the implication of the United States' imperialism: the depersonalizations, the humiliations, the diseases, and the unspeakable cruelty by the usurpers of the land. Archival photographs illustrate the results of the defeat and colonization of a people risking everything in order to preserve its traditions and its land.

Geronimo and the Apache Resistance contradicts popular notions promulgated by the mass media and the self-serving fiction created by those who gained from the subjection of Native-American people. The video further points out the ironic fact that Geronimo and other native people appeared in Wild West shows. It is regrettable that the full horror of this fact was not emphasized in the film. Geronimo and other Native Americans took part in humiliating show business events: they had to characterize themselves as virtual blood-thirsty savages; they had to reenact and fictionalize the events leading to their defeat, all for the aggrandizement of the Buffalo Bills and for the glee of multitudes. In addition, the still photographs used in the video were posed for the most part for white photographers at the turn of the century and show stoic faces, dehumanized and seemingly unfeeling, closed to the white man's gaze. As one of the Apaches' descendants mentions, we are allowed a privileged view into the reality of the myth surrounding Geronimo; but it is just a glimpse.

Regina W. Betts, Department of Theatre

GLRELCUL

Title:	# Hail Umbanda (Salve a Umbanda)
Producer:	Jose W. de Araujo
Director:	Jose W. de Araujo
Distributor:	University of California, Berkeley, Extension Media Center
Release Date:	1988
Technical:	46 min. / color / English with some Portuguese subtitled in English
Purchase Price:	$385
Rental:	$35
Presentation:	Documentary, including some interviews
Study Guide:	Discussion guide available

Content: *Hail Umbanda* provides an overview of Umbanda, the new religion established in Brazil early in this century (1908). Considered a blend of African cults, Catholicism, native Brazilian Indian beliefs and practices, and European spiritualism, Umbanda has since spread to all of the major cities of that country. The video provides a close view of activities at the Audaria Maria Spiritist Umbanda Center in the state of Ceara (in northeast Brazil), as well as scenes from ceremonies and rituals in Rio de Janeiro, São Paulo, and Brasilia. Materials obtained from the ceremonies, rituals, and consultations are used in the video to provide rare insights into the nature and functioning of Umbanda and into the role of religious leaders. Interviews with Umbanda priests and other adherents provide most of the narration of the film.

Classroom Use: The video is suitable for courses in African-American studies, Brazilian studies, Latin-American studies, comparative religion, folklore, and cultural anthropology.

A four-page classroom discussion guide, available with the video, provides useful background information, including the names and brief descriptions of Umbanda's principal deities, protectors, and guides. Recommended background reading includes: Diana DeG. Brown, *Umbanda: Religion and Politics in Urban Brazil* (Ann Arbor: UMI Research Pr., 1986).

Critical Comments: The following text is presented prior to the showing of images:

"Umbanda is the fastest-growing popular movement in Latin America today. In Brazil alone, Umbanda and its closely related spiritist movements represent 35 million followers. Though often pagan in appearance, the deities and rituals of Umbanda embrace and utilize the apostolic order of the Catholic Church."

"Umbanda has seven lines of development in its faith. Each line is divided into seven phalanxes. These, in turn, are subdivided into seven subphalanxes; each subphalanx branches into seven tribes. Each of the tribes is composed of seven sublegions, and the sublegions, in turn, are occupied by seven peoples."

Next comes a statement by Brazilian filmmaker Luis Paulinho dos Santos, expressing the belief that Umbanda is the most original, spontaneous, and authentic religion in Brazil because of its historical background in representing three different sources: the spiritual beliefs of the Indians, who were the first inhabitants of the country; the Judeo-Christian tradition, brought by the Portuguese colonists; and the animistic cults brought from Africa by the slaves, which are similar to Indian beliefs in that they are connected to nature and closely related to everyday life.

The opening scene provides views of a ritual at a crossroads as the director of this film, Jose W. de Araujo, explains what he had to do in order to gain access to Umbanda practices. The adepts of this religion are particularly wary of outsiders, in view of past experience with persecution by the Catholic church, repression by police and military authorities, and social discrimination. Araujo states: "In Brazil, before beginning any work, any project, any undertaking, one has to please the Eshus. The Eshus are the messengers of the Orishas, the masters of the crossroads, the bearers of tidings, and the lords of the pathways. As angels of good or evil, they represent us, simple humans, to the forces of the unknown. . . . One day, before arriving here, I spoke to the Father of the Gods to find out if it was possible to make this film. He said [it would be] all right, but that I had to ask the permission of the roadblock Eshu and make an offering at a forest crossroads at midnight. I looked for Roadblock, and he said he approved and had faith in this project, and that the Father of the Gods would teach us about Umbanda, the world of the spirits and the world of humans."

The next scene introduces the Father of the Gods (Pai de Santo) Jose Alberto Ferreira Nunes ("Painho"), of the Audaria Maria Spiritist Umbanda Center in Maranguape, Ceara, in northeast Brazil. This religious leader tells of his experiences as a medium, describes the organization of the Umbanda system of beliefs, and provides the names of the principal deities of his religion along with the general role of each, in addition to indicating the Catholic saints with which they have become syncretized. He talks about the current status of Umbanda, mentions persecutions suffered in the past, and tells of the benefits the religion brings to its followers. Throughout the remainder of the film, Painho continues to provide information on the beliefs and practices of Umbanda, and to describe how it helps those who practice it.

Hail Umbanda shows scenes from several ceremonies which include trances by the priest, his followers, or even members of the public attending the ceremony. The Umbanda devotee believes that trances result from possession of a medium's consciousness by one of the spirits, which include not only African deities (often syncretized with Catholic saints), but also "Caboclos" (spirits of unacculturated Indians), "Pretos Velhos" (spirits of Africans enslaved in Brazil), and a group of lesser entities.

A person in a trance exhibits the speech and other behavior considered typical of the possessing spirit. On being incorporated, the spirits demand their favorite food and drink, dress in their customary ritual clothing, and go around the center speaking to people in their typical ways. Singing, dancing,

and drum playing are common on such occasions, causing them to take on a festive aspect. Possession takes hold with a violent seizure followed by a state of trance. After the trance is over, the medium recalls nothing.

Umbanda functions as a kind of "therapy of the poor." People turn to the religion with their problems, and they find help. Following return from the state of trance, the dispossessed may acquire a sense of power and respect through association with the forces of nature. Social and family relationships may be readjusted as a result of this. Trances may help reintegrate the adherent's personality by permitting expression of repressed features during possession. In addition to describing the beliefs of practicers of Umbanda concerning possession by the spirits during trances, the film presents the concept of the trance as an alternative psychological and mental state, which some evoke under certain circumstances. Followers of Umbanda believe that mediums are born, that one does not acquire the capacity to enter into a trance.

Umbanda has become a powerful force in popular culture in Brazil. It provides inspiration for creative expression and its influence is found in literature, music, and the visual arts. Brazilian political leaders commonly pay visits to Umbanda priests during campaigns to receive advice and to attract votes. Similar related religious practices have spread throughout Latin America and are also found in the United States, such as "santeria" in New York, Miami, Los Angeles, and San Francisco, or as "rootwork" in New Orleans and Chicago ("santeria" and "rootwork" are religious practices in the Americas derived from African spiritual traditions).

Hail Umbanda provides information that can help change myths and misconceptions commonly held by outsiders with regard to other religions, particularly those of African origin or with strong African influence. In this film, practitioners and leaders of Umbanda explain what the religion means to them, how it has affected their lives, and how its practices work. By presenting scenes from actual ceremonies, the film shows the dramatic aspect of Umbanda gatherings, which the spirits are believed to visit, through the mediums, in order to eat and drink, sing and dance, and advise and help those who practice this religion.

Brian F. Head, Department of Hispanic, Italian, and Portuguese Studies

GLCULCLA

Title:	## Haiti: Dreams of Democracy
Producer:	Transvision Haiti
Directors:	Jonathan Demme and Jo Menell
Distributor:	Cinema Guild
Release Date:	1987
Technical:	52 min. / color / English voiceovers of French and Haitian Creole; subtitles for musical lyrics
Purchase Price:	$350
Rental:	$75
Presentation:	Documentary, including some media footage; vignettes of ordinary Haitian people; music performed by the Beggar Band, Manno Charlemagne, Group Foula, Freres Parents, and Group Samba

Content: This video covers Haiti after the fall of the Duvalier regime in 1986, featuring some media coverage of Jean-Claude Duvalier's departure and the public response—mostly celebrations—to the end of despotic rule begun in 1957.

The film proceeds by means of brief vignettes of people's lives, interspersed with appropriate commentary. For example, the film begins with street musicians setting up and tuning their cans, bottles, and plastic ''instruments.'' Later, a popular singer lip-synchs a song about Haiti's awakening. Another person featured is Abauja, a vodun musician and activist who explains vodun as Haiti's way of life, not as a religion of fear and strange rituals. Of course, many of the comments from people on the streets are criticisms of what still is not right in post-Duvalier Haiti, but these comments are understandable not only as an outpouring after so many years of censorship but also in terms of the impact of the international media. Other aspects of Haitian culture are given exposure, such as the colorful Tap Taps (privately owned small buses) and primitive or naive painting. Music looms large in most scenes, but this emphasis is understandable in terms of music's role as an instrument of resistance. A woman doctor offers a persuasive view of what is occurring in the country.

Classroom Use: This film is general enough in approach so that the educational or sensitivity level of the viewer should not be an issue. Whoever watches the film—except certain observers of Haitian history and culture—will be surprised at the positive images portrayed of common Haitians, who are most often portrayed as cowering in fear from their own culture and religion (vodun) and speaking a nearly unintelligible dialect (Haitian Creole). A professor who uses this film may wish to discuss some elementary Haitian history, but I don't think it is necessary to alert students to biases in the film. The biases, in fact, will come from the students watching the film, not from the film itself which, if it has a bias, is that it takes Haitians seriously. Obviously, the film is most useful to Caribbean studies and to anthropology courses.

Critical Comments: Most of the people in this film are common, everyday Haitians, as opposed to political and economic elites. Josh DeWind (Columbia University) is an American anthropologist who has worked in Haiti since the 1970s. Francois Duvalier, a black medical doctor with ethnological interests in rural Haitian culture, came to power in 1957, displacing the mulatto elites who have ruled Haiti during most of its history as an independent nation, especially since the U.S. occupation of Haiti between 1915 and 1934. In this sense, at least, Dr. Duvalier (''Papa Doc'') was a revolutionary in his time. Within a short time, whether due to the circumstances of consolidating power against longtime class enemies, or due to Haitian political traditions, Duvalier turned despotic, creating the hated Tonton Macoutes, a paramilitary squad that terrorized the Haitian people, extorting money for real and imagined infractions of the public order and torturing or killing those who resisted.

At the time of his death in 1971, Papa Doc Duvalier, who had named himself "President for Life," was succeeded—with the same title—by his 19-year-old son, Jean Claude Duvalier ("Baby Doc"), who remained in power until 1986. During his time in office, Jean Claude managed to reach rapprochement with Haitian mulattos, symbolized by his marriage to Michelle Benet, daughter of a mulatto businessman. Between 1971 and 1986, elite control over the Haitian masses was intensified, resulting in massive migrations (such as the Haitian "boat people") and, in the mid-1980s, unheard of demonstrations against the government.

Thus the departure of Baby Doc to exile on the French Riviera was cause for rejoicing and high expectations in Haiti. The subsequent struggle for power, which ended in 1990 in the stunning election of a Catholic priest (Jean-Bertrand Aristide) to the presidency of Haiti, exposed much of the enduring strength of Haitian character and culture and contradicted the prevailing pessimistic projections for Haiti's future. This documentary, covering the period of uncertainty after the fall of the Duvalier regime, is invaluable in demonstrating basic Haitian values and strengths. As noted, the senior producer, Josh DeWind, is an anthropologist, so one might expect primary attention to cultural issues rather than political or economic issues. Perhaps it is most accurate to say that the film is built upon the assumption that people find cultural ways of surviving even the most horrendous circumstances.

In a certain sense *Haiti: Dreams of Democracy* may seem an inappropriate choice for a "diversity" film, in that the film was not intended to facilitate the comprehension or appreciation of Haitian experiences in the United States. Rather, the concern is with contemporary expressions of Haitian culture and yearnings. Haiti, after all, is often referred to offhandedly as a "basketcase" and has been called "the land of limitless impossibilities." The people in the film, of course, are not those who have fled Haiti to reside permanently elsewhere, such as in the Bahamas, France, Canada, and the United States; they are the ones who have remained in or returned to Haiti. It would be misleading to suggest that Haitians residing in the United States are mere conveyors of the island's popular culture, since the migrants have had to adapt to vastly different conditions in this country. Perhaps the relevance of the film is to convey a sense of empathy for a grossly misunderstood people in their own habitat.

James Wessman, Department of Latin American and Caribbean Studies

USGENREL

Title:	**Half the Kingdom**
Producer:	Francine E. Zuckerman for Kol Isha Productions, with the National Film Board of Canada
Directors:	Francine E. Zuckerman and Roushell N. Goldstein
Distributor:	Direct Cinema Ltd.
Release Date:	1989
Technical:	58 min. / color / English, some ritual observances in Hebrew
Purchase Price:	$250
Rental:	$75
Presentation:	Documentary with interviews and live action footage; filmed in Canada, the United States, and Israel

Content: *Half the Kingdom,* a documentary on the themes of feminism and Judaism, examines the changes women and some men are demanding and effecting in present-day Judaism. Through the views and experiences of seven representative Jewish feminists, the film examines the areas in which changes are being made and areas where these women still perceive inequities and resistence to women's needs. Of the seven women, three are Canadian, two are American, and two are Israeli. They include Norma Baumel Joseph, an Orthodox educator; Naomi Goldenberg, a professor of religious studies; Michelle Landsberg, a journalist; the novelist E. M. Broner; Elyse Goldstein, a reform rabbi; Shulamit Aloni, a member of Israel's Parliament; and Alice Shalvi, an Israeli activist and educator. Each represents a different background and different approach, yet all are committed to feminism and Judaism and are working in various ways to transform what has been an essentially patriarchal tradition.

The film examines efforts to introduce Jewish ritual and spirituality into the events which are particular to women's lives in the context of a religious tradition which has not been particularly interested in the female experience. It looks as well at the political consequences of trying to bring about social change, especially in Israel where women suffer many disadvantages under religious law. Rabbi Goldstein notes the many important ways in which she functions as a model of female leadership for the members of her congregation and her colleagues. E. M. Broner de-

scribes her struggles, during a year of mourning for her father, to say daily prayers with a group of men who preferred not to acknowledge her presence, and Norma Baumel Joseph laments the difficulties of combining feminism with traditional Jewish practice.

Classroom Use: This film has obvious uses in Judaic studies courses which touch on the experiences of Jewish women, but I think its appeal is much broader. It could be used with valuable effect in sociology, anthropology, women's studies, and religious studies courses which deal with women and religion, religion and social change, or the varieties of feminist thought and experience.

Critical Comments: This is a moving and multifaceted film which is extremely sensitive to gender, class, and diversity concerns. It makes excellent and effective use of personal reflections (all from women), interspersed with live footage. Scenes depicted include synagogue worship, women's prayer and study groups, women's political activities both in North America and in Israel (including the ''women of the Wall,'' who are fighting for equal religious rights for Jewish women, and the ''women in black,'' who demonstrate weekly to show sympathy with the Palestinians' plight in occupied territories), and family ritual activities.

The views expressed in *Half the Kingdom* are diverse and reflect a wide spectrum of Jewish practice and self-definition. All the statements are highly personal yet, at the same time, all the speakers (an unusually articulate, sympathetic, and inspiring group) are activists who are making changes in their communities, each in her own way.

Judith Baskin, Department of Judaic Studies

USGENEXP

Title:	**Hearts and Hands: The Influence of Women and Quilts on American Society**
Producer:	Pat Ferrero, Ferraro Films
Director:	Pat Ferrero
Distributor:	Hearts and Hands Media Arts
Release Date:	1988
Technical:	63 min. / color, b&w / English
Purchase Price:	$350
Rental:	n/a
Presentation:	Archival materials and a collage format that includes authentic photographs and illustrations explicated with voiceover narration; written by Beth Ferris
Awards:	Blue Ribbon, American Film and Video Festival; Crystal Apple, National Educational Film and Video Festival; Best Fine Arts, San Francisco International Film Festival; Gold Plaque, Chicago International Film Festival; Ciné Golden Eagle

Content: This video presents the historical role played by American women and their textiles in the 19th century's great movements and events. *Hearts and Hands* explores the lives and accomplishments of many types of women, from anonymous quilters to activists such as Harriet Tubman, who was instrumental in the underground railroad and whose journeys were recorded in encoded quilting patterns. It illustrates how women of many racial, ethnic, and economic backgrounds made quilts whose beauty went beyond their utilitarian functions, and how they used needle and thread to express their views on the societies in which they lived. The video gives particular attention to Lucy Larcom, who worked in the textile mills of New England during the Industrial Revolution; Elizabeth Keckley, an African-American slave who utilized her needlework to buy freedom for herself and her son; Abigail Scott Dunaway, a feminist active in the movement to secure wo-

men's suffrage; and Frances Willard, founder of the Women's Christian Temperance Union. *Hearts and Hands* delineates the ways in which quilting has provided a medium for women to convey their concerns and political allegiances on a wide range of topics in varying historical circumstances, especially when other avenues of expression were unavailable to them. Filmmaker Pat Ferrero has directed and produced a number of superb documentary and historical films, including *Quilts in Women's Lives* and *Hopi: Songs of the Fourth World,* and this is one of her finest.

An excellent companion book, *Hearts and Hands: The Influence of Women and Quilts on American Society,* by Pat Ferrero, Elaine Hedges, and Julie Silber, is available from the Quilt Digest Press, P.O. Box 14127, San Francisco, CA 94114.

Classroom Use: *Hearts and Hands* is appropriate for classroom viewing at the university level, both undergraduate and graduate. It could be used in courses on diversity in the arts, folklore, women's studies, history, American studies, Africana studies, sociology, and political science.

Critical Comments: The video provides an engaging and insightful view of social history through the eyes of women and skillfully examines the complex relationship of women to the textile arts. Ferrero has carefully contextualized her investigation by considering the social, political, and economic factors that have influenced the creation of quilts, and she has crafted a beautiful and provocative visual record of the role of women in shaping American life. She includes a wide range of different types of women in her account—slaves, pioneers, political activists, Native Americans—noting the differing ways in which the needle arts were significant in their lives. She moves beyond many other studies by noting that textile arts have been used simultaneously by women on opposite sides of many issues, such as those who supported the Union and those who supported the Confederate campaign during the Civil War.

This video would be of use in addressing diversity issues in a variety of ways. It comments on alternative methods of expression that marginalized groups, particularly women, often use to convey their views when they feel that more direct forms of political action are inaccessible. The video addresses gender-related concerns in conjunction with racial diversity and provides knowledge of diversity as expressed through aesthetic and ideological endeavors. It focuses on the dynamics and mechanisms of alternative forms of social and political commentary used by women to express their views and discontent.

Linda Pershing, Department of Women's Studies

USETHSTE

Title:	**Heathen Injuns and the Hollywood Gospel**
Series:	Images of Indians (Program no. 4)
Producers:	Paul Lucas and Robert Hagopian, for KCTS-9/TV Seattle, and United Indians of ALL Tribes Foundation
Directors:	Paul Lucas and Robert Hagopian
Distributor:	Native American Public Broadcasting Consortium
Release Date:	1979
Technical:	28 min. / color, b&w film excerpts / English
Purchase Price:	$49.95
Rental:	$35
Presentation:	Narration by actor Will Sampson interspersed with interviews, archival Hollywood material, and occasional dramatization

Content: Framed by a dramatization of extraterrestrials assessing Western culture and ritual without really understanding it, this video goes on to show how Hollywood films have promoted misunderstanding and stereotypes of Native-American religious rituals and cultural practices. The pervasive impact of feature films upon mainstream culture, as they continue to be shown on television, is addressed, as well as the effects of media stereotyping upon native children and their understanding of their heritage. The first part of the film focuses on inaccuracies concerning the peace pipe, regional and local tribal practices, treatment and kidnapping of white settlers and their children, and misrepresentations of such famous Indian leaders as Crazy Horse. Film excerpts are interspersed with interviews of native actors and writers, white directors, and even a rodeo announcer who testifies on the negative effects of media on children.

The second part of the film focuses on interviews with a number of Indian women, some of whom are actresses, and the discussion centers on the depiction of Indian women and the opportunities for them in the theatrical industry today. According to one actress, Indian women are not called for professional or powerful roles, and only very young, attractive women or old, fat women are required for the unilaterally negative stereotypical roles that do exist. The women speakers challenge Hollywood's depiction of the relationship between Indian men and women as one that involves the abuse of the mindlessly subservient women. A more accurate portrayal of Indian women as equal partners in marriage and as powerful decision makers in tribal affairs is substituted. At this point, the women address the Hollywood invention of various legends and rituals and their superimposition onto native culture within the movies. Two examples of inaccuracies attractive to westerners are ceremonies involving the intermingling of blood and the legends of the scarlet horseman. At the end, the narrator returns to the alien spaceship and the counter-assessment of the dominant culture continues, making the point that language as well as images out of context can reduce any people to the status of savages.

Classroom Use: *Heathen Injuns* is appropriate viewing for classes in religious studies, film, American studies, cultural diversity, and anthropology.

Critical Comments: Before pointing out any difficulties with films in the *Images of Indians* series, it is important to emphasize that this is really the only resource available for examining stereotypes propagated by Hollywood through the movies—perhaps the most powerful form of public entertainment and cultural indoctrination. A variety of issues come up in the video. From the title *Heathen Injuns and the Hollywood Gospel,* it is clear that the focus of this program will be Native-American religion and ritual as depicted in the movies. The opening and closing frames with children dressed as aliens seems rather hokey, but the points are well-taken and the tables are turned upon the dominant culture for a change.

There is a curious divergence from the format in the middle of the film, when native women speak of their treatment at the hands of the motion picture industry. In a way it seems to fit in with the misconceptions of how Indians perform ritual, but women's issues probably require an entire segment themselves. Here they seem to be buried within a more general agenda which is returned to again toward the end of the program. The segment on women might be of particular interest to women's studies classes because of the delineated stereotypes within the movies and the plight of the contemporary actress in finding work in motion pictures. An interesting topic not brought up is the Native-American women's position between the women's movement and allegiance to the Indian Movement.

Jeanne Laiacona, Department of Art

USETHGEN

Title:	**Honored by the Moon**
Producer:	Skyman-Smith
Distributor:	Minnesota American Indian AIDS Task Force
Release Date:	1989
Technical:	15 min. / color, with b&w still photographs / English
Purchase Price:	$92
Rental:	$45
Presentation:	Documentary, mostly interviews; script development by Mona M. Smith; traditional flute music performed by Ricardo Rojas

Content: *Honored by the Moon* consists mainly of interviews with Native-American gays and lesbians who reveal the sacred place that gays have traditionally held in Native-American culture, particularly before the European invasion. The men and women featured in the video tell of the special status traditionally accorded them as leaders and as healers. They also explain that they were once considered a spiritual people whose "otherness" was seen as a gift from the Creator and who straddled the shadowy path between the supernatural world—which was the true reality—and the physical world—which was but its reflection. They alone completely understood both men and women and were the "connectors" between the genders. The film's participants perceived that the continued preeminence of Native-American gays in the arts and human services was evidence of their sacred status as healers and leaders. They further felt responsible for reversing the homophobia promulgated by the Europeans and for paving the way for a new generation of Native-American gays to regain their traditional place.

Classroom Use: *Honored by the Moon* can be a valuable aid in women's studies, Native-American studies, and in courses which deal with gender issues and homophobia. It can be particularly apt in human diversity courses since it reveals how gender identity and relations are regarded, and differences celebrated, in other cultures. The film may also be used to discuss questions concerning norms, and the homophobia which exists in the United States today.

The following books may be helpful in planning a course in which the video would be used:

Bess Brant. *Gathering Spirits*. Firebrand Books, 1988.

Jonathan Katz. *Gay American History*. Dutton, 1992.

W. Roscoe (ed.). *Living the Spirit*. St. Martin, 1989.

W. Williams. *The Spirit and the Flesh*. Beacon Pr., 1988.

Critical Comments: *Honored by the Moon* gives insight into the importance of a relatively unknown aspect of Native-American culture. The film reveals the respect that Native-American gays were once given, the regained consciousness of traditional roles, and the contemporary effort to overcome prevailing homophobia. It also undermines stereotypical views about Native-American men and women and pictures them instead as contemporaries concerned with some of the same problems as other gays in having to overcome the negative attitudes of mainstream thinking. But the film is often too impressionistic in not explaining fully the tradition of *berdache* (the term used by Native Americans to describe people in their community who are gay) which considered gay men and women as sacred. The emphasis on the spiritual aspects of Native-American gays and lesbians makes for a low-keyed approach which omits the important contribution that Native-American gays have had in the fight for equal rights and for AIDS research.

Regina W. Betts, Department of Theatre

GLGENCLA

Title:	**The Hour of the Star**
Producer:	Assuncao Hernandez
Director:	Suzanna Amaral
Distributor:	Kino on Video
Release Date:	1987
Technical:	96 min. / color / Portuguese, with subtitles in English
Purchase Price:	$79.95
Rental:	$175, 16mm only
Presentation:	Video of commercial feature film
Awards:	All twelve major awards at the Brasilia Film Festival; Best Film at the Havana Film Festival; Best Director at the International Women's Film Festival; and Best Actress at the Berlin Film Festival

Content: This film is a portrait of a poor, scarcely educated, 19-year-old woman from the underdeveloped northeast of Brazil, who has recently arrived in São Paulo, the country's industrial center, in the southeastern region.

Classroom Use: This video is recommended for use in courses on cultural diversity, Latin-American studies, women's studies, Brazilian studies, film, and literature.

Critical Comments: This is the tragic story of Macabea, a young woman who has migrated from the underdeveloped northeast Brazil to the highly industrialized São Paulo, far to the south. It is a painful portrait of her incapacity to cope with the normal demands of her socially and emotionally impoverished existence, due to the severe limitations of her background.

Poorly educated, Macabea works as a typist; although she strives to please her bosses, her work is tolerated only because she is willing to accept a salary below the legal minimum wage. But, because her work is so poor, she is barely hanging on to the job; advancement is, of course, inconceivable. Macabea shares a meager apartment of one room with several other girls attempting to survive in the big city. Although all are of humble origin, Macabea's primitiveness stands out: she changes her clothes

only when covered in bed (a result of her upbringing, as an orphan, by a prudish aunt), she does not bathe, she constantly wipes her nose on her dress, and she uses the chamber pot while eating. The lack of concern with basic personal hygiene is only part of her failure to take care of her person: she eats the cheapest food, and her makeup and dress are pathetically comical.

Yet, Macabea has a winsome basic charm: her naive, open smile has the capacity to illuminate her features, no matter how homely they are; she loves flowers, and she is emotionally moved by fine music; above all, she shows pluck, persisting—often cheerfully—in her efforts to cope with life. Macabea's social life is also primitive. For recreation she rides the subway, where she enjoys feeling the physical proximity of men. At one point she becomes excited because she thinks that a stranger at the lunch counter is looking at her, but it turns out that he is blind. Finally, she meets a metal worker who, like her, is a migrant from the northeast, but is somewhat more citywise and is a notch or two above her on the employment scale.

Her newly found acquaintance becomes her boyfriend, of sorts, but only under his own conditions: he offers to treat her to coffee, providing that she will pay the cost of having milk with it, in case there is any difference in price; he makes cruel fun of her, telling her that her name "sounds like a disease" and laughing at her naiveté; he becomes angry when she insists on asking questions he is unable to answer; and, finally, he jilts her in favor of a promiscuous coworker of hers.

But for all of his efforts to show his superiority, this man is also severely limited by his social and cultural background. To his pretentious-sounding first name of Olimpico the surname de Jesus is attached, indicating illegitimacy, according to the naming traditions of his culture. The product of a social, cultural, and geographic milieu where male supremacy is widely cultivated and accepted, Olimpico is compelled to show his dominance over the hapless Macabea, resorting to stupid manifestations of presumed, but baseless, masculine superiority. Like Macabea, Olimpico is socially marginal; he absurdly brags that he will someday become a congressman, even though he does not really understand what it means to be one. After he has rejected Macabea with the belittling putdown that she is like ''a hair in my soup'' in favor of her sexy, promiscuous coworker, he is in turn rejected by his new girlfriend, after one brief fling.

Whereas Macabea wins the viewer's sympathy and good wishes by her honest, though ineffective and ill-conceived, attempts to confront the challenges of life as she perceives them, Olimpico is basically dishonest and cruel.

The title of the film is the same as that of the short novella on which it is based (available in a paperback English translation published by Carcanet, New York, 1987), and derives from author Clarice Lispector's ironic particular concept of death, as shown in the final scene. The metaphoric nature of the literary ending need not distract attention from questions relating to the cultural origin and social destiny of the ''thousands of girls like this girl from the Northeast to be found in the slums (of major urban centers to the South),'' girls who ''aren't even aware that they are superfluous and that nobody cares a damn about their existence,'' in the words of the author.

Brian F. Head, Department of Hispanic, Italian, and Portuguese Studies

USETHCOM

Title:	**How Hollywood Wins the West**
Series:	Images of Indians (Program no. 3)
Producers:	Paul Lucas and Robert Hagopian for KCTS-9/TV, Seattle
Distributor:	Native American Public Broadcasting Consortium
Release Date:	c1979
Technical:	30 min. / color, b&w film excerpts / English
Purchase Price:	$49.95
Rental:	$35
Presentation:	Narration by actor Will Sampson interspersed with television programming, archival Hollywood materials, and occasional dramatization

Content: In the beginning of this video, a Saturday morning program for children called *Elbow Room* is examined for its glib account of westward expansion in the United States. The ideas of manifest destiny and divine right are questioned along with the inconsistency of European and U.S. officials buying and selling property that really did not belong to them in the first place. It is pointed out that Indians were seen as comparable to natural features to be overcome or conquered. The narrator turns off the television and instructs Indian children about the native people already living on the land when the westerners came, and about the extent to which the Indians helped and influenced settlers. When information is juxtaposed with a movie clip, the Western lack of consideration of the Indians as people or as owners of the land is painfully obvious. The epitome of this kind of Western thinking is apparent in a dramatic reenactment of a meeting between Andrew Jackson and the Indian people who were to be moved off their land through enactment of the 1830 Indian Removal Bill. Jackson assures them that they will be given recompense for the trip and the land lost, but they are unimpressed. Singer Johnny Cash tells about the collection and marching of the tribes to Oklahoma, a difficult and often fatal trip.

The next section of the video shows how movies have perpetuated the myth of manifest destiny. Some of the areas explored are: exploitation of conflict taken out of historical context; negation of separate tribal identities and customs; creation of stereotypical emotional reactions to images like ''lurking Indians''; and insensitivity to land claims. Hollywood's justification of its treatment of Indians leads to interesting issues that are beyond the scope of this film series. Interviews with directors and writers bring up the relationship of feature films to literature. While films were based upon novels, novels were often dependent upon restrictions of magazine serialization since authors were paid more for magazine publication than for a book format. Therefore, they could include no interracial marriages or sympathetic Indian treatment because of reader reaction. At the very end of the video, Indians and blacks confront each other in a scene from the movie ''Buck and the Preacher,'' one of the few sensitively executed portrayals of Indian people. Relationships between minority groups in American society reveal the complex mechanism of dominant culture hegemony over both groups.

Classroom Use: At least the first half of this video deals with a revision of U.S. history that overturns the basic assumptions of most Americans. It would be of interest to history classes and classes of a theoretical type, especially in terms of the extension of prejudice through popular cultural art forms. Political science or anthropology classes could deal with the influence of native systems of government upon the founding fathers of America. The issue of the social effects of the dominant culture's view upon minority children, who have been forced to identify against themselves, brings up questions in the areas of psychological development and educational strategies.

Critical Comments: A kind of awkwardness marks the dramatized portion of the program in which Andrew Jackson meets with Indian peoples. The Indians seem clearly anachronistic—not at all in keeping with the fairly authentic historical tone of the other figures. In contrast, the interviews in this program are moving and revealing. A complexity of consideration not evident in the title, *How Hollywood Wins the West*, is embodied in the interrelationships among history, movies, and literature that are emphasized in this video. Classes of film, literature, or cultural studies would find ample topics for discussion in this material. In a curious tacked-on fashion typical of this series, the relationship between African-Americans and Native-Americans is briefly touched upon and abandoned. Relationships among minorities in America deserve further attention and research.

Jeanne Laiacona, Department of Art

USRACGEN

Title:	## Ida B. Wells: A Passion for Justice
Series:	The American Experience (PBS)
Producer:	William Greaves
Distributor:	William Greaves Productions, Inc.
Release Date:	1989
Technical:	60 min. / color, b&w / English / close-captioned
Purchase Price:	$59.95
Rental:	n/a
Presentation:	Historical documentary and biography; narrated by David McCullough
Award:	Silver Apple, 1990, National Educational Film and Video Festival

Content: The anthology series *The American Experience* raises issues on American governance, racism, the economy, and the past personal triumphs and trials of U.S. citizens in hopes that they will enrich the current debate on significant national issues. *A Passion for Justice* examines the life of feminist and anti-lynching spokesperson, Ida B. Wells. On the eve of her death in 1931, Wells could look back over a career that spanned a critical transitional era in the African-American experience. She was born a slave during the Civil War in 1862, reared in a politically active family during Reconstruction, and educated at schools run by northern missionaries. She came of age at the turn of the century when the Jim Crow system was evolving and, along with W. E. B. DuBois, William Monroe Trotter, and others, she championed a strategy of protest in opposition to the ideology of accommodation espoused by Booker T. Washington.

A schoolteacher and journalist, Wells was a founder, but not one of the leaders, of the National Association for the Advancement of Colored People. A friend of Marcus Garvey, a social worker in Chicago's ghetto during the first wave of the great northern migration, and an activist in the initial political awakening of black northerners in the first quarter of the 20th century, Wells is best known today as the voice of the turn-of-the-century effort against lynching.

Who was Ida B. Wells? How many know of her—even among those who teach and write history? Almost no one does, concedes David McCullogh, and

he includes himself among the seriously uninformed. And yet, as historian McCullogh acknowledges: "By almost any measure, Wells was the kind of heroic figure we all should have grown up with in school. All of us should know her from books and films about great American achievements. That is if we really believe what we say about the value of human relations and justice in American life. She stood for, she fought for, everything we have been raised to hold most dear as the bedrock of the good society: fair play, freedom of opportunity, freedom from intimidation and the horror of mob rule. She had enormous courage; she was an investigative journalist before there was such a thing; she risked her life for her principles. She was everything, in other words, that we value in a hero. And in many history books, even today, she receives no mention at all. But then, you see, Ida B. Wells was a black woman in the nineteenth century."

Classroom Use: Recommended uses would include with courses dealing with the beginning stages of black activism during and after Reconstruction; American writers; African-American journalism; women's studies; and general courses on diversity in America.

Critical Comments: In her autobiography, *Crusade for Justice,* written shortly before her death in 1931, Ida B. Wells insisted that black youth, especially, were entitled "to the facts of race history which only the participants can give." Regrettably, she reported, the story of the black men and women who fought and died to maintain their rights as free citizens was all but "buried in oblivion." *A Passion for Justice* rescues from oblivion an important piece of the larger African-American past, a past which the traditional telling of American history has either omitted or seriously distorted.

In addition to making an important comment about the invisibility of blacks in the nation's history, the video convincingly drives home the point that African-American history cannot be understood apart from the broader national and even international developments of which it is an integral part. Indeed, as Robert Starobin, a professor of American history, recognized a quarter of a century ago, African-American history and American history form part of an indivisible whole; that the African-American experience provides a revealing context in which the whole of the history of the United States can be taught and studied. Finally, the centrality of the black experience is seen here as a result of the documentary examining not only "what was done to blacks," but "what blacks were able to do for themselves." Rather than portraying blacks as the passive victims of the actions of others, or simply a "problem" confronting white society, blacks were active agents in the making of Reconstruction as well as the turbulent history of the post-Reconstruction era.

As Wells's life and career make abundantly clear, the black quest for individual and community autonomy did much to establish the era's social, political, and economic agenda. A variety of themes are dealt with here: the disruption of black family life following the Civil War; the internal migration of blacks to southern cities, a prelude to the great northern migration; the emergence of a small black middle class during the short-lived "honeymoon" period of Reconstruction; the growth of the Ku Klux Klan; the proliferation of the black press (the *Conservator* in Chicago; the *Memphis Free Speech and Evening Star;* the *New York Age,* etc.); and the beginnings of the black Women's Club Movement.

The central focus, however, is the southern capitulation to extreme racism as seen in the intimidation and especially the physical violence directed against blacks following the Supreme Court's overturning in the early 1890s (the Slaughterhouse cases) of the federal laws that had provided protection for blacks. The violence, especially the lynchings, radicalized Wells, and this documentary focuses on her efforts, here and abroad, against this outrage. In her role as investigative reporter, and notably in her pamphlet *A Red Record: Lynching in the United States* (1894), Wells exposed the economic and psychological roots of the lynching mania of the period. Contrary to the white explanation given at the time—and since—that the lynchings were justifiable retribution for black sexual assaults against white women, Wells showed how the white hysteria might well have sprung from the suspicion that the relationship between black men and white women was far more mutual than whites, especially white men, were prepared to admit! (The documentary is not for the squeamish: a number of dramatic photographs of black men being hung and literally burned to death, are shown.)

Like any documentary that focuses on the life and career of a single individual—the same might be said of biographies—there is a tendency here to end up with a larger-than-life figure. Perhaps this can be said of Wells as her life and especially her career are dealt with. Nonetheless, as David McCullough reminds us, Wells's story fills an important void in our history, and serves to remind us that not all of our heroes have been white or male.

This documentary forms a piece with *Ethnic Notions* (see page 76), another documentary available for use in diversity courses. Where *Ethnic Notions* concentrates on how American racial attitudes were gradually formed by the iconographic environment of the period 1820–1960, *A Passion for Justice* throws a beacon of light on how those dehumanizing caricatures and stereotypes were an instrument of social, political, and economic oppression during the nadir of race relations in the United States, circa 1890–1930.

Topics dealt with in the documentary are considered in the following books:

Eric Foner. *A Short History of Reconstruction.* Harper, 1990.

Thomas C. Holt. "The Lonely Warrior: Ida B. Wells-Barnett and the Struggle for Black Leadership." In *Black Leaders of the Twentieth Century,* ed. by J. Franklin and A. Meier. University of Illinois Pr., 1982.

Joel Kovel. *White Racism: A Psychohistory.* Pantheon Books, 1970.

Gerda Lerner. "Early Community Work of Black Club Women." *Journal of Negro History* 59 (April 1974): 158–67.

Arthur F. Raper. *The Tragedy of Lynching.* University of North Carolina Pr., 1933/1970.

Ida B. Wells. *Crusade for Justice: The Autobiography of Ida B. Wells.* University of Chicago Pr., 1970.

Joel Williamson. *A Rage for Order: Black-White Relations in the American South since Emancipation.* Oxford University Pr., 1968.

Forrest G. Wood. *Black Scare: The Racist Response to Emancipation and Reconstruction.* University of California Pr., 1968.

George A. Levesque, Department of Africana Studies

USETHCUL

Title:	**I'isaw: Hopi Coyote Stories**
Series:	Words & Place: Native Literatures of the American Southwest (no. 4 out of 8 programs)
Producer:	Larry Evers, Department of English, University of Arizona
Distributor:	Norman Ross Publishing
Release Date:	1981
Technical:	28 min. / color / Hopi language with English subtitles
Purchase Price:	$157
Rental:	n/a from Norman Ross
Presentation:	Story narration and singing by Hopi woman Helen Sekaquaptewa to her grandchildren at her home in New Oraibi, Arizona

Content: The social group represented in the video is the Hopi Indians of Arizona, a Native-American culture that has been relatively successful in maintaining its land base, language, ceremonies, and cultural identity. The society is matrilineal and woman-centered; social life is strongly communal and kin-based.

Helen Sekaquaptewa is a highly respected Hopi elder and noted storyteller from Oraibi, which is probably the oldest continually inhabited settlement in the United States (Hopis have been there 800 years or more). The video was filmed in a modest private home (possibly Helen's) in an informal setting, with the collaboration of Helen's son Emory Sekaquaptewa, an anthropologist at the University of Arizona, and her daughter Allison Lewis, who transcribed the narrative and wrote the English subtitles. In essence, Helen is a woman who has man-

aged to bridge the gulf between tribal culture and life in the modern world. She has lived through and mastered the 20th century, and continues to fill the role of clan matriarch, transmitting traditional knowledge to her descendants, as she does in this film which took place on December 20, 1976 (I do not know whether she is still alive in her mid-90s).

The context is Hopi: bilingual Indians living on reservation land, economically marginalized but with a strong sense of cultural identity. The film begins with scenes of the landscape and of Helen working in her garden, with a soundtrack of her singing in Hopi. Most of the film is shot indoors, with Helen seated on a sofa and surrounded by children. She tells two stories in Hopi, a long one and a short one, both of which incorporate a song; the children respond and sing along. The stories are about Coyote, the Hopi (and other Western-Indian) trickster—an extremely popular and important figure in traditional and contemporary Native-American literature. Andrew Wiget, a major scholar of Native-American literature, has written a

Editor's note: See also the review of *Itam Hakim, Hopiit,* on Hopi storytelling, p. 110.

study of Helen's performance of this story, based on this videotape. He includes an English transcription of the story (closer to the Hopi original than the version given in the subtitles), a discussion of the story itself, and a detailed analysis of Helen's storytelling technique (voice, gestures, audience participation, etc.). His article "Telling the Tale: A Performance Analysis of a Hopi Coyote Story," is in *Recovering the Word: Essays on Native American Literature,* edited by Brian Swann and Arnold Krupat (University of California, 1987). There is also an autobiography of Helen Sekaquaptewa, *Me and Mine: The Life Story of Helen Sekaquaptewa,* edited by Louise Udall and published in 1969 by the University of Arizona Press.

Helen was born in 1898 to traditionalist parents, was forced to attend boarding school where she learned English, and as an adult joined the Mormon church; she claims that Mormon teachings helped her better to understand traditional Hopi teachings, and vice versa. Her children include businessmen and Hopi tribal officials in addition to her anthropologist son Emory and daughter Allison.

Helen and Emory also appear in the excellent PBS video *Hopi: Song of the Fourth World,* which may be available for classroom use. Along with the article by Wiget, these resources provide abundant contextual material for the storytelling performance on the video.

Classroom Use: The video is appropriate for any undergraduate level. In regard to classroom study of diversity, the video fits several disciplinary contexts: anthropology, folklore or oral literature, Native-American or U.S. ethnic studies. The type of diversity represented is cultural and artistic, concerning ethnic identity and the continuing survival of the traditional Native-American expressive culture.

For the classroom, some or all of the materials cited above could be used (by instructor if not by students) to provide context. There are also various studies of Coyote, in general and from specific cultures (including Hopi). A very good general study is an article by William Bright, "The Natural History of Old Man Coyote," in the same volume as the Wiget article.

Critical Comments: The video does require some introduction so that it is not seen simply as an old woman telling a cute story. The video itself gives no information about who and where the Hopi are, who Coyote is, and who Helen is. It is important to stress the significance of oral storytelling on the transmission of Native-American culture and language: the telling of stories, especially in the native language, is not simply for entertainment but is a major mode of teaching traditional values. This is evident in the longer Coyote story here. Long ago a group of birds (symbolizing the Hopi people) lived at Oraibi, and worked hard together to gather seeds. Coyote comes and attempts to befriend them only so he can later eat them. They see through his plot and, in the end, the trickster is tricked. The story encapsulates the relation of the Hopi to the outside world, which threatens their survival but from which they wisely take what they can use, rejecting the rest.

This video would work very well in conjunction with other videos from this series such as *Running on the Edge of the Rainbow: Laguna Stories and Poems with Leslie Marmon Silko* (see page 175). Here Silko, a younger woman from another matrilineal Pueblo culture, and an acclaimed poet and novelist in English, talks about incorporating traditional stories into her writing. These include Coyote stories, some of which she tells here; she even quotes something that Helen says in the other film. Silko also discusses how important the old stories still are to people today, in defining their identity and relating them to the group and its communal values. The older woman telling stories in Hopi, paired with the younger woman finding new ways to interpret and transmit such stories in English, would very effectively convey different modes of continuity and transformation in ethnic traditions. This could serve as the basis for a discussion of what tradition is and how diverse cultural traditions can be adapted and maintained in the present.

Louise Burkhart, Department of Anthropology

USIMMLAW

Title:	**Immigration Reform**
Series:	The Constitution, That Delicate Balance (no. 11) Annenberg/CPB Collection
Producer:	Jude Dratt, Columbia University School of Journalism
Director:	John Merdin
Distributor:	Intellimation
Release Date:	c1984
Technical:	60 min. / color / English
Purchase Price:	$29.95
Rental:	Varies (available from Penn State Audio Visual Services)
Presentation:	This video is based on a debate filmed for television, part of a thirteen-part telecourse on the Constitution; the commentator is Scott Friendly and the moderator is Benno Schmidt Jr., dean of Columbia University School of Journalism
Study Guide:	*A Guide to The Constitution, That Delicate Balance*, $12.25 from Intellimation

Content: This film was produced in June of 1983 when the House of Representatives was debating the bill on Immigration Reform. This bill was passed on June 20, 1984, by a small margin and later became known as the Simpson-Rodino Bill. The participants in the debate are major figures related to the immigration question as well as others who are reputable political, juridical, or academic representatives: U.S. court judges, presidents of universities, a civil rights lawyer, a representative of the U.S. Immigration and Naturalization Service, a U.S. district attorney, a representative of the American Civil Liberties Union, AFL-CIO leaders, Senator Alan Simpson, some Hispanic representatives, and some journalists.

Classroom Use: The video would be useful as a way of initiating discussion on a number of related topics, such as the consequences of the now-passed immigration reform law vis-a-vis the previous debates, as well as many issues that are relevant to U.S. migratory practices. It could be used in courses related to work, labor economics, migration, U.S. government, political science, and Latin America to offer the perspective of the receiving country on migratory matters. However, this is not an action film and therefore would be used most productively with more mature audiences for the sole purpose of gen-

erating discussion rather than providing information. Very little background information to the overall debate is offered and the viewers should be provided with a general introductory picture of migration issues in the United States.

Critical Comments: The debate is useful in that it raises many issues that are directly and indirectly relevant to U.S. migratory policies and that have major implications for the immigrant population. Some of those issues are the:

(a) different standards applied to different migratory waves;

(b) question of what civil rights should be extended to migrants;

(c) question of whether the Constitution protects the rights of migrants, even if they are illegal;

(d) distinction between refugees and migrants;

(e) issue of cheap immigrant labor versus American workers and unemployment;

(f) need to protect U.S. borders;

(g) consequences of a universal I.D. card; and

(h) issue of employer controls and the dangers of discrimination based on appearance and the probability of employing an illegal alien.

Liliana R. Goldin, Department of Anthropology

USETHEXP

Title:	# Itam Hakim, Hopiit
Producer:	Victor Masayesva Jr., IS Productions
Distributor:	Electronic Arts Intermix
Release Date:	1984
Technical:	59 min. / color, b&w archival stills / Hopi with English translation
Purchase Price:	$275
Rental:	$75 per screening
Presentation:	Documentary through storytelling

Content: Made on the occasion of the Hopi Tricentennial celebration, this video by a Native American Hopi is dedicated to Ross Mataya, an old man and traditional storyteller who appears in the film. The film begins with drastically cropped shots of the legs and feet of the storyteller as he does his daily chores on the Hopi reservation in Arizona. The view widens to take in the landscape, Mataya's modest home, and a group of children. Mataya becomes the narrator and storyteller, first of his own history and then of that of his people. Moving from the particular and personal to the mythical, Mataya tells the "Emergence Story" and the story of the "Bow Clan Migrations." The children gather to listen and are also entertained by playful songs. As the man speaks and sings, the camera shifts from the intimate interior gathering to the landscape, animals, and ritual and everyday activities of the Hopi people. An account of the Spanish intrusion and resultant atrocities occurs within the stories, provoking a condemnation of the Christian religion and its effects. Hopi language, English translation, and ceremonial singing merge to create a rich discourse that swells and accompanies a series of evocative visual images. Ross Mataya makes a final appeal for the continuation of the storytelling tradition at the end of the film as the way to keep Hopi culture vital.

(Editor's note: See also the review of *I'isaw: Hopi Coyote Stories,* p. 107.)

Critical Comments: Anyone with a class in photography or film cannot fail to address the way in which Native Americans have moved from being the object of the camera aimed by anthropologists, scientists, and tourists to being the wielders of the camera themselves. In the Hopi tribe especially, there are many photographers with a wide variety of approaches. Masayesva is one of the few who manipulate the medium for special effects.

Anthropologists may note the adoption of the camera and the transformation of that medium and the genre of documentary film into a contemporary form of oral tradition. The film's forthright indictment of Western influence and Christianity as destructive forces challenges history, and at the same time brings up complicated issues of ambivalence toward Western influence and technology.

In the choice of the English version of this film for educational purposes, some of the intent has been lost. Masayesva uses the Hopi language to make a statement about the importance of language in evoking a culture. It stands as a challenge to the scientific, observational documentaries made about Indians by westerners in a language foreign to the Indian people. Any course concerned with language would find a striking example of its importance in this presentation.

Jeanne Laiacona, Department of Art

USRACGEN

Title:	**James Baldwin: The Price of the Ticket**
Producers:	Karen Thorsen and William Miles, for Maysles Films, Inc., and WNET/TV, New York
Director:	Karen Thorsen
Distributor:	Resolution, Inc./California Newsreel
Release Date:	1989
Technical:	87 min. / color, b&w / English
Purchase Price:	$295
Rental:	$95
Presentation:	Documentary, interviews, and narration
Award:	Red Ribbon, American Film and Video Festival

Following is the first of two reviews of
James Baldwin: The Price of the Ticket.

Content: This documentary traces the life history and accomplishments of James Baldwin, the great American writer. The film begins with his funeral and then focuses on issues of being poor, African American, and homosexual and the links between books and the lives of their writers. Born in New York's Harlem in the mid-1920s, Baldwin was one of nine children who spent much time at the library, trying to make a connection between books and life. He talks at length about his relationship to his father—how structured and dominated by fear it was, how he was forced to go to church though the church turned him into a writer. His experiences with racial segregation in the United States led him to move to France in 1948. At the time he was trying to write "everyone's protest novel," but his racial experiences in America forced him never to lose sight of being an American and to examine the French prejudice against Algerians in his work *No Name in the Street* (Dial, 1972).

The film then moves to his life in Switzerland as part of a gay couple and talks about the writing of one of his most famous books, *Go Tell It on the Mountain* (Dell, 1985). He details the difficulties of getting Knopf to publish his work in 1954 and talks about life in the Paris expatriate community that led him to write *Giovannni's Room* (Dial, 1956). He describes this period as one in which he learned to "say yes to life," wrote *Another Country* (Dial, 1962), spent time with other writers at William Sty-

ron's guest house, and traveled in Turkey. He summarizes this period by saying that "another set of assumptions can teach you a lot about your own civilization and your own assumptions."

His return to the United States was prompted by the beginnings of the civil rights movement. Having discovered at age five or six that he was not white, that the flag had not pledged allegiance to him, that there was no place for him, he wrote *The Fire Next Time* (Dial, 1963) upon his return. He saw the book as a plea—to tell white Americans what it's like to be black. He admits that he doesn't know what whites "feel," he can only infer it from the state of institutions in white America. This work was followed by *Blues for Mister Charlie* (Dell, 1985), a drama of race and class struggles. In it, Baldwin reflects on the hatred around him, the assassination of Martin Luther King Jr., and the riots of the 1960s. Baldwin was a controversial figure then because he was attacked by Eldridge Cleaver for his loathing of violence and his view that all men are brothers. This led him to return to the south of France, record his bitterness in *If Beale Street Could Talk* (Dial, 1974), and ponder the difference between bitterness and anger. The movie ends (as it began) with his funeral and the idea that "we can all become better than we are but the price is enormous and people are not yet willing to pay."

Classroom Use: This film is more appropriate for upper-class students than first year ones, though it will require some setup by the instructor for all classes. Some familiarity with the work of Baldwin is essential, such as an introductory lecture placing him in the context of African-American writers. It would also be a good idea for the students to read one of the books talked about in the film, preferably before they view it. The film is very long and without knowledge of the power contained in Baldwin's writings, it will seem to drag. The film does not do a very good job of explaining why one should be interested in Baldwin—one is assumed to have already gotten that from his writing.

This film would be of more relevance in humanities diversity syllabi than in social science courses. This is in part due to its length, but also because it focuses on the role of being a writer, and then adds the complexities of race and homosexuality. Many students in social sciences do not see themselves as writers and so might have trouble relating to the film in the context of social science diversity courses as they are sometimes taught.

Critical Comments: The main strengths of the film are that it covers multiple diversity issues (race, class, and homosexuality) and that it relates an ''individual-level'' story, thus helping students to identify with the historical events going on. However, it does presume knowledge of the main civil rights events, as well as knowledge of Baldwin's work. In short, it is a powerful and extremely well-done film that I enjoyed tremendously but I would urge instructors to view it before using it in a classroom.

Nancy A. Denton, Department of Sociology

See also below.

Content: James Baldwin (1924–1987) was at once a major 20th-century American author, a civil rights activist, and, for two crucial decades, a prophetic voice calling black and white Americans to confront their shared racial tragedy. Returning to a theme he had explored 35 years earlier, he wrote in ''Here Be Monsters,'' an essay published only two years before his death, and with which he chose to conclude his collected nonfiction *The Price of the Ticket:* ''Each of us, helplessly and forever, contains the other—male in female, female in male, white in black, black in white. We are part of each other.'' *James Baldwin: The Price of the Ticket* is a haunting, beautifully made biography which captures on film the passionate intellect, the courageous, controversial, and, at times, agonizingly conflicted writing of a man who was born black, impoverished, gay, and gifted.

Black-and-white archival footage evokes the atmosphere of Baldwin's formative years in Harlem in the 1930s, and the emigré demi-monde of post-war Paris to which Baldwin fled in 1948. Newsreel clips from the 1960s and still-life photos record Baldwin's involvement with the civil rights movement and reveal the extent to which, following the publication of *The Fire Next Time* in 1963, he was exalted as the voice of black America. Baldwin, by choice it seems, was forever surrounded by friends and hangers-on. His art and his output no doubt suffered as a result, but the loss is offset by an unprecedented film record of what were, for Baldwin, quiet retreats in Paris, the south of France, Istanbul, and Switzerland—retreats where he was able to write without the distractions of racial tensions in America.

Among those remembering Baldwin and commenting on his life and work are writers Maya Angelou, Amiri Baraka, William Styron, Ishmael Reed, and biographer David Leeming; friend (and lover) Lucien Happersberger, who was only 17 when he met Baldwin in Paris in 1949; Bernard Hassel, Baldwin's personal assistant; and his brother, David Baldwin. Happersberger, Hassel, and David Baldwin were with ''Jimmy'' when he died in the 18th-century house he had purchased just outside the tiny, ancient walled village of St. Paul de Vence on the Mediterranean.

Finally, the film skillfully incorporates excerpts from Baldwin's major works—including *Go Tell It on the Mountain* (Dell, 1985), *Notes of a Native Son* (Dial, 1963), *Another Country* (Dial, 1962), *The Fire Next Time* (Dial, 1963), *Giovanni's Room* (Dial, 1956), *Blues for Mister Charlie* (Dell, 1985), and *If Beale Street Could Talk* (Dial, 1974).

Classroom Use: Just as reading Baldwin's marvelously long sentences, bristling with commas and qualifications, requires some effort, some stage setting is necessary if students are to absorb the fascinating melange of history, ideas, and biography which the film brings together. This background is best obtained by having students read Baldwin's fiction (e.g., *Go Tell It on the Mountain*) and, perhaps, his most famous essay, *The Fire Next Time*. Baldwin himself was keenly aware that the ''social reality'' approach to understanding black history—''the beast in our jungle of statistics'' approach, he called it—was more shadow than substance. But without a good background understanding of post-World War II black history, the connection between Baldwin the belletrist and Baldwin the ideologue, will be missed. For use in humanities courses, then, background on the civil rights movement might well be necessary while social science courses may require getting students to read from Baldwin's literary output. Diversity offerings will find the film a rich vehicle for exploring race, race relations, comparative history, class, homophobia, and homosexuality.

Critical Comments: A number of themes are brilliantly interlaced in this film biography. One of these, perhaps the most important, is the question of what relationship, if any, the artist bears to the revolutionary. If Baldwin had a central political argument, it was that the destinies of black and white Americans were inextricably interwoven. ''[M]y own experience,'' he revealed in *Notes of a Native Son,* ''proves to me that the connection between American whites and blacks is far deeper and more passionate than any of us likes to think. . . .'' But these were hardly the words to inspire or move along a cause. They certainly did not mesh with the slogans of self-affirmation that liberation movements require. Moreover, as a writer, Baldwin was at his best when he explored his own equivocal sympathies and clashing allegiances. His role was to ''bear witness'' he said, not to be an ideologue. Those who hope to inspire a cause must have a firm grasp on their role, and an unambiguous message to articulate. Baldwin had neither, a fact Eldridge Cleaver exposed in *Soul on Ice* in 1968. ''I began to feel uncomfortable about something in Baldwin,'' Cleaver wrote. ''A rereading of *Nobody Knows My Name* cannot help but convince the most avid of Baldwin admirers of the hatred for blacks permeating his writings.''

Cleaver attacked Baldwin not only for his presumed racial self-hatred, but because of his sexuality—that is, his homosexuality. Given the determined sexual chauvinism ingrained in the black nationalism of the late 1960s, ''Baldwin bashing'' became something of a rite of passage, and it was not uncommon to hear Baldwin referred to as Martin Luther Queen by young militants. How large a role black homophobia played in the estrangement of James Baldwin, and what role this forced marginalization as a spokesman for the cause had on his recantation of his earlier ''black and . . . white, deeply need each other'' credo, is unclear. The documentary broaches the homosexual theme, but with little or no hint that it played a role, however significant, in Baldwin's pathetic attempt to convince naysayers that he was not irrelevant to the revolution then raging in the streets of America.

It was at this time, as William Styron recognized, that Baldwin was being torn by a ''terrific, almost schizoid wrenching—being pulled in one direction by the demands of his art, and the other direction by his moral need to do what he was also good at—which was to preach, to preach the gospel of equality.'' If there is a failing in this film, it is the unwillingness of its creators to use Baldwin's career to make clear the costs involved—the price of the ticket, as it were—when the talents of an artist are made to serve those of the ideologue—and especially the reluctant ideologue. Desperate to resume his role as the darling of the movement, Baldwin changed his message from one of compassion to one of rage. Just how far the author of *The Fire Next time* (1963) had come is revealed in *No Name in the Street,* a book he published in 1972. ''It is not necessary for a black man to hate a white man, or to have particular feelings about him at all, in order to realize that he must kill him,'' Baldwin wrote in the later work. Those who knew Baldwin realized that he was merely trading on the populist slogans of the H. Rap Browns, the Stokeley Carmichaels, and others who are now, mercifully, forgotten. Nothing is more tragic than a ''Jeremiah without convictions,'' and that is precisely what Baldwin had become.

Amiri Baraka was among those who eulogized Baldwin at his funeral in Notre Dame Cathedral. Baraka, who had earlier joined in the chorus of Baldwin-bashing by calling him ''the Joan of Ark of the cocktail party'' whose ''spavined whine and plea'' was ''sickening beyond belief,'' now praised him for being ''God's black revolutionary mouth.'' Baraka's tribute was hypocritical and, what is more, in 1987 it was an anachronism. The unfortunate pronouncements of his later years are not representative of the message Baldwin should be remembered for. Nor do they acknowledge that in his last writings Baldwin returned to his central conviction: ''We are part of each other,'' he wrote in 1985. ''Many of my countrymen appear to find this fact exceedingly inconvenient and even unfair, and so, very often do I. But none of us can do anything about it.''

Thirty years ago, Baldwin believed that an effort by the handful of ''relatively conscious'' blacks and whites might be able to avert the prophecy of the old Negro spiritual: ''God gave Noah the rainbow sign. No more water, the fire next time!'' If he were alive today Baldwin would be appalled by the celebration of ghettocentric culture by the media as well as by the extent to which that scientific silliness called Afrocentricity has made inroads in the academy. The embalming of dead genius in libraries is hardly an American invention; but the strong strain of anti-intellectualism in the American character makes us especially prone to seal the lips of our best prophets and soothsayers. This is regrettable generally, and especially unfortunate in the case of James Baldwin, whose central message was to remind us of our common humanity.

George A. Levesque, Department
of Africana Studies

USGENSTE

Title:	**Just Because of Who We Are**
Producer:	Toni Dickerson, Heramedia Collective
Director:	Toni Dickerson
Distributor:	Women Make Movies, Inc.
Release:	1986
Technical:	28 min. / color / English
Purchase Price:	$195
Rental:	$60
Presentation:	Documentary with interviews, working tapes, and photographic stills
Awards:	American Film and Video Festival, finalist; Global Village Documentary Festival, honorable mention; San Francisco Lesbian & Gay Film Festival

Content: *Just Because of Who We Are* consists for the most part of lesbians' first-hand accounts of homophobic attacks upon their persons. Most of the interviews in the film took place in 1983, at a time when the passage of a gay rights bill was being debated in New York's City Hall, a bill which finally passed in 1986. The film illustrates the types of pressures that society, religion, and family have brought to bear on lesbians. It further shows the women's struggle for freedom of choice and their militancy in their fight for gay rights. The women in the film recount the degrees and types of violence they have had to suffer; a violence which they see as existing in society at large and which allows for their persecution. They detail their experiences with physical and psychological abuse at the hands of strangers and family members, on the street and sometimes at home. Examples abound of the vilification that lesbians have to suffer: the name-calling and hate mail; the rapes and death threats; the police harassment and the deprivation of their children. However, the women see that the expansion of the gay rights movement has given them strength in unity. Ironically, according to one of the women interviewed, visibility has proven to be a double-edged sword at times: on one hand, attracting more support, and on the other, drawing more hatred.

Classroom Use: *Just Because of Who We Are* would be valuable to women's studies and sociology. It is an important aid in human diversity courses because it deals with questions of sexual identity and gender relations and because it shows clearly the problems that marginalized groups who choose non-traditional lifestyles may have to face in contemporary America. *Just Because of Who We Are* may also dispel students' preconceived notions about lesbians.

The following books would be helpful when planning courses in which the videotape is used:

Audrey Lorde. *Sister Outsider.* Crossing Pr., 1984.

Cherrie Moraga. "Pesadilla." In *Cuentos: Stories By Latinas.* Edited by Alma Gomes, Cherrie Moraga, and Marianal Romo-Carmona. Kitchen Table: Women of Color Pr., 1983.

—— and Gloria Anzualdua (eds.). *This Bridge Called My Back.* Kitchen Table: Women of Color Pr., 1981.

Critical Comments: This video is particularly interesting because it features writers Cherrie Moraga and Barbara Smith, who speak of their own experiences with homophobia (Moraga in her short story "Pesadilla" has written about an incident similar to the one she speaks about in the film: a burglar not only took all of her and her lover's possessions, but also defiled their living space with racial and sexual slurs). Because first-hand accounts in the video are so specific and the emotions with which they are told are so honest, *Just Because of Who We Are* is more than a mere documentary about homophobia.

The video clearly exemplifies the way racism, sexism, and homophobia are intertwined. However, it also shows that the gay rights movement unified and gave strength to individuals' demands for dignified treatment and for legislative changes.

Regina W. Betts, Department of Theatre

GLECOGEN

Title:	**La Operacion (The Operation)**
Producer:	Ana Maria Garcia
Director:	Ana Maria Garcia
Distributor:	Cinema Guild
Release Date:	1982
Technical:	40 min. / color, b&w sequences / English narration, Spanish with English subtitles
Purchase Price:	$295
Rental:	$75
Presentation:	Documentary, including narrative and interviews
Awards:	Merit Award, Latin American Studies Association; Documentary Prize, Festival of New Latin American Cinema
Study Guide:	Available

Content: This film discusses the policy of systematic sterilization of women in Puerto Rico, concentrating primarily on the post-World War II period. It describes the Puerto Rican experience with rapid economic growth and development after the war, describes the conditions which led to government promotion of mass sterilization to stem population growth on the island, and interviews women who were subjected to this method of population control.

Classroom Use: This short film is appropriate for courses dealing with gender issues, as well as those that consider demographic aspects of economic development.

Critical Comments: *La Operacion* illustrates attempts by Puerto Rican and U.S. governments to reduce population growth on the island via a policy of female sterilization. The basic belief on the part of governmental authorities was that unless population growth in Puerto Rico was reduced, living standards would remain low. Thus, to achieve higher income levels, explicit policies such as sterilization of women and mass emigration were promoted.

A major issue that arises throughout the film is the extent to which "The operation" was voluntary. Clearly, from the perception of public health authorities and many doctors, the procedure was viewed as entirely voluntary on the part of those who agreed to undergo it. What also becomes clear from the interviews is that many of the women were misinformed as to the nature of the procedure; they did not realize that it is a virtually irreversible process. The combination of easy access to medical facilities, little cost to the patient, limited knowledge about alternative procedures, and misinformation as to the effects of the surgery effectively led to a dramatic number of operations.

Another issue that arises in the film involves the role of the Roman Catholic church and a male-dominated society in determining that female sterilization was an appropriate instrument of public policy to reduce population growth on the island. Abortion and contraception were viewed as unacceptable alternatives in a largely Catholic society, but there was little opposition from religious circles to the sterilization of women who were mostly poor. Also, vasectomies and condoms, certainly less radical methods of birth control, were not viewed as options on the part of many men.

The narrative puts into perspective the Puerto Ri-

can development process, and the interviews of physicians, public health officials, and former patients brings to reality the motivations for and consequences of a policy of female sterilization to reduce population growth. *La Operacion* is critical of the use of this type of policy for demographic control and argues convincingly that the sterilization of Puerto Rican women as public policy was experimental in nature and that many of the subjects participated without full knowledge of its implications.

Carlos E. Santiago, Department of Latin
American and Caribbean Studies

GLCULEXP

Title:	**Land of Look Behind**
Producer:	Alan Greenberg, for Solo Man Production
Director:	Alan Greenberg
Distributor:	Facets Video
Release Date:	1990
Technical:	88 min. / color / English, with some "standard" English subtitles for the Rastafarian and rural Jamaican speakers
Purchase Price:	$79.95
Rental:	$10 for members of Facets Video Club
Presentation:	People telling their own stories; narration by residents of both rural Look Behind and urban Kingston; occasional footage of formal ceremonies; and island music—reggae, Christian, African—as a background score

Content: Black Jamaicans present a politicized vision of their culture that contrasts with the pristine image that tourists view from their hotels. Rastafarian culture is highlighted in order to show how these Jamaicans confront racism, poverty, urban violence and squalor, materialism, miseducation, and neglect. The film celebrates the music, language, and spiritual systems that the Jamaican people have nurtured during centuries of political struggle. Filming was conducted during May and July 1981, but the majority of scenes are evocative of many different times. I give the film high marks for the ways in which it presents Jamaicans telling their own stories

against the backdrop of a country whose politics they themselves do not entirely understand.

Classroom Use: In presenting Jamaicans of African descent, the film raises issues that relate directly to African-American history and culture. In particular, the lingering psychological effects of enslavement and the survival tactics arising from that period can be discussed in conjunction with this film. Bob Marley, King of Reggae, the "Bob" whom so many of the speakers adore, is frequently compared to Marcus Garvey and Dr. Martin Luther King Jr. Before screening the video, viewers should be familiar with the roles of Garvey and King in African-American folk culture as well as our politics and civil rights activities.

Because of the many Rastafarians represented, I recommend some prior introduction of college-level classes to this movement (see resource list below) and to its spiritual leader, Haile Selassie.

Critical Comments: The film's strongest appeal is that it relies entirely upon the Jamaicans themselves to comment on their lifestyles and aspirations. With the exception of reggae stars Lui Lepke and Gregory Isaacs, the speakers are ordinary black Jamaicans—farmers, market vendors, tailors, poets, singers, street preachers, con artists, and even prisoners. Beginning in the treacherous district of Look Behind, with its forbidding forests, sinkholes, and cliffs, and traveling to the traffic jams and reggae clubs of Kingston, the camera presents a parade of speakers who represent many levels of wealth, influence, and schooling. The Ras Tafari movement is presented as proposing natural lifestyles to replace technocentric ones, communal lifestyles to replace competitive ones, an emphasis on meditation and individual creativity, and a philosophy that art, particularly music, connects us to the gods. Rather than present Ras Tafari spirituality as a panacea, the film uses music and poetry to expose the Rastafarians' own biases and points of compromise.

Although "translations" of the speakers' English are occasionally provided, they are shown merely to aid unfamiliar viewers. Very much explicit in the video is the assumption that the dialect of the speakers is neither illiterate nor substandard. In this way the video connects with the current debates in the United States about whether to establish a national language, whether black English is really a language, and whether to provide bilingual classrooms. Also, the video calls attention to African continuities in the English that African Americans speak. The black Jamaicans display much similarity to African Americans in their fondness for naming, wordplay, proverbs, puns, rapping, and worrying the line. Viewers should have some prior exposure to the coded spirituals that Africans developed during enslavement, for this use of code is evident both in the reggae songs and the religious sermons included in the film.

The video calls attention to several aspects of human diversity. In addition to its political and linguistic content, the film has potential applicability in discussions of literature and storytelling technique. Both wildlife and water recur throughout the film to call attention to the Jamaicans' concerns about survival, spirituality, urbanization, and escape. These motifs present another opportunity to show how the black Jamaicans often speak of experiences similar to many of America's racial and ethnic groups.

For background on the sociopolitical struggles of Jamaicans, and particularly the Ras Tafari movement, I suggest:

Michelle Cliff. *Land of Look Behind*. Ithaca, N.Y.: Firebrand, 1985.

Jack Johnson-Hill. "Unheard Voices: Jamaica's Struggle and the Multinational Media." *Caribbean Quarterly* (June-Sept. 1981): 1–16.

"*Reggae International:* Spiritual Balm for a Trembling World." *Caribbean Review* (Spring 1983): 32–33.

George Simpson. "Religion and Justice: Some Reflections on the Ras Tafari Movement." *Journal of Caribbean Studies* (Fall 1986): 145–53.

Michael Thelwell. *The Harder They Come*. New York: Grove, 1980.

Barbara McCaskill, Department of English, now at the University of Georgia, Athens

GLCLAGEN

Title:	**Les Bon Debarras (Good Riddance)**
Producers:	Marcia Couelle and Claude Godbout
Director:	Francis Mankiewicz
Distributor:	International Film Exchange
Release:	1981
Technical:	114 min. / color / French dialog with English subtitles
Purchase Price:	$79.95
Rental:	n/a
Presentation:	Dramatization
Awards:	Winner of 8 Canadian Academy Awards

Content: *Les Bon Debarras* is the story of a dysfunctional family living in a rural area of Quebec. Michelle, along with her 13-year-old daughter, Manon, and her alcoholic brother, Guy, who is brain-damaged as the result of a childhood bout with meningitis, eke out a living selling firewood to local residents. Geographically far removed from any social services, Michelle is the sole caretaker, both financially and emotionally, of her brother. These demands, coupled with her own need for a relationship with a man, allow little time for her daughter. This lack of parental guidance leaves Manon free to determine what direction her life will take. With no positive role models to emulate, it is not surprising that she chooses a self-destructive lifestyle which includes truancy from school, smoking cigarettes and marijuana, drinking, and sexually precocious behavior.

Like most children in dysfunctional families, Manon yearns for a normal family life through fantasy. In her fantasy world, her mother meets a rich, handsome man in a sportscar who rescues the two of them from their dismal existence. However, in the stark reality of her real world, Manon realizes that the best relationship she can arrange for her mother is with Gaetan, the pot-smoking local mechanic and school bus driver. Before Manon can make her fantasy family a reality, though, she must eliminate the two men presently in her mother's life—her brother Guy and Maurice, the local police chief who is the father of her mother's unborn child. This she manages to do through deceit and manipulation.

Classroom Use: This film would be appropriate for classes dealing with the issues of classism, sexism, and cultural diversity. The social issues raised, along with the complexity of the characters' lives, should generate a great deal of classroom discussion.

Critical Comments: This film poignantly portrays many of the social problems inherent in the dysfunctional family, including poverty, child abuse, alcoholism, low self-esteem, and parent/child role reversal. Manon, like many children in her situation, is forced to assume adult responsibilities beyond her years. She is more concerned with her mother's well-being than with her own and desperately wants to make her mother happy in every way. This longing to please and feelings of guilt over a parent's unhappiness are also symptomatic of the dysfunctional family.

The film also deals with issues of class. In French, as in English, a person's socioeconomic class can often be determined by his or her use, or misuse, of the language. Those familiar with the French language may find themselves unable to understand some of the French spoken in this film. The use of "joual," the language of the working class, immediately establishes the class of the characters. Class differentiation is also apparent when Michelle's lifestyle and living conditions are juxtaposed against those of one of her wealthy customers.

Gender issues, such as sexual harassment, are also dealt with, as when Gaetan tries to force himself on Michelle as payment for having freed her van from the mud. A woman's right to control her own body also becomes an issue when Maurice tries to pressure Michelle into getting an abortion. Despite her perceived weakness when it comes to men, Michelle does not allow her convictions in these areas to be swayed by Gaetan and Maurice.

From an artistic and technical point of view, the director, Francis Mankiewicz, successfully uses location, sound, and light to set the mood for the film. The landscape, which would be considered beautiful under different circumstances, is lonely and depressing against the pervasive gray sky. His use of annoying background noise in the form of barking dogs, chain saws, and police car sirens, establishes a mood of tension and anxiety, much like that which often accompanies a life of poverty. These sounds of chaos and confusion are especially effective when they are contrasted with the soft, calming music which can be heard each time the trio delivers firewood to the neat, orderly home of the rich customer. The actors in this film are perfectly cast and are convincing both in performance and appearance. There is no Hollywood hype or glitz in this film—just real people with real problems and no solutions.

Christine Pearce, Department of French Studies

USETHCLA

Title:	**Les tisserands du pouvoir (The Mills of Power)**
Producer:	Claude Fournier for Ciné Les Tisserands, Inc.
Director:	Claude Fournier
Distributor:	Malofilm Video
Release Date:	1988
Technical:	116 min. / color / French with English subtitles
Purchase Price:	$70
Rental:	n/a
Presentation:	Dramatization (historical fiction)
Study Guide:	Text by Claude Fournier, Les tisserands du pouvoir (Montreal: Edition Quebec/Amerique, 1988)

Content: Treated here are the migration and adaptation by some 10 percent of the Canadian population to the northeastern United States—the largest continental migration in North America. It is illustrated through the Lambert family's struggle to maintain its French-Canadian identity, language, and culture in Woonsocket, Rhode Island. Class conflict is portrayed through the rise of a French industrialist in the United States as compared to the economically disadvantaged Franco-American laborer. The time is post-World War I, at the height of industrialization in a highly competitive industry seeking to maximize labor's potential.

The film opens with an appeal for continued French-language programming on the local television network by a now-old Jean-Baptist Lambert. His loss of connectedness with native language reflects the cost of assimilation in an adopted land. Using flashbacks, the film portrays the primacy of class interests, when mill workers are denied company time for the observance of the French-Canadian national holiday, the feast of St. John the Baptist. The mill owner, a wealthy French industrialist from northern France, refuses, sparking controversy. This in turn causes a labor stoppage on the feast day. The angered owner issues an ultimatum: work or be fired. The viewer becomes acutely aware that class interest takes precedence over laborers' cultural traditions.

Classroom Use: *The Mills of Power* will provide students of world cultures, ethnology, or sociology (particularly labor relations) vivid, first-hand insights into the social drama of the French-Canadian migration to the United States at the turn of the century. Culture study classes can explore the social impact of assimilation on traditions, language, and ethnic identity. The labor struggles of an ethnic group in an industrialized society can also be analyzed.

Critical Comments: *The Mills of Power* is a dramatization of the economically and socially disadvantaged French-Canadian Lambert family. It is the story of discrimination and exploitation by one ethnic group, the French industrialist Roussel family, of another ethnic group, the Franco-American mill worker in Woonsocket, Rhode Island. This film, of Franco-American life between the two world wars, is represented from a Quebecois perspective.

An unsparing indictment of class conflict is seen when the wealthy French industrialist sends his young son, Jacques Roussel, to live and study in Montreal. Jacques's internal knowledge of the French-Canadian mentality later enables him to understand and exploit the economically and culturally disadvantaged Woonsocket laborers. Jacques's subsequent marriage to Simone Fontaine, a French-Canadian opera singer, highlights the distinctions between social milieus and the disparity between social classes.

The contrasts between the Lambert and Roussel families unveil the cultural differences, preconceived notions of class and society based on ethnicity, and the primacy of class interests over those of language and culture.

Patricia Sutliffe, Department of French Studies

GLGENEXP

Title:	**The Life and Poetry of Julia de Burgos**
Producer:	Jose Garcia Torres, for Sandino Films, San Juan, Puerto Rico; shown here as a segment of the PBS program ''Realidades'' (WNET/TV, New York)
Director:	Jose Garcia Torres
Distributor:	Cinema Guild
Release:	1979
Technical:	28 min. / color, b&w archival footage, photographs / Spanish with English subtitles, some English
Purchase Price:	$295
Rental:	$65
Presentation:	Docudrama: Documentary, with dramatic reenactments of Julia's life and archival footage

Content: The film focuses on the life and poetry of Puerto Rico's most venerated female artist, Julia de Burgos. It relies on her own journals, journalism, and correspondence to show her active pursuit of Puerto Rican nationalism, fair labor laws for factory and sweatshop workers, and respect for the Puerto Rican campesino or peasant farmer. Included is a rare audiorecording of Julia herself reading from her most acclaimed work, ''Rio Grande de Loiza.''

Critical Comments: In a fine manner the film avoids the dryness of typical documentary and uses music and poetry to enliven Julia's story.

Born to a poor farming family in Carolina, Puerto Rico, Julia learned early to take pride in her people and her island. During the 1930s, while studying to become a teacher at the University of Puerto Rico, she began to channel this intense patriotism into La Republica, the country's nationalist movement. Because her poetry very much revolves around this theme, college-level audiences might benefit from some prior introduction to the history of Puerto Rico, in particular the strong-armed interventionist role of the United States government in suppressing this nation's independence. Julia sustained long friendships with such socialist intellectuals as Nicolas Guillen and Juan Bosch, and the theories of socialism are evident in two of her political poems recited in the film, "Palm Sunday" and "Responsory in Eight Parts."

This film focuses especially upon gender-related concerns as well as those of racial and ethnic diversity. For example, Julia's founding of the Daughters of Liberty, a military arm of the Puerto Rican Nationalist Party, is applicable to class discussions of gender roles. Useful for discussions of race and stereotyping are poems recited that address color consciousness ("Ay, Ay, That I am kinky and pure black!"), self-determination ("Workers! Bite the fear. Yours is the naked earth"), and master-slave relationships ("If being in servitude is to have no rights, being the master is to have no conscience"). Two symbols that recur throughout her verses—llantos (tears) and brazos (arms)—might also prove a catalyst for the discussion of diversity issues.

Barbara McCaskill, Department of English, now at the University of Georgia, Athens

USGENCLA

Title:	**The Life and Times of Rosie the Riveter**
Producer:	Connie Field
Director:	Connie Field
Distributor:	Direct Cinema Ltd.
Release Date:	1980 (motion picture by Clarity Productions); 1987 video
Technical:	65 min. / color, b&w / English
Purchase Price:	$350
Rental:	$100
Presentation:	Documentary with archival footage, interviews, and narration (in-depth interviews with five women)
Award:	New York Film Festival 1980

Content: *Rosie the Riveter* documents the expansion of women's work into nontraditional jobs in the defense industry during World War II. These jobs were a direct result of military necessity. The film also explores the process by which women were removed from the work force with the demobilization of the armed forces.

Classroom Use: This film is appropriate for high school and college-level students. It will be useful for classes in United States history, women's studies, labor studies, public policy, and sociology. Companion references for this film include:

Phillip Sheldon. *Women and the American Labor Movement.* Free Pr., 1979.

Darlene Clark Hine, Lillian S. Williams, Elsa Barkley Brown, and Tiffany Patterson. *Black*

Women in United States History. Carlson, 1990.

Leila Rupp and Verta Taylor. *Survival in the Doldrums.* Oxford University Pr., 1987.

Critical Comments: Women's labor was critical to the support of the United States' war efforts in the 1940s. The United States conducted a propaganda campaign to persuade women to abandon their traditional jobs for the well-paying industrial jobs that had been vacated by male laborers who joined the armed forces. It was women's patriotic duty to join the labor force and the government paid for their training. These job opportunities provided women with a liveable wage and new-found independence. In essence, a social revolution was effected. *Rosie the Riveter* documents the whole process: the important contributions women's labor made to the war effort, the impact that meaningful work had on their lives, and the systematic campaign of the government and the media to compel women to return to their traditional race/gender roles following the war.

Through a series of in-depth interviews with five women, the film successfully juxtaposes the goals of government propaganda campaigns and the realities of both black and white women's experiences and expectations as workers. It provides an accurate depiction of race, class, and gender issues. Race and gender determined the positions that women secured in the defense industries, with black women employed in the least desirable jobs. Simultaneously, race governed the relationships among workers.

Workers, however, occasionally overcame these barriers and engaged in collective activities to protect their interests. Black women joined other racial minorities and sometimes provided the leadership in their quest for equality on the job. The film accurately portrays this history. The experiences of *Rosie the Riveter* show the extent to which government policy, indeed, can effect social change. Because of military necessity the United States government established training programs and day care centers for working mothers, policies that today either have been severely curtailed, or are being debated by Congress.

Lillian S. Williams, Department
of Women's Studies

USGENSOC

Title:	**Longtime Companion**
Producer:	Stan Wlodowski, for American Playhouse Theatrical Film
Director:	Norman Rene
Distributor:	Facets Video
Release Date:	1990
Technical:	96 min. / color / English / close-captioned
Purchase Price:	$89.95
Rental:	$10 for members of Facets Video Club
Presentation:	Videocassette release of 1990 motion picture; script by Craig Lucas; Academy Award nomination for Best Supporting Actor, Bruce Davison

Content: This film depicts in powerfully evocative ways the response of a segment of the gay male community to AIDS. The setting is the gay urban subculture in the 1980s and the stories of several gay men who are linked to the same friendship network are told. The film explores the way these men respond to AIDS. It is, at one level, a story of how the gay community comes together to fight AIDS and the social discrimination that is intensified with the epidemic.

Critical Comments: Stereotypes abound about gay men. They are frequently portrayed as promiscuous, amoral, and deviant. In some respects, AIDS has intensfied these stereotypes and the discrimination that accompanies them. This film challenges these stereotypes in an emotionally compelling yet subtle way. Gay men are presented as ordinary in many respects. They are seen as involved in relationships, friendships, families, and careers. Moreover, even though this film focuses on white, mostly middle-class men, they are portrayed as diverse. Some are businessmen or lawyers, others are salesmen, health workers, writers, etc. They are all presented in positive, self-respecting ways. These are characters that the viewer can identify with regardless of sexual orientation. Being gay is seen less as a sexual preference than as a social identity. It is the friendships and a common culture made up of a shared language, dress codes, etc., that define these gay men.

The theme of the film revolves around how this circle of gay couples and friends respond to AIDS. AIDS is described as caused by a virus and its spread among gay men is seen as largely accidental, at least not as a punishment for homosexuality or a result of that lifestyle. None of the gay men who get AIDS is said to have lived a fast-lane lifestyle. AIDS is presented, though, as potentially devastating to the gay community. It threatens to destroy the web of love and friendship that knits the community into a coherent whole. It threatens to rob this community of many of its creative figures and leaders. On a more personal level, the film tries to show the threat to individual personal lives. AIDS threatens lovers and friends; it injects a constant anxiety into the community.

This is, however, a film of AIDS victimizing the gay community. Indeed, what is emphasized is the response of these men to AIDS: the compassion they show for each other; the sacrifice they make for each other; and their sense of personal and community pride. These are not men who are passive or self-doubting; they are sure of who they are and defiant and proud in the face of the suffering brought by AIDS. In the end, AIDS is depicted as helping to shape a new community; the old one that circled around sexual joy, coming out, the retreat into the ghetto, gives way to a new community based on stronger feeling and social and political commitments. This I take as the film's utopian or ideological message to the gay community and perhaps to the straight population as well.

This is a well-done and important film. There are very few serious films about gay men that preserve the integrity and complexity of their lives; there are even fewer that integrate the theme of AIDS as well. The portraits of people with AIDS are compelling. Most importantly, people with AIDS are not presented as victims. The film's politics are largely submerged and subtle, not interfering with the dramatization of gay male life. But it is not without flaws. Most obviously, lesbians are absent. The men are almost all white, middle class, and stereotypically handsome. These characters are purged of almost all character blemishes, which renders them a bit one-dimensional. At its best, the film is a glimpse into one segment of the gay male culture of the 1970s and 1980s. This is a film that will definitely appeal to students. It should prove very useful as both a vehicle to discuss gay male culture in the 1980s and as an introduction to AIDS.

Steven Seidman, Department of Sociology

USETHCLA

Title:	**Los Sures**
Producer:	Diego Echeverria, for Terra Productions and WNET/TV-13, New York
Distributor:	Cinema Guild
Release Date:	1984
Technical:	60 min. / color / English with some Spanish easily understood
Purchase Price:	$595
Rental:	$100
Presentation:	Documentary which focuses on six people's lives
Awards:	Blue Ribbon, American Film and Video Festival; Special Jury Award, San Francisco Film Festival

Content: The subjects of the film are the Puerto Ricans who live in the Williamsburg area of Brooklyn, New York, known as Los Sures (literally, the people who live on the south side of Brooklyn). The context is the mid-1980s, when Puerto Ricans in the United States confronted a series of seemingly insurmountable problems.

The six subjects are Tito, a young man in his twenties who works in a chop shop, dismantling stolen cars and selling the parts; Marta, a single mother who lives on welfare and food stamps; Cuso, who runs his own construction business; Evelyn, a community organizer; and Ana Maria, a middle-aged woman who is active in a spiritualist church. The film follows each of these people in their daily routines and provides ample opportunity for each to comment on their lifestyles.

Classroom Use: The film is presented at a fairly straightforward level, which requires little preparation for students viewing it. On the other hand, it may be relevant to mention that Puerto Ricans have been U.S. citizens since 1917, so that students don't confuse them with other Hispanic groups in this country. (It is amazing how many people in this country don't know Puerto Ricans are citizens by birth.) Viewers might be made aware of the fact that the people whose lives are depicted in the video are ones who are visible in public life in Williamsburg,

The six Puerto Ricans profiled in *Los Sures* live (as U.S. citizens) on the south side of Brooklyn, N.Y. In different ways they face the "seemingly insurmountable obstacles" of that setting. Here, 20-year-old Tito (second from left) stands with friends at a corner where Tito's brother was killed. (Courtesy Cinema Guild)

not professionals or business people who do not frequent this impoverished area of Brooklyn.

Critical Comments: The film does not try to prove some theoretical point. Its evident goal is to present an empathetic view of people who live in poverty, without romanticizing the poor nor blaming them for their plight. This is a fine line to traverse and I believe the film does a good job of it.

The primary focus of the film is upon people in different social roles within this community. As such, it gives as well-rounded a perspective as one might hope from this limited coverage. If it is understood that this film deals only with certain poor people who are Puerto Ricans, it can be a useful film for the purposes of the diversity requirement. I have had criticisms of it from students who thought that only "losers" were portrayed, but I consider the film to be more positive about the Puerto Rican poor in the United States—positive in the sense of their comprehension of how they came to be poor and what life chances they might enjoy—than other films of this kind I have seen.

James Wessman, Department of Latin American and Caribbean Studies

USETHSTE

Title:	**Los Vendidos**
Producer:	Luis Ruiz
Director:	George Paul
Distributor:	Teatro Campesino
Release Date:	1972
Technical:	27 min. / color / English
Purchase Price:	$250
Rental:	$55
Presentation:	Television production of KNBC/TV, Burbank, Calif., based on a 1967 skit presented for the first time at the Brown Beret junta, Elysian Park, East Los Angeles
Awards:	Emmy Award, 1973; the San Francisco Broadcast Media Award
Study Guide:	Los Vendidos, by Jorge Huerta. See under Classroom Use, below.

Content: The film focuses on the various stereotypic representations of the Chicano: the revolutionary, the farm worker, the zoot-suiter, the ladies' man, the pachuco (young, tough guy), the vato loco (tough guy crazed by drugs), and so on. Luis Valdez is the Chicano creator of the Teatro Campesino, a company born out of the struggles of the Chicano farm workers. The film satirizes the Anglos' prejudices due in part to their ignorance of the Mexican-Americans' historical and cultural roots. It also shows the degree of acculturation that Chicanos and Chicanas have to undergo in order to be accepted by the dominant society, which often perceives them only as objects of mirth and cheap labor.

The videorecording of *Los Vendidos* opens with a skeleton wearing a striker's headband dancing among the archetypal characters portrayed by the members of El Teatro Campesino which include: the farm worker, the sellout, the soldier, and the corrupt farm labor contractor as the coyote. The characters surround an Aztec calendar stone out of which emanates a voice which announces: "The Farmworkers' Theatre of the Universe." The action then moves to Honest Sancho's Used Mexican Lot, which displays models of Mexican types. Miss Jimenez, an anglicized Chicano secretary from Governor Ronald Reagan's office, has come to purchase a Mexican type to window-dress his all-white Anglo adminis-

tration. The secretary is shown an Indio with his maiden; a farm worker who will never go on strike; a Pancho Villa-type who resembles the "frito bandito"; a pachuco complete with a switchblade; and a drugged-up vato loco. But Miss Jimenez wants a man whose skin is not too dark, who is hardworking, sophisticated, English-speaking, romantic, and who can be manipulated. In other words, she wants a "beige" white man. Finally she is shown a fair-skinned Mexican-American with a buttoned-down business suit, close-cropped hair, English-speaking, super-patriotic, and who reveals his ethnicity to a minimum degree. Overjoyed, Miss Jimenez has found the ideal for the governor's office and she purchases him.

In addition to writing *Los Vendidos* and numerous other plays, Luis Valdez is the author of *The Shrunken Head of Pancho Villa* (*Necessary Theatre: Six Plays about the Chicano Experience,* ed. Jorge Huerta. Arte Publico, 1989) and the creator of the films *La Bamba* and *Zoot Suit.*

Valuable for the study of Chicano contributions to the performing arts and to the understanding of the work of Valdez are:

John Chavez. *The Lost Land: The Chicano Experience in the Southwest.* University of New Mexico Pr., 1984.

Jorge A. Huerta. *Chicano Theatre: Themes and Forms*. Bilingual Pr., 1982.

Alfredo Mirande and Evangelina Enriquez. *La Chicana: The Mexican-American Woman*. University of Chicago Pr., 1979.

El Teatro Campesino: The First Twenty Years. El Teatro Campesino, 1985.

Luis Valdez. *Pensamiento Serpentino: A Chicano Approach to the Theatre of Reality*. El Teatro Campesino, 1973.

Classroom Use: Beside the study of theater and drama, *Los Vendidos* would be an asset in the social sciences, political science, Hispanic studies, and Native-American studies. It presents several concerns related to diversity courses. It deals with the social, economic, and political problems that face Chicanos today in the United States. It can lead to discussions regarding the way stereotypic representations tend to reify and dehumanize the "other." It can be used to examine the rich culture that has existed among the people who occupied the land that is now known as Mexico and the southwestern United States, prior to Columbus's "discovery," the invasion by the Spaniards, and the advent of Manifest Destiny.

A supplemental study guide written by Jorge Huerta is available free of charge. *Los Vendidos* is published by the Teatro Campesino in *Actos: El Teatro Campesino*. The volume also contains scripts stemming from the company's involvement with the United Farmworkers, the Vietnam War protests, and the reclamation of the Chicano cultural heritage.

Critical Comments: El Teatro Campesino is the brainchild of Luis Valdez. The group's work started in 1965, together with the inception of Cesar Chavez's struggle to organize farm labor into the United Farmworkers of America. What began with field hands performing revolutionary skits for fellow strikers has evolved into a respected world-renowned, nonprofit theater company "dedicated to the creation and advancement of Chicano heritage in the performing arts." The company presents propaganda pieces in a style influenced by Brecht's theories concerning political theater. Luis Valdez explores questions of discrimination and assimilation; seeks to reclaim the spiritual and cultural heritage of the Chicano in Aztec and Mayan roots; spurns the usual Spanish antecedents; and illustrates the manner in which migrant workers are exploited and degraded.

Valdez's look is ironic and his tone sardonic as he presents us with the many familiar stereotypes of Mexican-Americans. *Los Vendidos* also illustrates the humiliating process of "whitewashing" that the Chicano has to undergo in order to get even a modicum of attention. But for Valdez, any attempts at acculturation, physical makeover, and denial of "indio" roots amount to a sellout. Instead, he appeals to the group identity by representing social realities which are all too familiar, and calling forth the Chicanos' and Chicanas' common spiritual heritage.

Regina W. Betts,
Department of Theatre

GLCULREL

Title:	**Machu Picchu**
Producer:	Educational video written by Sidney and Mary Lee Nolan
Distributor:	Educational Video
Release Date:	c1987
Technical:	18 min. / color / English narration
Purchase Price:	$39.95
Rental:	30-day preview
Presentation:	A series of stills translated into video format
Study Guide:	Verbatim transcript of the narration accompanies the video

Content: The focus of the narration is upon the mountain city of Machu Picchu in southern Peru. A very brief history of its "discovery" by Hiram Bingham is provided, and, as one moves from scene to scene, interpretations are offered of its significance for the Incan civilization. The interpretation seems to be aimed at those unfamiliar with the site or its religio-cultural significance. The narrator is concerned with the possible significances of Machu Picchu for the Incas, and the Inca are the primary cultural group here. But the Spanish invasion and colonization of the Incan empire also receive some interpretation, as do the modern "discovery" and attempt to interpret Machu Picchu. At least one of the producers seems to specialize in Meso-American history. There is a slight amount of Andean pena music accompanying the slides, although it does not receive any interpretation.

Classroom Use: The script is minimal, adequate mainly for use with high school students, though a college instructor might find the slides useful as a preliminary introduction to the site, or as a point of departure for a fuller discussion of the site and its possible significances.

Critical Comments: This reviewer did not expect a videotape solely of slides. The tape would be most valuable to someone who is quite familiar with the site but for some reason has no slides of their own. The interpretations offered definitely require supplementation, if used on the college level. Because Machu Picchu is such a stunning site, students are likely to be engaged by even a very brief exposure to this tape, and in this sense it is a very valuable resource for involving students in the study of Incan culture and Hispanic history in Peru. In this case, the value of the videotape is relative to the resources of the teacher and his or her in-class strategies. Its most likely users are faculty providing survey courses who have little time to provide in-depth study of Incan societies. Those well-informed on Peruvian histories are likely to have access to more developed materials, perhaps of their own making. But a knowledgeable instructor without such visual resources could make good use of this brief production.

Robert M. Garvin,
Department of Philosophy

USAGEGEN

Title: **Maggie Kuhn, Wrinkled Radical**

Producer: Howard Weinberg, for WNET/TV, New York and PBS

Distributor: Indiana University Audio Visual Center

Release Date: 1977

Technical: 30 min. / color / English

Purchase Price: $220

Rental: $15.90, 16mm only

Presentation: Documentary interview; also issued as a motion picture

Content: This is an interview of Maggie Kuhn, the founder and leading spirit of the Gray Panthers, an activist organization concerned with public policy issues affecting the aged in our society and with the treatment of the ''old'' in America. The interview is conducted by Studs Terkel. Interspersed are some action scenes of Kuhn and Gray Panther activism, and some home shots of Kuhn and the two younger women who live with her and who are also Gray Panther workers. The film is interesting, educational, and moving.

Kuhn, who was 69 years old when the film was shot, has a history of political activism, starting with her work in the Women's Trade Union Movement as a young woman. We see Kuhn demonstrating in Chicago some years ago against the American Medical Association for its stand on national health care policy (or lack of it), and we see her more recently speaking to a nursing association on that and other age-related health questions. We also see the work of some of the Gray Panthers staff helping people in nursing homes and helping them get out of those homes through legal aid.

Critical Comments: The film would have been a better one had Terkel done a little more homework or asked Kuhn a few more follow-up questions. However, to his credit he does not try to dominate a la Ted Koppel, but mostly lets Kuhn speak for herself. She does so wittily, charmingly, and very informatively. I recommend this film; it is well-done and thoughtful in its approach to ageism, political activism, and feminism. Kuhn—whose female relatives served as her role models—obviously can be a role model for other women, both in demonstrating to older women how vibrant and vital older age can be, and for showing younger women that, indeed, older women can have wisdom to offer and can have a challenging and interesting role to play in activist politics.

Joan Schulz, Department of English

GLGENSOC

Title:	**A Man When He Is a Man (El Hombre, Cuando es el Hombre)**
Producer:	Valeria Sarmiento
Distributor:	Women Make Movies
Release Date:	1982
Technical:	60 min. / color / Spanish with English subtitles
Purchase Price:	$350
Rental:	$90
Presentation:	Documentary with extensive interviews
Awards:	Rotterdam Film Festival; Taipei International Film Exhibition; Berlin Film Festival; Films de Femmes, Sceaux, France

Content: This documentary discusses men's and women's attitudes toward their sex roles in Costa Rican society.

Classroom Use: It is recommended for courses dealing with gender roles, especially in Latin America, and the concept of machismo.

Critical Comments: Using interviews of men and women of different age groups and social classes, this documentary illustrates how Latin-American men and women still tend to view or define themselves and their relationships within a patriarchal frame of reference. While men remain the primary figures of authority at home and in public life, and are free to do as they please, women's primary role continues to be defined in terms of their functions as devoted mothers, obedient daughters, and faithful wives. The subordination of women, expressed through the prevailing sexual double standard, is constantly perpetuated and reinforced through socialization and in societal institutions.

The film is quite effective in illustrating how the church, schooling, the mass media, prevailing moral values, and child-rearing practices all contribute to maintaining a sexual double standard, relegating women to the domestic sphere and limiting their participation in government and public life. The subjects interviewed illustrate the many contradictions shared by different generations of men and women regarding their own sense of identity within the family and society.

Although the film was made with Costa Rican male and female subjects, its content is generalizable to other Latin-American contexts. When released, this documentary was the subject of controversy in Costa Rica, since it was intended as a denunciation of sexism and as a consciousness-raising tool. Ultimately, it served to open up a public dialog and debate about issues concerning the general status of women and the need for change.

Edna Acosta-Belen, Department of Latin American and Caribbean Studies

USGENCLA

Title:	**Martha Mitchell of Possum Walk Road: Quiltmaker**
Producers:	Jack Peterson and Melvin R. Mason
Director:	Dick Rizzo
Distributor:	KAMU/TV, Texas A&M University
Release Date:	1985
Technical:	30 min. / color / English
Purchase Price:	$40
Rental:	No rental, no preview
Presentation:	Documentary using voiceover narration (both by Mitchell and a male narrator) and recordings of Mitchell's own commentary as she works

Content: This video is an examination of the life and work of Martha Mitchell, a white, 81-year-old quilter from Huntsville, Texas. It provides an unusual, contextualized glimpse of quilting as one of many creative activities in the life of a woman.

Born in 1902, Martha Mitchell learned as a girl how to quilt and do many other types of needlework. She gradually received public recognition for her quilts and became something of a celebrity in Huntsville, Texas. This video traces her recollections about and reflections on her life, childhood, work, and artistic practices, with an emphasis on her award-winning quilting. The viewer sees not only her quilts, but also the social environment in which they were created. Mitchell leads a tour of her house, the small town in which she lives, her garden, and the contents of her hope chest, providing a fuller sense of the significance of quilting in the life of the maker. Sometimes Mitchell did the quilting for quilt tops that had already been pieced together by others. In the video she also displays and demonstrates her own quilts and unique quilting techniques, while sharing her own perceptions about life and her philosophy of living. This is a woman who took great pride in her work and whose attention to detail was manifested in many aspects of her daily routine. At the age of 81 (she died in 1985), Mitchell was doing all her own yard work and gardening on a two-acre plot of land, in addition to her needlework, cooking, and housekeeping. The video also offers fascinating insights into women's perceptions of history, the domestic arts, and the aging process.

Classroom Use: *Martha Mitchell of Possum Walk Road* is appropriate for classroom viewing at the university level, both undergraduate and graduate. This video could be of use in addressing diversity issues in a variety of ways. It places a heavy emphasis on the importance of contextual factors in interpreting artistic expression. It also introduces issues of ageism and common misconceptions about older people and the aging process. It could be used in courses on or having to do with gender, folklore, aging, diversity in the arts, women's studies, American history, American studies, anthropology, and sociology.

Critical Comments: At times Mitchell's narration sounds overly practiced and awkward, as though it were read aloud, but the video offers a refreshing examination of needlework (and artistic creation more generally) in context. Toward the end of the video there is a helpful discussion of the ways in which folk artists combine elements of tradition and innovation in their work in order to create their own personalized means of expression. Students who do not understand or appreciate needlework as an art form, or who perceive rural Americans or older people as unsophisticated or boring, may have a difficult time appreciating this video, as it accentuates the everyday routine that structured Mitchell's life in a small country town in Texas. A thorough introduction to the video and prior discussion of these issues would improve its reception among contemporary, urban-dwelling students.

This video relates directly to the history of the United States and addresses gender and age-related concerns. It provides knowledge of diversity as expressed through aesthetic and ideological endeavors.

Linda Pershing, Department of Women's Studies

GLRACCLA

Title:	**Master Harold . . . and the Boys**
Producer:	Iris Merlis
Director:	Michael Lindsay-Hogg
Distributor:	Warner Home Video Inc.
Release Date:	1986
Technical:	90 min. / color / English
Purchase Price:	$59.95
Rental:	n/a
Presentation:	Originally produced in 1984 as a motion picture version of Athol Fugard's play, which premiered at the Yale Drama School in 1982 and was thereafter successfully mounted on Broadway with the same cast
Awards:	The three actors appearing in this video—Matthew Broderick, Zakes Mokae, and John Kani—received Tony Awards for their performances when the play was produced on Broadway

Content: The action is set in a small tea room owned by a white family in South Africa. It deals with the relationship between a young white man and two black servants. Athol Fugard is a white South African playwright, who has written extensively and has received wide acclaim for his work about the problems of apartheid in his native land. Master Harold is set in the 1950s in a middle-class setting within the larger political, economic, and social arena of institutional racism.

Harold, the young, white adolescent reminisces about the special friendship and closeness that has existed between him and the family's black servants, Sam and Willie. But upon learning that his alcoholic father is about to be released from the hospital, Harold, in his unhappiness, fear, and frustration, turns viciously on his servants. For a moment, the possibility of mutual respect and friendship seemed to prevail. But the illusion is shattered, and the "master" reasserts his prerogatives.

The play is published by Viking Penguin and is obtainable from bookstores and libraries. Theater periodicals contain numerous studies on Fugard and his work. Background on apartheid is, of course, widely available.

Classroom Use: In addition to theater and drama courses, the film would be useful to Africana studies, political science, and social sciences. It provides a valuable teaching tool because of its depiction of black and white relationships and the way that they are irremediably affected by racism. In this reviewer's experience, students watched the film after having read the script. At the time, the topic under discussion was institutional racism and its implications in the United States. The representation was instrumental in helping the students perceive the pathology of racism and in moving them to see its personal ramifications.

Critical Comments: *Master Harold . . . and the Boys* has a profound impact on its viewers because of its powerful dramatic qualities. Implicit in the presentation is the assumption that if the white world insists on its stance of innate superiority and if it rejects opportunities for the correction of existing inequities, it will eventually find itself forever isolated, as the young man in the play does, on a "for whites only" bench.

This faithful and powerful adaptation of the stage production graphically shows the syndromes of the white master/black servant relationship with its humiliations, beatings, mockeries, and the literal "spitting in the face" from one who sees himself endowed with moral, social, and political superiority. This videotape is particularly moving since its structure is dramatic. It abstracts and focuses on climactic moments where confrontations between South Africans are particularly poignant. For example, the spittle that Harold directs at Sam, his servant, can be seen not only as a humiliation but also as hurtful as a knife-thrust.

The following concerns related to human diversity are inherent in *Master Harold . . . and the Boys:*

it can easily be compared to the institutional racism which presently exists in the United States and be related to the students' personal experiences as members of the mainstream or as victims of prejudice. It can help show the impossibility of positive and "normal" intercourse when categories of race, gender, ethnicity, or sexual preference are established and serve to subjugate and deny others their personhood because of some sense of superiority. It gives an insight into the impact of apartheid on the daily lives of individuals, and shows that it may not be possible to live in a "world without collisions," if the hand of reconciliation is not accepted. It provides a chance for discussion and for a comparison to the American experience. It presents an opportunity to discuss and understand the struggles and angers of African Americans. The fact that the action is set in South Africa creates a distance which helps Americans see the devastating effects that domination has both on the master and on the slave.

Regina W. Betts, Department of Theatre

USGENSOC

Title:	**Men's Lives**
Producers:	Josh Hanig and Will Roberts
Distributor:	New Day Films
Release Date:	1974
Technical:	43 min. / color / English
Purchase Price:	$275
Rental:	$15
Presentation:	Thematic exploration of male identity in American culture, conducted through brief excerpts of interviews and live coverage of everyday social interactions between men and women, boys and girls; the directors narrate their own search for definitions of masculinity and manhood
Awards:	Best Student Documentary, Academy Award (1975); Gold Ducat, Mannheim International Film Festival; Blue Ribbon, American Film and Video Festival

Content: This video explores the pressures on, competition among, and conditioning of American men in the 1970s. Hanig and Roberts, both in their early twenties when the video was made, examine their own upbringing and socialization through critical eyes. The movie features brief interviews with school teachers, grade school children, teenage boys and girls, parents, and people in the community, conveying a range of ideas about what it means to be male in American society. The video emphasizes how men have been taught and are expected to be strong, in control, competitive, unemotional, afraid of intimacy, aggressive, and the primary wage earners for their families. In turn, it examines the considerable pressures and unrealistic expectations that this places on men to succeed and how men spend much of their time and effort trying to "prove" themselves, with an enormous fear of failing to live up to societal expectations about their male prowess.

Classroom Use: *Men's Lives* is appropriate for classroom viewing at the university level, both undergraduate and graduate. It is a useful tool for generating discussion about socialization and gender identity. Many students will be able to identify with some aspect of what they see presented as typical occurrences in the everyday lives of boys and men.

This video can be of use in addressing diversity issues in several ways. It comments primarily on gender relations and differences; however, it also raises useful issues concerning the interrelationships of gender, race, and class through comments made by men and boys of color (detailing the pressures they feel to achieve status through prestigious jobs and wealth) and working-class men (noting the drudgery and dehumanization of factory labor). It can be used in courses on gender and the study of folklore. It can also be used in women's studies courses or courses about diversity in American life.

Critical Comments: *Men's Lives* raises interesting questions about the ways in which we learn gender roles and the strengths or weaknesses of highly divergent notions of what it means to be male and female. The video was made in the 1970s and it is somewhat dated both in the appearance of the peo-

ple (e.g., haircuts and clothing styles) and in the discussion of women's roles (there is little recognition that many women work outside the home). Nonetheless, one of its striking features is that, all in all, so little has changed, encouraging the recognition that today many boys and men still feel pressured to conform to the norms outlined in the video.

Although *Men's Lives* deals with the enormous pressures men feel to conform to conventional notions of masculinity (and the consequent toll this takes on them), it never seriously addresses the privileges that men enjoy in American society. To some degree, men are featured as victims whose emotions and potential as human beings are constrained by society, rather than as perpetrators or benefactors of male privilege, and this is a weakness in the theoretical assumptions implicit in the video. There is, in addition, the suggestion that capitalism is linked to the drive for men to find self-esteem through monetary success and material possessions and the devaluation of women's domestic work. This notion is introduced through interviews with men and boys who claim that having a successful, high-paying job and being able to buy an expensive car or house makes them "real" men, whose work counts for something meaningful. The term *capitalism* or the discussion of its effects on gender relations is never addressed explicitly, however.

This video relates directly to the contemporary United States (although it's a little dated) and addresses gender-related concerns. Indirectly and peripherally it also addresses racial and class-related diversity. It provides knowledge of diversity as expressed through sociopolitical and ideological endeavors and assists students in understanding some of the sources and manifestations of gender-related conflicts and cultural norms. It also focuses on the dynamics and mechanisms of gender relations that often limit men and subjugate women.

Linda Pershing, Department of Women's Studies

USIMMRAC

Title:	**Miles from the Border**
Producer:	University of Southern California Center for Visual Anthropology
Director:	Ellen Frankenstein
Distributor:	New Day Films
Release Date:	1987
Technical:	15 min. / color / English (background Spanish, usually translated)
Purchase Price:	$175
Rental:	$40
Presentation:	Documentary (first-person narration and voiceover)

Content: This short documentary portrays aspects of the life of an immigrant Mexican-American family in Fillmore, California—an agricultural community—from the perspective of the eldest sister and her brother. The film opens with a 1965 snapshot of the family still in Mexico and immediately shifts to Fillmore in 1986, where we learn that this is a "sleepy, and I mean sleepy town," where nothing seems to be happening except for a "hidden division" between Anglos and Mexicans—now becoming stronger because of new arrivals. We never do learn the name of the sister, who does most of the narration and who teaches in the English as a Second Language and bilingual program of a local high school, though we learn a great deal about how she sees her life and her family. The brother, whom we also meet, works with preschool children and their families and is a championship runner.

We see images of the town, the fields, the high school band, and the sister in her classroom as she discusses her students, her initial experiences when she first arrived, and her visions of upward mobility. We meet the brother and see him on the track and teaching children in their home as he describes his feelings of frustration when he arrived from Mexico, was placed in kindergarten, and had to tolerate other kids calling him "dumb." The sister talks about the constant separation of Anglo and Mexican students, and describes her strong desire to learn prompted by the differences in resources between her old village in Mexico and her new home in Fillmore. She discusses her differences with her contemporaries who did not learn English and now

work in factories, who used to call her a traitor because of her desire to do well in school. She does not see herself as a traitor and maintains an active pride in her people and culture. The brother talks about a high school counselor who refused to let him into college preparatory courses, but accepted him as "one of us" when he won an athletic championship.

Finally, the sister talks at length about the impact of her younger sister, Rosa, on the family. Rosa went to Yale University, but in her senior year developed schizophrenia and died a year later. The ensuing fragility and sense of loss felt by the family becomes a metaphor in the narration for the difficulties inherent in adapting to a new country ("When we come to a new culture or a new language, part of us dies in some way") and living in two different worlds. The film ends by capturing some of the sister's ambivalence as she struggles to define herself and to help others do the same. We hear her counseling a college-bound student regarding the implications of this for the family, we listen to her describe the strength she has derived from her grandfather's dictum never to forget where you come from, and watch her address her class of recent arrivals on the importance of learning English.

Classroom Use: Ultimately, the film does a decent job of presenting one view of immigration and acculturation from the perspective of the individual who is experiencing these processes. But it only dances around the more difficult questions regarding how best to interpret these experiences in the larger context of the intergroup relations and social processes that surround them. I can imagine the take-home message all too easily as something like, ''Immigration was and is difficult, but if you try hard, you can make it.'' In a classroom situation, perhaps these faults can be turned to virtues by using the film as a screen on which to project students' perceptions and assumptions. I believe that most learning can occur by generating discussion regarding not only what is in the film but what is left out.

Critical Comments: The film incorporates many important themes relevant to immigrant families in general and Mexican-Americans in particular. Through the images and the narration, we are introduced to reverberations of discrimination and intergroup tension, to strains and stresses of acculturation, to dangers of marginality, to pain and pleasure of biculturalism, and to tensions brought about by social mobility and immobility among immigrant Mexican agricultural and factory workers.

After watching this short video, we get the impression that we now know much more about the experience of Chicanos in the United States and that we have more insight into what it's like for Mexican-Americans as they struggle to find their individual identities in a largely hostile Anglo-dominated world. Indeed, we do get a clearer picture of some of the conflicts that can arise between the pursuit of economic advancement and the pressures of cultural alienation. We hear of one woman's vision of success, as defined by her struggles to balance learning English and pursuing academic achievement with maintaining pride in her origins and cultural background. Yet her story is tainted by the painful experience of her sister's death and her uncertainty about how much she will really be accepted. We get glimpses of the patterns of change and social mobility experienced not only by this family but also by many others. And we get a vivid sense of the stresses brought about by living in two worlds. To this extent, the film provides rich raw

material to provoke discussion and to complement course readings and lectures in a variety of courses, especially those on Hispanic or Mexican-American cultures or on ethnic relations.

However, the film has important gaps that make it an incomplete treatment of the Mexican-American experience in general or even of one family's experience in particular. Nevertheless, these are issues that can be addressed in discussions and through readings and other films. Because of the film's brevity and its relatively undigested format, it does not address many details about the family and the world around it that would help frame the experiences described by the sister. For example, a recurring theme seems to be the importance of learning English for success in the new life. The sister discusses how many of her peers who arrived at the same time saw doing well in school as traitorous, did not learn English, and now have fewer opportunities.

In this situation and in others, one can easily come away with the impression that the primary factor in ''success'' is individual effort. In spite of learning of the difficulties faced by newcomers, the separation of Anglos and Chicanos, and the potentially alienating effects of establishment universities, we never hear the words ''racism'' or ''discrimination.'' We learn that Anglos and Mexicans are completely divided, but the factors that maintain those divisions are barely addressed. We see a woman struggling to be part of a system that doesn't fully accept her, but we never get to hear her reflect on this and other paradoxes. We learn about ambivalence on the part of both brother and sister regarding the benefits of coming to the United States, and we hear of the sister's commitment to maintaining her ties with the past. But beyond listening to her speak Spanish in the classroom and seeing her mother cook a tortilla at home, we don't get any insight into what the family most values about its Mexican culture.

Bernardo M. Ferdman, Departments of Psychology and of Latin American and Caribbean Studies

USRACCOM

Title:	**A Minor Altercation**
Producers:	Jackie Shearer, Terry Signaigo, and Mary Tiseo
Director:	Jackie Shearer
Distributor:	Women Make Movies
Release Date:	1977
Technical:	30 min. / color / English
Purchase Price:	$225
Rental:	$60
Presentation:	Dramatization

Content: The film is about an integrated school setting and segregated communities in an urban New England city in the late 1970s. The social groups represented are working-class, African-American, and Irish-American families.

The video dramatizes a real-life incident involving a fight between two high school girls, one white and one African-American, over placement in a special computer class. The video depicts the reactions of the girls and their families, illustrating various perceptions of racism. Both families' efforts to investigate the incident between the two girls reveal the institutional racism that was at the root of the initial conflict.

Classroom Use: Undergraduate and graduate students are appropriate audiences for this video. The experiences and perspectives depicted are realistic and reveal no biases for or against any specific racial or ethnic group. The stereotypes and prejudices that members of each group hold about the other are portrayed impartially and non-judgmentally. School administrators are depicted as impersonal, racially biased, and insensitive. Inexperienced viewers should be informed that the latter depiction, while realistic, is not representative of all school administrators.

Critical Comments: The underlying theoretical assumptions of the video are: (1) institutional racism can be at the root of conflicts between individuals of different racial or ethnic groups; and (2) prejudice, stereotyping, and racism serve to constrain people's ability to understand conflict and limit their problem-solving abilities.

This video would make a valuable contribution in the classroom to explore intergroup conflict; institutional factors that contribute to racism, discrimination, prejudice, stereotyping, and social stratification; and how racial/ethnic prejudice and racism are communicated and perpetuated through language.

Salome Raheim, Department of Communication

USETHGEN

Title:	**Mitsuye and Nellie: Asian American Poets**
Producers:	Allie Light and Irving Saraf
Distributor:	Light-Saraf Films
Release Date:	1981
Technical:	58 min. / color, b&w / English
Purchase Price:	$100
Rental:	No rental; no preview charge
Presentation:	Documentary with archival footage, interviews, and narration

Content: *Mitsuye and Nellie* is a powerful film that chronicles the immigration and adaptation of several generations of Chinese and Japanese Americans to life on the west coast of the United States. Through the eyes of the families of poets Mitsuye Yamada and Nellie Wong, the film depicts the unique cultures of these groups and the impact of race, class, and gender upon their adaptation processes.

Classroom Use: This film is appropriate for high school and college students. United States history, ethnic studies, women's studies, American literature courses, and U. S. social history courses will find this film invaluable.

Critical Comments: *Mitsuye and Nellie* chronicles the experiences of three generations of the poets Mitsuye Yamada and Nellie Wong's families. It provides a compelling depiction of the U.S. social climate in which they found themselves as young immigrants in the 1930s and 1940s. The film provides detailed accounts of government policy that resulted in discriminatory treatment of Asians, who were considered temporary settlers rather than permanent residents. Asians could not become citizens and were not permitted to bring their families to the United States. Their access to jobs was restricted to the lowest paying and most arduous positions. It soon became evident to these immigrants that the American Dream was for whites only. The internment of the Japanese in camps during World War II and the reaction of other (non-Japanese) Asian-Americans to their incarceration further substantiated their beliefs. All of these events are depicted in

forceful ways, for the documentary shows the impact of these atrocities on real families with whom the audience can empathize. Despite the harsh realities of discrimination, these people retained their indigenous cultures that enabled them to live, love, and survive the atrocities they experienced in the land of opportunity.

The film also deals with gender issues. It shows how women and men experienced immigration differently and the ways in which they coped with their stay on Angel Island, California, the port of entry for Asians. It presents an honest portrayal of sexism, especially within the Chinese-American culture, and its stultifying effect upon the growth and development of girls. Three generations of women discuss their hopes, dreams, and realities as women of color in the United States. Both Yamada and Wong used their poetry as a vehicle for self-actualization as well as educating others about their cultures.

Mitsuye and Nellie is an example of social history at its best. It is predicated upon works by historians Ronald Takaki, Sucheta Mazumdar, and others. This passionate film shows intergenerational conflicts between mothers and daughters and breaks down stereotyped images of Asian-American women. Companion references are:

Maxine Hong Kingston. *The Woman Warrior.* Vintage International, 1989 [c 1976].

Ronald Takaki. *Strangers from a Different Shore.* Little, Brown, 1989.

Lillian S. Williams, Department of Women's Studies

GLECOPOL

Title:	**Mr. Ludwig's Tropical Dreamland**
Producer:	WGBH/TV (Boston) and BBC (London), for the NOVA series
Distributor:	NOVA
Release Date:	1979
Technical:	57 min. / color / English
Purchase Price:	no longer available for purchase
Rental:	$38, 16mm only; available for rental from the media centers of several major universities, such as University of Washington
Presentation:	Documentary, with limited interviews
Study Guide:	A transcript of the NOVA program presented in this video is available from Journal Graphics, 1535 Grant Street, Denver, CO 80203

Content: This film covers the early history of a project to produce wood fiber on a vast tree farm in the heart of the Amazon jungle.

Classroom Use: It is recommended for use in courses dealing with cultural diversity, Latin-American studies, Brazilian studies, and ecology.

Critical Comments: In 1967 American businessman Daniel K. Ludwig purchased an area of four million acres (approximately 20 percent larger than the state of Connecticut) from a consortium of Brazilians and launched the largest forest industry project ever undertaken by private enterprise, known as the Jari Project (the property being located on both sides of the Jari River, a major tributary of the Amazon). Due to its immensity and its audacity, the Jari Project attracted worldwide attention. For developmentalists, the project raised hopes for the futures of both the area (or the Amazon region, in general) and Brazil, long considered a "sleeping giant" due to its major untapped resources. For many Brazilian nationalists, the project fed suspicion that the Amazon region was being taken over by foreign interests, with the connivance of the military regime which ruled Brazil from 1964 to 1984. Moreover, as cutting and burning of the native forest proceeded at the rate of approximately 12,500 acres annually during the first few years of the project, environmentalists became increasingly concerned over the fate of the native forest. According to research by Brazil's National Institute for Amazonian Research (INPA), approximately half of the atmospheric water vapor of the region is a direct result of transpiration from the Amazonian forest; thus, the ongoing large-scale deforestation could have profound effects on the local rainfall, thereby endangering the ecology of the entire region.

The video provides a balanced presentation of the Jari Project during its early years, with attention both to its goals and expectations and to obstacles of various types. It documents contrasting views of the project; differences in social conditions between the Brazilians and the Americans and other non-Brazilians working on the project; failures on the part of the project's managers to understand some of the customs of the Brazilian workers (as well as their biases) and to make appropriate adjustments in their demands or expectations; failures on the part of planners to take into account some of the basic features of the environment and the ecology of the region; and failure to heed some of the lessons of other economic ventures by foreign companies in the Amazon.

Such failures in the planning and execution of the Jari Project are not explicitly labeled; it is up to the viewer to identify them. Thus, the video can serve as the basis for practice in critical, analytic observation. Moreover, since the documentary does not present the entire history of the Jari Project—its coverage extends only to the late 1970s—it is interesting to consider subsequent directions taken by the project with a view toward identifying lessons that can be learned about such projects in the Amazon and other forest regions of the world. After all, some of the arguments both pro and con have been used many times, in various contexts; a critical review of the history of the Jari Project can help assess the validity of some of them.

Brian F. Head, Department of Hispanic, Italian, and Portuguese Studies

GLCULREL

Title:	**Music of the Devil, the Bear, and the Condor: Spirits of the Andes**
Producer:	Nick Doff, for Skater Keeni Films, with TSI Video Productions
Director:	Mike Akester
Distributor:	Cinema Guild
Release Date:	1989
Technical:	59 min. in 2 parts / color / English narration; Spanish and Aymara recording with subtitles in English
Purchase Price:	$350
Rental:	$90
Presentation:	Documentary

Content: The focus of the film is largely upon Aymara-speaking peoples living on the altiplano in southern Peru and northern Bolivia, with some material on the cities of La Paz and Puno. Campesinos (indigenous, pre-Hispanic native peoples) and mestizos (people of Hispanic and Indian ancestry), studied separately and in their interactions, are interpreted. The film begins with an introduction of the gods and spirits that have been important to the Aymara peoples at least since the time of the Incan conquest. The sun god, moon goddess, earth goddess, Marani (Lord of the Year), the spirits of the dead, the god of war, village saints, and the Virgin are the main sacred realities introduced, with some historical references to the importance of the sun and the moon and the earth goddess for the Incas.

There is some marvelous pena music, with exquisite shots of the musicians (the film has some very fine artistic/aesthetic moments, and the brief coverage of some of the musicians is superbly done). At least four of the songs sung in the film are translated in the subtitles, which adds a great deal to the value of the film. There are brief studies of campesinos planting potatoes, carrying out rituals to ensure a generous harvest, and dividing the harvest with mestizo landlords. There is a study of an 81-year-old campesino who is visited by the spirits of the dead at night, and who agrees to divide his lands among his daughters, with appropriate rituals. The interactions between mestizos and campesinos in the villages of Iyata and Vitocola, including the school children, are presented; the visit of the school children to a medical clinic is studied with the rather grim revelation of their various illnesses; there is marvelous coverage (in part) of several festivals with magnificently costumed campesinos; and there are a few comments on the political conditions in Peru and Bolivia at the time of the film (c. 1987).

Classroom Use: This is an above-average film, technically, anthropologically, and educationally. Faculty dealing especially with peoples of the altiplano region of southern Peru and northern Bolivia, or perhaps dealing comparatively with these peoples and others, could make excellent use of this film both in class and in media centers where the student might review the film. It touches upon traditional cultural life, economic conditions, political realities, religious practices, music, and festivals, and the interaction of Hispanic and Indian cultures.

Critical Comments: The narrator provides intelligent interpretations of the content of the film, but no hermeneutical issues (in anthropology, history of religions, etc.) are explored or discussed. This makes it possible for the instructor to use the film with high school students, at the upper levels; but its best use is more likely to be in upper-class courses in a university. It is the kind of film that might appear on PBS, but there is no effort made to relate the cultures in the film with those of North Americans, even though it lends itself readily to an intelligent effort to do that. The film is basically sympathetic to the campesinos, but some of us will detect some of that aristocratic distance and condescension that oftentimes appears among the upper classes in South America towards the ''Indios.''

Robert M. Garvin, Department of Philosophy

USRACGEN

Title:	**Never Turn Back: The Life of Fanny Lou Hamer**
Producers:	Bill Buckley and Tracy Sugarman
Director:	Bill Buckley
Distributor:	Rediscovery Productions
Release Date:	1983
Technical:	58 min. / color, b&w / English
Purchase Price:	$150 (60 minutes); $90 (30 minutes)
Rental:	n/a
Presentation:	Documentary with archival footage, interviews, and narration
Award:	1984 Ciné Golden Eagle Award

Content: *Never Turn Back* documents the life of Mississippi human rights activist Fannie Lou Hamer. It focuses upon the civil rights years—1964 until Hamer's death in 1977—and includes an interview with her, comments from individuals who knew her, and scenes of her work in civil rights efforts.

One of 20 children born to a sharecropping family in the Mississippi Delta, Hamer experienced firsthand the deleterious impact of structural inequities on the social, political, and economic development of African Americans and poor communities. With little formal education, Hamer used her indomitable spirit and dogged determination to fight this oppression, and that helped to catapult her and the struggles of Mississippians into the national limelight. Although she concentrated her efforts on alleviating the oppressive forces that rural Mississippians experienced, she perceived racism as a corruption in American life. She dedicated her life to eradicating this cancer from American society and she lectured throughout the country to win support for the self-determinationist efforts of blacks. She believed that peonage and a lack of political power condemned African Americans to second-class citizenship.

Classroom Use: This film is appropriate for high school and college students. It is useful for classes in United States history, African-American studies, women's studies, and political science. It addresses issues of race, gender, and class, and gives accounts of social reform and self-determination.

Critical Comments: *Never Turn Back* documents Fanny Lou Hamer's efforts to empower blacks and the poor and, in the process, fills a major void in available resources that present the reform activities of "the inarticulate masses." It also rescues from oblivion the activities of black women civil rights fighters, a group that heretofore received little attention, yet whose contributions to the movement were critical to its successes. (See, for example, the book *Women in the Civil Rights Movement* by Barbara Wood, Vicki Crawford, and Jacqueline Rouse. Carlson, 1990.)

Unlike many biographies that depict their subjects as larger than life, this video accurately portrays Fanny Lou Hamer and places her in proper historical perspective. Born in 1918, Hamer was alive for the major events that affected 20th-century Americans—migration, world wars, depression, the civil rights years, etc. Hamer joined the formal civil rights movement under the auspices of the Student Non-Violent Coordinating Committee in Mississippi, 1962. Like so many of her predecessors, it was her religious faith that provided the foundation for development of her political ideology. One cannot fully understand the reform efforts of black Americans outside of the context of their religion.

As a child Hamer learned the concept of agape or mutuality in her family. Love and faith sustained her during famine and episodes of violence inflicted upon blacks who dared to question the legitimacy of U.S. apartheid. The producers of this video understood well this aspect of the culture of black Americans. Consequently, their product chronicles the experiences of rural Mississippians, as well as the life of Fanny Lou Hamer. Within this context it also becomes evident why Hamer stressed economic development for poor blacks and whites, while she campaigned for political rights for blacks. She was instrumental in establishing communal gardens and kindergartens which are still in existence today.

But her political activities in the Mississippi Freedom Democratic Party are what made her most widely known. In this film Ella Baker, Anne Braden, Charles McLaurin, and other contemporary activists discuss the significance of Hamer's contributions to the movement. The producers also compare the rural and urban reform movements and depict the vitality of the former at a time when the urban movement had become moribund.

This film is well-done for it not only describes the life of Hamer, but also provides the historical context that created her and her contemporary reformers. For further information on this topic refer to the following books:

Vicki Crawford, Jacqueline Rouse, and Barbara Woods. *Women in the Civil Rights Movement.* Carlson, 1990.

Darlene Clark Hine, Lillian S. Williams, Elsa Barkley Brown, and Tiffany Patterson. *Black Women in United States History.* A ten-volume series. Carlson, 1990. Includes several articles on black women in the civil rights movement and other areas of women's reform.

Anne Moody. *Coming of Age in Mississippi.* Dell, 1976.

Robert Weisbrot. *Freedom Bound.* Norton, 1990.

Lillian S. Williams, Department of Women's Studies

USIMMETH

Title:	**The New Puritans: The Sikhs of Yuba City**
Producers:	Ritu Sarin and Tenzing Sonam
Directors:	Ritu Sarin and Tenzing Sonam
Distributor:	National Asian-American Telecommunications Association/CrossCurrent Media
Release Date:	1985
Technical:	27 min. / color / Punjabi dialog, English subtitles and narration
Purchase Price:	$150
Rental:	$50
Presentation:	Documentary; some traditional Sikh music

Content: The "new Puritans" are Sikhs, some of whom came to the United States around 1900 when economic and political conditions were very difficult in India. They and those who came after them settled in the Sacramento Valley near and in Yuba City, California. The narrator traces the history of Sikhs in this area from the first migrations of the early 1900s to 1985 (when the film was made). By 1910 over 1,000 Sikhs were in this area; by 1924, when further immigration was closed, there were over 6,000. These early immigrants were mostly men who eventually assimilated to American culture, many marrying Mexican women and raising their children Roman Catholic. But with the change in the immigration laws in 1946, new immigrants arrived who were especially attracted to orchard farming (labor-intensive, but profitable). With the more open policy implemented by President Johnson in 1965, immigrants arrived in sufficient numbers to make it plausible to preserve their cultural and religious identity in the United States.

The narrator traces the relations between the early and later immigrants and then focuses upon ways in which the latter have maintained their cultural and religious identity. For obvious reasons, much of this exploration focuses upon current marriage practices, and several generations of Sikhs present their views of traditional practices. There is a good deal of dialog on how different individuals feel about maintaining traditional Sikh culture in the United States, how they see themselves in relation to political struggles in the Punjab, and why they find themselves committed to maintaining traditional identities in this country. Considerable footage deals with a wedding and associated rituals.

The narration includes occasional references to the history of Sikhs in India that provide a minimal historical interpretation of this very important Indian minority.

Classroom Use: This video can be used with young people in high school; it also lends itself to more sophisticated usage in university-level courses. Since there is not much visual material available on the Sikhs (except to those of us fortunate enough to have made some of our own), many persons dealing with minorities in the United States, or teaching courses on Indian history, culture, and society, or a course on world religions, could profitably use a brief film like this as a basis for class discussion, as an incentive to particular student projects, or as a helpful supplement to lectures.

Critical Comments: The video is clear, generally accurate, sympathetic to the Sikh immigrant viewpoint, and presents enough glimpses into Sikh culture and information about Sikh life and history to further student interest and guide them toward some beginning understandings. Of course, there are many limitations of such a short film dealing with the Sikhs in the American cultural context. Such a limitation can also be an asset for the knowledgeable instructor. The video is especially provocative in terms of issues having to do with nurturing, accepting, or living with "cultural diversity," and the persons interviewed present significant viewpoints from an "insider" perspective.

Robert M. Garvin, Department of Philosophy

USETHECO

Title:	**Northern Lights**
Producers:	Bob Nilsson and John Hanson
Distributor:	Facets Video
Release Date:	1978
Technical:	90 min. / b&w / English
Purchase Price:	$19.95
Rental:	$10 for members of Facets Video Club
Presentation:	Docudrama, with reenactments
Awards:	Winner of the 1979 Cannes Festival Palm d'Or for best first feature film; Blue Ribbon, American Film and Video Festival, 1980

Content: This film is a fascinating depiction of rural populist/socialist organizing among Norwegian immigrant farmers in the North Dakota prairie from 1915 to 1917. As a study of the Non-Partisan League (NPL) and the politics of the organization and its members, the film offers a rich view of the links between the "personal" and the "political." Further, as a slice of life among an ethnic group that remains relatively obscure in the United States, *Northern Lights* offers a valuable opportunity for viewers to understand the varieties and commonalities of American ethnic experience. Though it might at first seem odd that the actor who played the Jewish Henry Goldbloom in *Hill Street Blues* plays a Norwegian-American farmer in this film, it actually helps the viewer begin to comprehend the flexibility of ethnic identity.

Critical Comments: While it takes chances with the problematic docudrama approach, the film more than succeeds. It is a highly ethnic, yet quintessentially American film dealing with perhaps the core contradiction of the American identity: that the hyper-individualism of this culture exists on a highly contested terrain next to needs for communal identity and collective action. The central conflict which drives the film is the need for commitment beyond the individual in order for people to construct broader and more effective meanings to their lives.

The Norwegian-American farmers face lonely and isolated self-deception and decline as they conceive of their plight as specific to themselves. Once they begin to recognize that they are not alone in their desperation and that they can organize to gain control over their collective future, things do not seem as grim. Though the story is about the victimization and resistance of ethnic farmers facing powerful banks and agribusinesses, it could just as easily be about African Americans in the South facing racist local elite, or even housewives in the suburbs facing the problem without a name. Commitment gives meaning to life, even if it demands the sacrifice of a modicum of privacy and individual autonomy.

The main character, Ray Sorenson, cannot find the opportunity to marry his beloved, Inga, because both are busy with Non-Partisan League organizing; but their marriage had earlier been precluded by the dire economic straits of both of their families.

Lest one believe, however, that this portrait is so universal that it gives little content to the specifics of Norwegian-American culture in the northern prairie, beware. The characters are classically Scandinavian in their reserved demeanor, their paucity of words, and meagerness of expression. What is not said speaks more loudly than the screams of the dying. Brother faces brother in stony silence, unable to relieve or even express shared pain; lovers are incapable of expressing their love. And, above it all, the frigid wind screams unceasingly across the treeless plain. The black and white of the print underlines the starkness of the physical and social landscape of the vast prairie as it lends a simultaneous timeliness and timelessness to the story.

And what a story it is. More than a tale of redemption through collective action, it is a tale of

Norwegian immigrant farmers in North Dakota organize to control their future in *Northern Lights,* ''a highly ethnic, yet quintessentially American film.'' Though very much a portrait of Scandinavians in its particulars, the themes of isolation, victimization, and resistance could as well pertain to African Americans or even suburban housewives, says reviewer Robert L. Frost. (Courtesy First Run/Icarus Films)

coming to consciousness, of personal and collective empowerment. The long winters of the northern prairie can be conducive to alcohol, suicide, or worse—one is reminded of Bob Dylan's song ''Hollis Brown''—yet the harsh environment can also invite people to cuddle together for warmth. Similarly, the exigencies of the banks and agribusinesses can drive farmers to isolated, unhappy deaths, as happens with both Ray and Inga's fathers, or they can push people together. There are always the outsiders— the WASP bankers, the honkie cowboys (as opposed to the Scandinavian ''sodbusters'')—but outsiders are there by their own choice. The NPL has an ethnically inclusive agenda, for it talks to its constituencies in their own language, within their own cultural frame. It neither lauds nor denigrates the ethnic otherness of its people. It does respect the differences and recognize their importance for collective identity. In a memorable scene, one of the local male heads of a (micro-) clan tells a trite ''Ole and Lena'' joke—such jokes are an important, if informal, part of Scandinavian-American ethnic identity—and those around the table laugh not because it is funny, but because it underlines their quiet solidarity.

Northern Lights also offers an intimate look at the material culture which frames the lives of the farmers and NPL activists. The class differences and commonalities based on technology are reflected by the highly restricted access to a steam-powered thresher and the wide and popular access to the Model T. Ironically, both are used ultimately for communitarian ends: the limited availability of the thresher compels the locals to work frantically together to maximize use of the rare asset—men freeze in the flying snow as women prepare the massive meals (a gender division of labor which erodes as political activism increases)—while the Model T allows organizers to hurry from one isolated farm to the next. Technology can liberate or oppress, and the NPL activists and their communities used the available machines to meet collective, yet liberatory, ends. By contrast, the warm fur coat of the Anglo banker insulates him from the hatred directed toward him because he dispossessed those who worked to live and struggled to survive.

Northern Lights is an economic testament as well. In an odd way it affirms the now old Braudelian notion of economic cores and peripheries, showing how, in a sense, Dakota farmers have more in common with Columbian coffee farmers than with

Minneapolis grain traders or the purchasing agent at the local grain elevator. Just as the powers that be could use the mystifyingly blind (in)justice of the market against the farmers, they could use the arbitrary power that goes with wealth as a way to penalize the NPL activists. All of the farmers were plagued by falling prices for their crops, but special measures—a refusal even to buy Sorenson's crop— were used against the radicals. Similarly, a decision to foreclose was a judgment call on the part of the banker, and he was more prone to call in loans on activists than he was on others.

The film does have a few shortcomings. The period clothing, almost sepia-toned film, and anti-artsy techniques perhaps give too much the illusion of period material. Subtitling Norwegian conversation with white-toned English text against snowy backgrounds sometimes renders the text illegible. Recounting the ultimate election victories of the NPL in rolling text at the end of the film renders the narrative catharsis anticlimatic. It also glosses over the very real differences between the urban socialist and the rural non-partisan movements. But these are minor blemishes in an otherwise powerful film.

As a film for inclusion in the diversity agenda, *Northern Lights* has much to offer. It gives real depth to the ethnic specificity of a given group, keeping far from stereotyping, yet giving a sense of both the cement which holds the Norwegians together and of the commonalities between their experience and that of other white immigrant groups. By showing how people discovered the links between individual and collective identities, between ethnic specificity and broader, cross-cultural commonalities, this film celebrates difference and shows its empowering potential. It perhaps too blithely implies that gender differences fade as the needs of the collective struggle predominate, but it at least suggests that gender differences, socially constructed as they are, remain quite real. In short, *Northern Lights* would be a fine film to include in the diversity agenda.

Robert L. Frost,
Department of History

GLCULEXP

Title:	**Orfeu do Carnaval (Black Orpheus)**
Producer:	Sacha Gordine, for Lopert Films
Director:	Marcel Camus
Distributor:	Home Vision/Public Media Video
Release Date:	c1959 (original copyright)
Technical:	100 min. / color / Portuguese with subtitles in English
Purchase Price:	$29.95
Rental:	Preview available
Presentation:	Dramatization
Awards:	Grand Prize, Cannes Film Festival, 1959; Academy Award, Best Foreign Film, 1959

Content: The film focuses on Afro-Brazilians in Rio de Janeiro at carnival time in the 1950s. It was made from a 20-year-old popular film which is still shown on television during carnival (the period between Epiphany and Ash Wednesday). It is relevant to the theme of cultural diversity in that, as an adaptation of a classical Greek myth in the context of modern Rio de Janeiro, it relates to two different cultures.

Classroom Use: The film is suitable for use, with appropriate caution, in courses dealing with stereotypes, classical culture, Greek mythology, cultural anthropology, Latin-American studies, or Brazil. Depending on their backgrounds, students should receive orientation or instruction on the myth of Orpheus and Eurydice and on Brazilian culture prior to viewing this film.

Critical Comments: The story line is quite simple. Eurydice, a gentle, naive girl from inland Brazil, goes to Rio de Janeiro to stay with her cousin during carnival time. There she meets Orpheus, an athletic young man who plays the guitar and sings. Orpheus is already engaged, but the two soon fall in love. When they dance together in the parade of samba groups on the culminating night of the carnival celebration, a stranger who has been following Eurydice sees her. She flees from him, and Orpheus runs after them. Eurydice is killed and the stranger, who is wearing a costume representing Death, knocks Orpheus unconscious. When he revives, Orpheus goes looking for Eurydice. After trying several places, he finds her body at the morgue. Later, Orpheus is carrying Eurydice in his arms and singing to her when his jilted fiancée sees them. In anger, she throws a stone at Orpheus, which strikes him on the head and causes him to lose his balance: the two lovers fall over a precipice and tumble to the bottom, where they come to rest in each other's arms.

There are several parallels with the original myth in this adaptation of the classical tale of love between Orpheus and Eurydice. In the film, Orpheus plays the guitar, rather than the lyre, and he jokingly claims to children that he is able to make the sun rise by playing at dawn, similar to the classical Orpheus, who can control nature with his playing. Like the original Orpheus, the Orpheus of the film goes looking for his deceased beloved and also descends to the land of the dead when he goes down a long, winding set of stairs which lead him to the ground, where the land of the dead is represented by a candomblé (a Brazilian religion) worshipping place. When he tries to enter, he is confronted by a dog with the classical name Cerberus. Eurydice returns to Orpheus by speaking to him through a medium at the candomblé ritual but, as in the mythical version, the modern Orpheus loses contact with the deceased Eurydice when he tries to look at her. Students of the classics will doubtlessly notice other parallels between the original myth, as known through Greek and Latin sources, and this modern adaptation.

The cultural interest of *Black Orpheus* is not to be found solely, or even primarily, in its adaptation of the classical myth (which, after all, has been represented in many other, much richer versions in op-

era, drama, narrative fiction, and the plastic arts). A major cultural feature of this film is its presentation of Afro-Brazilian music and dance in authentic scenes from the cariocan carnival as celebrated a quarter of a century ago. Moreover, the film had a major impact on the world of contemporary music by making the Brazilian bossa nova widely known outside Latin America, as millions of copies of the soundtrack of this popular movie have been sold.

Unfortunately, much of Brazilian (or Afro-Brazilian) culture and society that is represented in this film is distorted by its view of an idealized setting or by the perspective of stereotyped characterization. The favela (slum) is portrayed as a joyful place; the poor are depicted as carefree and happy. Stereotypes abound, from the oversexed, rather stupid black lover of Eurydice's cousin (who even devours watermelon, a fruit not particularly typical of Brazil, but called into play nevertheless for representing the stereotype) to the naive, all-submissive, beautiful Eurydice. Since none of the main characters—all of whom are black—is shown to have any significant psychological or intellectual depth, the film can actually reinforce the all-too-common ethnocentric view of members of other groups, especially minorities, as childlike.

Yet, perhaps the most generally offensive feature of this dramatization is its view of life (that is, the lives of poor Brazilians of African origin) as having little value, a notion undeniably—although only implicitly—emphasized in the closing scene, in which a little boy picks up the guitar of his fallen hero and becomes the new Orpheus by starting to play for a small girl who dances happily to the rhythm of the music. The filmmaker seems to say that the tragic deaths shown earlier are not really very important, since there is someone else to keep on playing and someone else to keep on dancing—just as he has shown us, throughout his adaptation of myth to the selected context in Brazil, that what really matters to those happy, playful, childlike Afro-Brazilians is song and dance (along with love and food, of course).

It also should be noted that *Black Orpheus* must not be considered a product of Brazilian cinema: it was a joint international production with a French director and an American leading actress (dancer Marpessa Dawn). But where it differs most strikingly from Brazilian films is in its view of the country, its institutions, and its people, not only through the above-mentioned idealization and use of stereotypes, but also in its negative presentation of candomblé religion, the centralizing force within Afro-Brazilian culture. In contrast, several Brazilian films have dealt with life in the slums, Brazilian Negroes, carnival, candomblé, and other features of Afro-Brazilian culture, in much more perceptive, substantive, and authentic presentations. Such films represent the views of "insiders"—people who belong to the respective cultural environment—while *Black Orpheus* reflects the notions of people clearly from outside that environment, in terms of both experience and depth of understanding.

To viewers whose notions of Brazil in general, and of carnival in Rio in particular, have been shaped more by tourist brochures and the mass media than by serious comprehensive study or significant personal experience relevant to the context of the film,

Black Orpheus may be enjoyable and perhaps seem harmless. Students of the classics who view the film primarily for its interest as a modern adaptation of a classical Greek myth should be forewarned of its deficiencies as a representation of contemporary Brazilian culture and society. Knowledgeable students of Brazil are likely to enjoy the scenes from carnival, as well as the music and dance throughout the film—and to take issue with the stereotypes and overall social perspective.

Brian F. Head, Department of Hispanic, Italian, and Portuguese Studies

USETHCUL

Title:	**Our Hispanic Heritage**
Producer:	Earl E. Smith
Director:	Earl E. Smith
Distributor:	Merco International Films
Release Date:	1979
Technical:	60 min. / color / English
Purchase Price:	not available
Rental:	not available
Presentation:	Documentary

Content: Narrated by Orson Welles, this historical documentary provides an overview of the presence and contributions of Spanish/Latino cultures in the Americas.

The film traces the Spanish presence in the territories that later became the Americas more than a century before the arrival of the Pilgrims at Plymouth Rock. It emphasizes their historical role as conquerors and settlers of the North American Southwest and Florida, and the overall contribution of people of Hispanic descent to the building of U.S. society. The film begins with an overview of the pre-Colombian Indian cultures, the European conquest, the introduction of the African culture through sla-

very, and the resulting amalgamation among these three cultural and racial groups that now constitute the people of the Americas.

Critical Comments: This plurality of cultures is analyzed in reference to the emergence of the United States as a nation and the presence of Latinos in this territory both as descendants of the old settlers and as immigrants/migrants during more recent times. Extensive examples of the cultural, linguistic, social, and economic influences of Latino cultures to U.S. society are provided. Notable Latino figures are mentioned in areas such as government, arts and literature, and sports.

This documentary offers a comprehensive historical overview for any social science or humanities course that wishes to introduce or underscore the Latino presence in the United States. The major differences in the historical experience of each of the major Latino groups in U.S. society (Mexicans, Puerto Ricans, and Cubans) are also presented.

Edna Acosta-Belen, Department of Latin American and Caribbean Studies

USGENSOC

Title:	**Out in Suburbia: The Stories of Eleven Lesbians**
Producer:	Pam Walton
Distributor:	Filmakers Library
Release Date:	1988
Technical:	28 min. / color / English
Purchase Price:	$295
Rental:	$55
Presentation:	Documentary with interviews
Awards:	Gay & Lesbian International Film Festival, 1989; American Film and Video Festival, 1989; National Educational Film and Video Festival, 1989; Women in the Director's Chair, 1989; Best Documentary, San Francisco Lesbian & Gay Film Festival, 1989; National Council on Family Relations, 1989
Study Guide:	Available

Content: *Out in Suburbia* presents eleven women who speak honestly about their families, friends, and loves. They speak of their initial awareness of being lesbian, their struggle for self-acceptance, and the ways they deal with homophobia, discrimination, and stereotyping. These women are self-respecting, articulate, and speak frankly and with passion about their lives. Being a lesbian is presented as a lifestyle alternative; the emotional and social aspects of the women's lives are highlighted. This video presents: several women who feel they were born lesbian; one woman who was married for 22 years before she realized she was a lesbian; one mother who is accepting of her lesbian daughter and another who is not; one lesbian couple's decision to have children; some lesbians' feelings about men; one lesbian's struggle with religion; a lesbian high school teacher's dilemma; the pain of family rejection; and issues of gender role-playing.

Classroom Use: The average college student holds many stereotypes about gay people and these images contribute to inhibiting public discussion about homosexuality. Bringing up the topic of homosexuality in a college classroom is often as difficult for the instructor as for the students. Lesbianism is even more difficult to introduce and discuss, in part because there is so little realistic material available about it. This film helps to meet this challenge. It brings the issue of lesbianism into the classroom in a way that encourages an open and fruitful discussion.

Critical Comments: The video is well-done, upbeat, and will prove quite useful for classroom instruction. Women are presented who speak earnestly and with candor about their lives as lesbians. Lesbians appear as quite ordinary, yet heterosexism and discrimination is not denied. The major short-coming of the video lies in its focus on middle-class, suburban, relatively conventional lesbians. It neglects women who define their lesbianism in a more political way. To its credit, the film does present women ranging in age from 23 to 67, and includes women of color.

This film can be very effective in undergraduate courses. It exposes students to self-respecting lesbians who live lives of integrity and complexity. It is also very useful in combating prejudices that continue to be targeted toward this group.

Steven Seidman, Department of Sociology

USETHSOC

Title:	**Picking Tribes**
Producer:	Saundra Sharpe
Director:	Saundra Sharpe
Distributor:	Women Make Movies
Release Date:	1988
Technical:	7 min. / color / English
Purchase Price:	$200
Rental:	$40
Presentation:	Documentary with still photos and animation
Awards:	Newark Black Film Festival, Paul Robeson Award; Black American Cinema Society, First Place; National Black Programming Consortium, Prized Pieces; Films de Femmes, Creteil, France

Content: *Picking Tribes* describes the dilemma of a young woman of African-American and American-Indian ancestry who is confused by her multiple identities. She denies her African heritage until the social revolution sweeping the country in the 1960s forces her to embrace that heritage.

Classroom Use: This film is suitable for high school and college students. While the theme of self-identity has universal appeal, those in psychology, African-American studies, and women's studies will find *Picking Tribes* particularly useful, even in its brevity.

Critical Comments: *Picking Tribes,* with its stills and animation, is a humorous depiction of one woman's quest for self-identity. She celebrates her Indian ancestry and rejects her African heritage. The tenacity of the African-American struggle for freedom in the 1960s and the vibrancy of the accompanying cultural movement compel her to confront her African background. Subsequently, she removes the feather from her headpiece so that she can sport an Afro and a dashiki. The film addresses the multiple layers of identities that determine who each individual is. Through its portrayal it shows the absurdity of dichotomizing one's heritage. Therefore, it implicitly rejects an epistemology that embraces such notions.

Lillian S. Williams, Department of Women's Studies

USETHECO

Title:	**Place of the Falling Waters**
Producers:	Native Voices Public Television Workshop, Montana Public Television, and Salish-Kootenai College
Directors:	Roy Bigcrane and Thompson Smith
Distributor:	SKC Media Center, Salish-Kootenai College
Release Date:	1991
Technical:	90 min. (three 30-min. segments) / color / English and native languages
Purchase Price:	Personal, $39.95; Institutional, $99.95
Rental:	n/a
Presentation:	A reflective documentary comprising a three-part cycle; videorecorded oral accounts by Flathead Indians, filmed in Bozeman, Montana
Study Guide:	Included with text of video, full identification of speakers, and further information on history and issues covered; this is a valuable feature not to be missed as a supplementary guide
Awards:	Anthropological Film Festival, Native American Studies; Silver Apple Award

Content: This film focuses on the question of how the Kerr Dam in Montana has affected the Flathead Indian tribe and the continuation of its culture.

The conception of this video project as a whole is quite ambitious. In choosing to present the material in a three-part series, the producers of the program emphasize the fluidity of time and the continuous adaptive survival techniques of the tribe. Such a formal organizational technique subtly, but effectively, challenges both western notions of linear time, and stereotypes that locate Indians rigidly in the past, or as an extinct species of exotica. The chosen format of presentation clearly extends a cyclical model for contemplation as the Flatheads receive back the land they had originally lost to western economic development. At the same time, the whole question of "ownership" and transferral of land rights is exposed in native people's ambivalence toward imminent control of the dam and its implications for their culture. The video segments have the practical classroom advantage of being used separately, if necessary, because each part is introduced enough to function individually.

This video series is suitable for classes in anthropology, history, environmental science, multicultural issues, economics, business, and perhaps education.

Critical Comments: Part I: Before the Dam. This first segment of the program begins with a question about how the Kerr Dam has affected the Flathead Indian tribe. The beginnings of each successive segment, and the end of the series, reflect and repeat that same question. Having obtained legal rights to the dam effective in the first part of the 21st century and monetary compensation until the change of ownership occurs, Native Americans could very well have made a self-congratulatory video about their plans for the future. Instead, the entire enterprise seems to be part of a larger reflective process and assessment that patiently and wisely precedes action. Opinions from many sources are elicited and valued in interviews with elders, young people, educators, laborers, activists, and historians.

Those of us operating from a western perspective might expect from the title of this section an anthropological or archaeological account of the life of native people in Montana. Such an approach is pointedly eschewed in favor of a mingling of fact and myth that refuses to measure duration of time by western standards. Language and the oral tradition maintain precedence over analytical techniques as accounts of the old ways of the tribe are given informally, in a mixture of English and native languages. Respect for the elderly, characteristic of Native-American culture, virtually emanates from the screen in the dignity accorded individuals and their accounts.

The account of Indian-white relations and the systematic loss of Flathead land that follows is controlled and relentless. A Native-American female historian offers a revisionist historical interpretation of events. The separate factions of Flatheads, now confederated, are identified and distinguished: Salish, Kootenai, and Pend d'Oreille. Constrictions imposed by the 1855 Treaty of Hellgate led to a mixing of previously separate cultures on reservations.

One interesting and moving part of this segment is the treatment of Christianity. Since 1841 Jesuit missionaries have worked to convert the Flathead Indians. That they largely succeeded is exemplified by the complex and emotional testimonies of elders about mission-run schools. Most of the speakers either are, or have been, devout Catholics so they are careful to distinguish between good and bad "blackrobes" (Jesuits). In a move unprecedented for this project, the Reverend Dumbeck is interviewed about his missionary work and his responses are juxtaposed with Native-American accounts. The resource manual suggests that the priest even expressed regret for the cultural loss he helped to promote.

Part II: The Road to the Dam. The second section of the series documents federal attempts to assimilate the Flatheads into developing America. Beginning with the Allotment Act of 1904, natives were forced into accepting individual ownership of reservation property as opposed to communal usage. Unfortunately, this same law allowed white settlers allotments on reservations as well. A massive irrigation system supported the allotments by providing much-needed water for agriculture. The water functioned as a bribe to plant crops and a commodity for which individuals then accumulated debts. Many Native Americans lost their allotments through water debts or debts owed to local stores. It is pointed out that many prominent white citizens were guilty of conflict of interest in their dual political and capitalist roles. What native resistance there was is mentioned, but it seems futile in retrospect. The dam itself changed the physical characteristics of the land that provided sustenance for the Flatheads and allowed self-sufficiency.

A slow change from native independence to dependence upon a cash economy was given impetus by the Great Depression which forced many natives to depend upon what, for them, were unsavory government rations. At this time, as the ruined farmers served by the irrigation project were scheduled to

pay for its costs, Montana Power Company joined forces with Anaconda Mining Company in a bid for expansion and power designed to harness the sacred waterfalls of the Flathead people. The poverty-stricken people on the reservation were bought with cash handouts and groceries in such a way that necessity all but silenced dissenting voices. Actual footage of power company officials and tribal leaders at the falls is shown in the video along with photos of the stages of dam construction. The lack of legal protection for Native Americans was compounded by a lack of proper remuneration. Finally, John Colliers, an attorney working on behalf of the tribe, won the tribe close to $150,000 in annual rental fees and job preference for natives on the dam site. In fact, what sounds like a decent amount of money was only a fraction of the entire profit of the operation, and Native-American workers were given the most dangerous construction jobs. Predictably, deaths resulted from the lack of safety precautions.

Given the previous video segment in which the priest spoke for the Eurocentric viewpoint (that the indigenous people should be Christianized), this indictment stands without response from either the Bureau of Indian Affairs or the Montana Power Company. It is difficult to judge whose choice dictated that absence. Even in so grim a story, native humor glimmers through the bleak poverty of the Depression as the government rations—bacon too salty for tribal taste, used for firewood, and the flour boiled in water to stave off hunger pangs—become matters for laughter because of their incongruity.

Part III: The Dam and the Future. The saga of the dam continues from its completion in 1938 to its fate in the next century. In naming the dam after the Montana Power Company president Frank Marion Kerr, the native spiritual legacy was erased from the place as events continued to be reinterpreted from a western point of view. Immense changes in tribal identity and unity occurred after World War II and inhibited resistance to the situation, but the 1960s and 1970s brought a resurgence of interest in reclamation and traditionalism among younger tribal members.

In 1984 tribal people gathered at the dam site in an encampment designed to guard the sacred area and protest its use. Accounts by the elders of betrayed promises—like free power for natives—fueled the demonstration and bolstered communal resolve. The ensuing legal action challenged the Bureau of Indian Affairs, the Federal Energy Regulatory Commission, and the Justice system of the United States as well as big business. Payment to Flatheads for use of the land was increased from thousands of dollars to millions but, even so, a change of control was delayed until the year 2015.

This final section deals with native people's reactions to the results of their activism. Some people are primarily interested in the short-term monetary gain accorded the individual and the tribe by the decision. Others see the money as simply more assimilation into the cash economy of capitalism and the philosophy of materialism. Some want to finance a repurchase of traditional homelands and promote a revival of traditional lifestyles. Others feel that such a socialistic, communal system would never work today for people also imbued with American individualism. Still others express the importance of financing education in the mainstream and native cultures to allow the next generations of Flatheads to cope with life in America. Pessimism and optimism mingle in the startling candor and unashamed divergences of opinions expressed.

The poignancy of the end is charged again with humor as young and old joke about Indians having too many children and flying the flag on the Fourth of July. It is easy to see the techniques of living and philosophy that have ensured Native-American survival through the centuries. That in itself creates hope for the future and gives the viewer a clear view of contemporary Flathead culture as an antidote to western stereotypes. Probably the most interesting part of this segment is the idea that there are only a very few people who question whether the dam should exist at all.

Jeanne Laiacona, Department of Art

USRACIMM

Title:	**Pockets of Hate**
Producer:	Henry Singer
Director:	Henry Singer
Distributor:	Films for the Humanities
Release Date:	1988
Technical:	25 min. / color / English
Purchase Price:	$149
Rental:	$75
Presentation:	Documentary with archival footage, stills, interviews, narration

Content: *Pockets of Hate* explores the nature of contemporary racism and the wave of violence it has engendered in urban centers in the United States. It observes that African Americans and Jews have been the traditional targets of hate, but now the new immigrants are the victims. While citing the death of a black man in the Howard Beach incident and the death of African-American Yusef Hawkins in the white Bensonhurst area of New York, the film focuses upon the murder of an Asian Indian in Jersey City and that community's experiences. *Pockets of Hate* seeks to explain this post-civil rights resurgence of racism.

Classroom Use: This video is useful for classes in U.S. history, sociology, psychology, social work, and racial/ethnic studies.

Critical Comments: *Pockets of Hate* documents the dramatic increase in the number of racially motivated hate crimes in the United States in the 1980s. It asks if such incidents as the murder of Yusef Hawkins in Bensonhurst or the slaying of a young Asian Indian in Jersey City were aberrations or a new trend in racial violence. It also provides an engaging and insightful overview of the history of racial violence in this country. While noting that the obvious indicators of racial segregation—the laws and the physical demarcations—have been removed, the justification for these attacks by the perpetrators of racial violence remain remarkably consistent. One interviewee, for example, contended that the Indians in Jersey City were unassimilable and were interested in white women.

In another interview, professor Lenwood Gunther of Rutgers University argues that the incidents of racial violence are connected and that they are indicators of notions of territoriality, as well as the vestiges of racism. Gunther also sees a relationship between the economic slump and racial violence. Since the heavy industry that dominated working-class towns like Jersey City has been virtually shut down, working-class and lower-middle-class white residents blame the new wave of highly successful immigrants for their economic decline. Unlike the immigrants who arrived in the cities at the turn of the century, these newcomers are well-educated professionals who have been able to purchase housing in areas of gentrification. In contrast, the older residents, often recent high school graduates, are likely to be unemployed, and their outlook for the future suggests that they will not achieve the status of their parents. These groups often comprise the violent gangs that prey upon the urban newcomers, for they mistakenly perceive the newcomers to be the beneficiaries of affirmative action programs that have passed their own members by. One gang member expressed this concern and said that the Indians were taking "their jobs." *Pockets of Hate* documents how these perceptions have no basis in reality, for the people about whom the gang member spoke were medical doctors or other professionals and were not members of a protected class. The producers do attempt to clarify the definition of affirmative action.

This videotape also discusses other facets of racial violence, such as that which occurs on university campuses. It argues that the campus is a reflection of the community and, because of the increase in segregation, students seldom interact with people from diverse ethnic or class backgrounds until they reach college. Interestingly enough, this documentary suggests that, while racial awareness has been heightened as a result of the civil rights movement, racism has increased. In addition to the economic factors stated above, the film contends that the laissez-faire policies of the Reagan-Bush administrations and their persistent use of the "race card" have fueled such acts of violence.

The intent of this film is to illustrate the cause, as well as the impact, of racial violence and it provides an excellent overview. Its strength lies in its ability to explore the underlying views and assumptions racists use to justify their actions. Viewers who wish to pursue the topic further should refer to the following:

Companion video: *Racism in America* (see review, page 162).

Related published works:

John Hope Franklin. *Race and History: Selected Essays, 1938–1955.* Louisiana State University Pr., 1989.

George Fredrickson. *White Supremacy.* Oxford University Pr., 1981.

Andrew Hacker. *Two Nations: Black & White, Separate, Hostile, Unequal.* Scribner's, 1992.

David Roediger. *The Wages of Whiteness.* Verso, 1991.

Peter I. Rose. *Violence in America.* Random, 1969.

Studs Terkel. *Race: How Blacks and Whites Think and Feel about the American Obsession.* New Pr., 1992.

Lillian S. Williams, Department of Women's Studies

GLGENPOL

Title:	**Portrait of Teresa (Retrato de Teresa)**
Producer:	Evelio Delgado
Director:	Pastor Vega
Distributor:	World Video, New Yorker Video
Release Date:	c1979, 1990
Technical:	103 min. / color / Spanish with English subtitles
Purchase Price:	$69.95 (World Video)
Rental:	n/a
Presentation:	Dramatization; videorecording of motion picture produced by the Instituto Cubano de Arte e Industria Cinematográfica (ICAIC) in cooperation with the Center for Cuban Studies

Content: This film focuses on how traditional male and female roles are changing in post-revolutionary Cuba and the conflicts that arise within the marriage and family of a young working couple. It also points to the contradictions between a revolutionary ideology of equality between the sexes and the machismo and sexism still found at all levels of Cuban society.

The protagonist, Teresa, is a factory worker and her husband is a TV repairman. Her increasing involvement in the political and social activities of her union begin to incur the wrath of her husband, since it is limiting the time she dedicates to him, the house chores, and the care of their two boys. Teresa has become the coordinator of the amateur artistic group established by her coworkers. As the group gets ready to participate in a national competition, Teresa's late arrivals become the source of frequent arguments at home and resentment from her husband who still expects her to assume the primary responsibilities in the household. Teresa also feels the demands and expectations placed upon her by her coworkers who feel they need her initiative and leadership qualities in order to be successful in the competition. As she gradually develops consciousness of her subordination and of the contradictory demands placed upon her, she begins to take charge of her own life, a course that ultimately leads to the disintegration of her marriage.

Unable to understand Teresa's behavior and her further unwillingness to follow him to a new job pro-

motion that will take him to another province, her husband has an affair with another woman, and the husband and wife ultimately go their separate ways.

Classroom Use: The film is appropriate for courses dealing with sex roles, family relations, socialization in Latin America, and the machismo cultural concept, or for any course dealing with women's dual roles. It also provides a view of Cuban society two decades after the revolution.

Critical Comments: Recognizing the importance of film in its new socialist society, the Cuban government created the Instituto Cubano de Arte e Industria Cinematográfica (ICAIC) in 1962 to oversee the development of a new film industry. Since then, Cuban cinema has attempted to examine the formation process and ideological changes in post-revolutionary society, and contribute to conciousness-raising.

When first released, *Portrait of Teresa* was considered controversial for its honest and self-critical look at the ways new socialist values contradict the sexist attitudes that still dominate many aspects of Cuban daily life, particularly within marriage and family relations. The film is a moving character study of Teresa, her increasing awareness of her domestic subordination, and her ultimate self-assertion and independence as an individual. It depicts the disintegration of Teresa's marriage with balanced authenticity, and is also very effective in showing the social, political, and economic inconsistencies regarding the position of women in

Cuban society and underscoring the need for further change.

Edna Acosta-Belen, Department of Latin American and Caribbean Studies

USIMMRAC

Title:	**The Price You Pay**
Producer:	Christine Keyser
Director:	Christine Keyser
Distributor:	National Asian-American Telecommunications Association (NAATA)/CrossCurrent Media
Release Date:	1988
Technical:	29 min. / color / Voiceover narration in English
Purchase Price:	$150
Rental:	$50
Presentation:	Documentary with newsclips and interviews
Award:	American Film Institute National Video Festival Award

Content: This film looks at refugees from Vietnam, Laos, and Cambodia resettled in the United States after the Vietnam War. Since 1975 more than half a million refugees from these three countries have emigrated to America, over 40 percent of them have settled in California. The film gives the background of emigration and some history of the Vietnam War.

The film stresses that these people are dislocated as a direct result of U.S. military involvement in the region, and that those who were able to leave initially could do so primarily because they were supporters of the United States (they had provided military intelligence to U.S. forces and their lives would have been jeopardized had they stayed on). The film then focuses on the very negative reception these immigrants received once they arrived in the United States, where they were perceived as taking away benefits from African Americans and other "bona fide" Americans. In fact, as the film points out, very little help has actually been given to the

Southeast Asian refugees. The contradiction between the stated U.S. creed of welcoming the homeless and the reality of how that creed is practiced is a theme that runs through the film.

The film also discusses the racial stereotyping of Asians: from the paternalistic ("hardworking, polite, and cheaper than Americans") to the negative ("Southeast Asians eat cats and dogs" and can never be assimilated). Other interviews look at popular forms of resentment against the refugees, e.g., that the U.S. government has no business taking care of refugees when American-born people on welfare are not being helped, and fears that they will take away American jobs.

The film then focuses on how the immigrants are coping and trying to rebuild their lives. In conclusion, there is a brief discussion of the contributions made by this newest group of Americans to American society. There is also some footage of how the Vietnamese, Laotian, and Cambodian communities are trying to preserve their cultural heritage and pass on aspects of this culture and history to their children, for there is very little formal support outside the community which would help preserve their culture. Some thoughtful segments show how wedding ceremonies and religious worship are conducted in the various communities.

Classroom Use: The film is very accessible and the short length leaves ample time for discussion. It can be used for both lower-level and upper-level courses. The film should be useful in classes on American foreign policy, social welfare, public administration, and psychology. In addition, it should be useful in courses on ethnic and race relations, and intercultural communication, as well as for teachers of ESL programs (English as a second language).

I think the film makes a very good point in that the connection between U.S. military involvement overseas and the increase in immigration from that region is usually not made in the media or in the minds of the public. This suggests a need to make people aware that Southeast Asian immigrants were largely ''involuntary'' immigrants. Ultimately, the ''price'' paid for immigrating to the United States is also high when people come as war refugees. The video also challenges the stereotype that all Asian Americans are rich and part of the ''model minority.''

Sucheta Mazumdar, Department of History

GLCULEXP

Title:	**Puerto Rico**
Series:	Dances of the World (no. 15)
Producer:	Folk Dance Videos International
Distributor:	World Video
Release Date:	1988
Technical:	60 min. / color / English
Purchase Price:	$45
Rental:	n/a from World Video
Presentation:	Narrated documentary: filmed at the North Carolina International Folk Festival; performances and interviews with professionals of the Folkloric Guateque Ballet, Corozal, and the Folkloric Company, Las Muesas, of Cayey

Content: The film features performances of Spanish, African, and Indian dances. Having differing professions and occupations, performers represent a variety of social populations. Dances reflect diverse ethnic and regional customs and values. The video opens with a colorful dance involving a male performer; a female ragdoll guides viewers to the site of subsequent dance performances. These sequences include the African-influenced bomba of the interior; the plena, from Ponce, which blends Indian, Spanish, and African traditions; three versions of the seis; the Maria la Colora; and the machete, a dexterous rivalry between male performers. Excerpts from interviews, interwoven with a narrator's continuous commentary, describe the dances and create a historical and sociopolitical frame for understanding dance sequences, while supplying background information on sponsoring institutions. Specialists interviewed are Joaquín Nieves Caldero, anthropologist and director of the Guateque group; Nelida López, dance instructor; and Brunilda Vázquez, a drama teacher from Cayey.

Classroom Use: This film is appropriate for nonspecialists in dance who have an interest in an introductory presentation on Puerto Rican, Caribbean, or Latin-American cultures. In an introductory literature class, the polyrhythms of the poetry of Nicolás Guillén and of Luis Pales Matos could be explained within the context of the sequence on the bomba. The video could stimulate essays in an intensive composition class, lending itself readily to classifications of the dance forms, an analysis of a particular form, comparisons and contrasts of choreographers, performers or costumes. In a Spanish conversation course, it could inspire a consideration of narrative tone, or spark a contrastive discussion of the classification of race by phenotype in North America and the notational social criteria used for racial classification in Latin America and the Caribbean.

Critical Comments: A special introduction focusing on Taino pre-Columbian history or on African civilizations preceding slavery and their transformations and diffusion in New World diaspora communities would temper the Eurocentric perspective that taints the historical frame, dance descriptions, and images of ethnic minorities in the film. The narrator tends to overvalue Spanish cultural influences, and to diminish the significance of the contributions of other groups. For example, the narrator never refers to the Indians of Puerto Rico by name. One of the internal narrators asserts that the Indians refused to be conquered or enslaved, and that they were all annihilated. These resisting Indians were not at the same cultural level as those of other regions of the New World. History substantiates the immediate Taino resistance to the advance of Spaniards, and individual warriors, such as Gurimex and Urayoan did distinguish themselves. Yet, the decimation of the Indian population resulted not only from warfare but from their vulnerability to diseases contracted from contact with European and African immigrants. It was Arawakan slave labor that sustained the gold mining industry of Puerto Rico until the depletion of the mineral supply at the end of the 16th century caused a shift to agriculture. Studies of Taino belief systems encoded in petroglyphs, their cacique system of governance, their language, and the federation they formed with neighboring Caribs to resist the advance of Spaniards demonstrate that Taino culture was adequate enough to meet their needs.

Similarly, narrators distort the image of Africans in historical allusions that emphasize a passive acceptance of subjugation that left them to do the work that others refused. Africans were introduced in large numbers towards the end of the 18th century, when Puerto Rico's role in sugar production became clear. As in other areas, slave conspiracies and rebellions have been documented. Free coloreds were at the vanguard of the abolitionist campaigns in the 1860s. Slaves took advantage of the ruling that proffered automatic emancipation in exchange for enlist-

ment to fight the Spaniards in independence wars of the 1870s. Somehow, the film overlooks the struggle for independence altogether in a historical frame that began with the conquest by Spaniards and ended with the establishment of Puerto Rico as a possession of the United States in 1952. Its interpretation of public dance festivals as instruments of control is somewhat limited. Doubtless, such events were intended as distractions and escape valves to thwart rebellions and to sustain the Spanish hegemony. However, the governor's sudden decision to "throw off" these festivals in 1825 may just as well have been an attempt to avoid the spread into Puerto Rico of independence campaigns that had liberated most of Latin America by that time.

Additionally, whatever the intentions of those that governed, New World Africans exploited the public dances and used them to adapt traditions to new environments and to mask the worship of divinities. To this day there is evidence of religious syncretism among African descendants in the isolated community of Loiza in Puerto Rico, where the bomba and the plena are danced annually in honor of Santiago. A broader contextualization would have resulted in a discussion of the calenda dance mentioned in the video and its diffusion in areas that range from the southern River Plate countries to the southern United States. The bomba could have been explained within this context, rather than the descriptions accomplished principally by emphasizing its differences from other dance forms and its lack of acceptability among the Spanish, followed by an abrupt transition to European polkas and mazurkas which the narrator praises as exemplary refinements of the motherland. This editing technique juxtaposes the two dance forms, and the narrator's personal language and explicit praise of the European style implicitly condemns the more vigorous choreography of the bomba. The video offers no information on the fabrication of the drums and maracas used in the bomba sequence, but gives much attention to the artisanry involved in carving the guiro, which, ironically, is a Taino instrument. There is some mention of the competition between dancers and drummers, perhaps to suggest improvisation—which is one of the distinctive features of African-influenced music. Even though elsewhere the plena has been attributed to the black musical tradition—because of its antiphonal interplay between the soloist and chorus, and the satirical lyrics—here it is said to derive from the blend of the three ethnic groups that comprise the Puerto Rican heritage.

Edith M. Jackson, Department of Hispanic, Italian, and Portuguese Studies

GLETHCLA

Title:	**Quilombo**
Producer:	CDK/Augusto Arraes
Director:	Carlos Diegues
Distributor:	New Yorker Video
Release Date:	1986
Technical:	114 min. / color / Portuguese, with subtitles in English
Purchase Price:	$79
Rental:	Preview possible, no rental
Presentation:	Feature film; fictional version of colonial historic period

Content: This is a fictional version of part of the history of Palmares, the largest and most famous of the democratic communities known as "quilombos," which served as havens primarily for runaway black slaves, but also for poor whites and Jews, in Brazil during the colonial period.

Classroom Use: The film is suitable for use in courses on cultural diversity, Brazilian studies, Latin-American studies, and African-American studies. An introduction should be provided on the history of slavery in Brazil, with special attention to the quilombo community of Palmares, which was the first democratic society to be established in colonial America and which lasted for more than a century.

Critical Comments: This video, which is simply the presentation of an original feature film through another media, must not be mistaken for a historical documentary. Instead of attempting to present a filmic report on the history of Palmares, the director uses this quilombo as the symbol of utopia in the saga of blacks in Brazil. His epic view is that of a great symbolic drama, stunningly portrayed as an expression of ethnic pride through a synthesis of history, customs, and enduring ideals among Brazilians of African origin.

This is not to say that the story told by the film is solely, or even primarily, fictional. Surely the principal events narrated here are a well-known part of the history of slavery in colonial Brazil: the founding of democratic, African-like communities by runaway slaves; the prominence of Palmares as a center of successful resistance to enslavement in northeast Brazil; the growing concern on the part of Portuguese colonizers and increasing efforts by the colonial government to eliminate the quilombos; the conflict of different strategies for resistance between the leaders Ganga Zumba and Zumbi, resulting in division within the community of Palmares, and the subsequent massive invasion of the community by Paulistan troops led by Domingo Jorge Velho. The film tells this story, but its focus is not so much on the recounting of events as on their inspirational symbolic value, linking aspirations of the past to the values and justifiable reasons for pride among contemporary blacks in Brazil.

There are many myths surrounding Brazil, some of which are held by outsiders and by many Brazilians themselves. The notion of Brazil as a racial paradise is surely a distortion, held not only by foreigners with a superficial knowledge of the country, but also conveniently cultivated by Brazilians, especially by members of the more favored social classes, political leaders, and intellectuals interested in maintaining the status quo. (If it's a paradise, why change it?) It is significant to note that the first centennial, in 1988, of the formal abolition of slavery as a legal practice was not so much viewed among Brazilians of African origin as a time for celebration as it was considered an occasion for reflection and development of increased political and social awareness and action.

The film *Quilombo* does not tell the story of the invasion of Palmares as just one more example of the crushing defeat of the oppressed, but as the survival of an ideal, in spite of loss in battle.

Prior to showing the film's title and the initial credits, a text is screened, stating: ''The first Europeans to arrive in Brazil, in 1500, the Portuguese brought slaves from Africa to work the sugar plantations, the colony's greatest wealth. Absolute masters to their slaves, they subjected them to forced labor, and inflicted often fatal tortures. Some slaves escaped and hid in country areas, forming free communities called 'Quilombos.' The most famous of these was the 'Quilombo of Palmares,' founded at the end of the 16th century in the northeast of Brazil.'' The subtitle at the beginning of the first scene places the action at a sugar mill in the state of Pernambuco in 1650, during the war between the Portuguese and the Dutch colonists. The opening scene shows the lady of the plantation ordering torture of a slave (contrary to the notion that the Portuguese slaveowners were benevolent); she becomes annoyed when, contrary to her expectations, the slave dies during the ordeal. Successive scenes represent a rebellion of slaves on the plantation, their flight to Palmares, conflicts between the runaway slaves and the bounty hunters, life and political differences at the quilombo, treachery on the part of the Portuguese by making false promises in order to trap the runaway slaves, and the invasion of the community in 1694 by troops brought from São Paulo. Throughout the story, scenes expressing beliefs and showing practices typical of African religious cults reinforce the spirit and tone of successive events. A kind of auditory metaphor links the past to the present through alternation on the soundtrack between traditional forms of African music and modern compositions by Gilberto Gil, whose lyrics praise the quilombo as a ''black El Dorado.''

During the invasion of Palmares, even as the inhabitants are being defeated, their leaders proclaim that Palmares is eternal. Of course, both this claim and Gilberto Gil's lyrics are not to be taken literally: they refer to an ideal, not to actual facts. Yet, it must be noted that, as a center of resistance, Palmares lasted a remarkably long time: not only had it been in existence for a century before the invasion represented in this film, but it continued to serve as a focal point for opposition to oppression by the colonists for many years afterward. A text shown at the end of the video states: ''Camuanga [a survivor of the 1694 invasion] became a leader of the Palmares resistance, until 1704, when he was killed in battle with the Portuguese. Other warriors took his place. Colonial forces never managed to exterminate Palmares totally. In the region, resistance was last heard of in 1797, more than a century after the death of Zumbi [leader of the quilombo at the time of the 1694 invasion].''

While this film is appropriate for use in courses on Brazilian and Latin-American studies, and, from a comparative perspective, in courses on African-American studies, it is questionable whether students in the United States will identify with the tone, spirit, and pageantry of the idealistic presentation. Because of this, it is strongly recommended that adequate historical information be presented prior to showing the video, as well as appropriate comments on the objectives of Diegues's interpretation, as indicated by the composition and spirit of the film itself. This film was favorably reviewed by Vincent Canby in the *New York Times* (March 28, 1986).

Brian F. Head, Department of Hispanic, Italian, and Portuguese Studies

USRACCOM

Title: # Race against Prime Time

Producer: David Shulman

Director: David Shulman

Distributor: California Newsreel

Release Date: 1985

Technical: 60 min. / color / English

Purchase Price: $195

Rental: $75

Presentation: Documentary with newsclips and interviews

Content: Since 1968 Miami has experienced three major riots. This documentary takes us behind the headlines of prime time news to analyze the riots of May 17, 1980. The video—filmed two weeks after the riot—tries to sensitize the viewer about how news reporting is done and the ways in which the subjective considerations of the journalists, TV news crew, and other biases are transferred to the reporting of news. Problems of representation are analyzed along with the history of events.

Taking the verdict of the Arthur McDuffie case, when four white Miami policemen were acquitted (by an all-white jury after a three-hour deliberation) of all charges in the beating death of the black McDuffie, which precipitated the events of May 17, 1980, the documentary looks at how the events were covered by the major TV networks (ABC, NBC, and CBS). It shows that none of the networks initially even tried to examine the background of the riots. With the exception of CBS, which carried one three-minute segment once, the news coverage had no discussion of the history of police brutality against the African-American community and the growing frustration of that community with the judicial system. For example, the McDuffie case was only the most recent of four other cases in which white policemen had been involved but had been acquitted without charges. Examples of such cases included the "wrong-house drug raid," when a highly respected African-American school teacher and his son were beaten while racial slurs were heaped on them by the police. Only later did the police realize that they had the "wrong house," and no apology was ever

given by them. Another case concerned the killing of an unarmed black youth by an off-duty white policeman; again there was no indictment. Yet another case concerned the sexual molestation of a 11-year-old black girl by a white highway patrolman; again there were no charges filed.

The documentary points out that the media have very poor links with the African-American community, so that in a crisis situation, as in the May riots, they turned to the police for information! The actual news coverage of the riots focused on negative images of the black neighborhoods: images of chaos and violence and sensational, action-oriented events. The broader response of the African-American community was totally ignored as were the responses of poor whites who live in a neighboring area and were sympathetic to the frustration and anger of the blacks. Instead, as the documentary shows, a rather crude black-against-white version of the events was promoted. Violence by blacks against whites was played up while the greater degree of violence by white vigilantes against blacks during the riots was completely neglected.

The last portion of the documentary focuses on how the media create "spokespersons"— individuals who, because of their social position, are considered "authorities," while poorer community residents are prejudged as inarticulate and therefore unsuitable for media sound bites.

Classroom Use: This film would be very useful in all diversity courses, American history courses, sociology of race relations, and communications courses.

Critical Comments: *Race against Prime Time* is a very powerful film challenging any notion of ''objective'' TV news. However, the documentary is too involved with the specifics of the story, and does not explore the basic question it raises: how can this gross injustice continue year after year (one thinks of the 1992 Los Angeles riots)? There is no public policy analysis or discussion of how the political agencies should be made answerable. No local politicians or police were interviewed, so the documentary remains concerned with the mechanics of how news is covered.

Sucheta Mazumdar, Department of History

USRACETH

Title:	**Racism in America**
Producer:	Jan Petroff
Director:	Bob Morris
Distributor:	Films for the Humanities
Release Date:	1988
Technical:	28 min. / color / English
Purchase Price:	$149
Rental:	$75
Presentation:	Documentary with archival footage, interviews, and narration

Content: *Racism in America* documents the resurgence of racial violence in the United States during the 1980s and seeks to explain its causes. It shows that commentators can no longer focus exclusively upon the working-class or lower-middle-class communities as purveyors of this new racism, but they must examine upper-class communities as well.

Classroom Use: This film is appropriate for both high school students and college students. Those in history, sociology, psychology, social work, ethnic studies, and multicultural classes will find *Racism in America* useful.

Critical Comments: *Racism in America* is the result of an African-American news reporter's attempt to understand the racial violence that her mother experienced in her upper-middle-class New Jersey community. Her investigation revealed that racial hate crimes were on the rise in the early 1980s, and increased by 23 percent from 1987 to 1988 alone. Moreover, these crimes occurred across the nation, with several especially notable incidents in Chicago, the New Jersey cities of South Orange and Maplewood, and Indianapolis. What appeared to be unique about this violence is that it targeted upwardly mobile blacks who had actually achieved the American Dream, and that it occurred in the middle-class or upper-middle-class white communities where the blacks had purchased houses.

While this type of violence seemed to be inexplicable, there were precedents. Historian Kenneth T. Jackson documented the increase in membership in the Ku Klux Klan in the 1920s and its increasingly middle-class composition in his book *The Ku Klux Klan in the City, 1915–1930* (Oxford University Pr., 1967). The film notes that while there have always been those opposed to black progress, the attitudes of the 1960s seemed to support the notion of racial equality; yet during that decade, membership in the Klan increased quietly in both the North and the South. The video also shows that no community is free of racial violence, regardless of the socioeconomic status of its residents.

Racism in America tries to explain the source of this new wave of violence. To accomplish this goal it interviews several prominent scholars and activists including: Althea Simmons, chief lobbyist for the NAACP, Peter Salins, Manhattan Institute for Policy Research, Donald Tucker, Commission on New Jersey Black Issues, F. Scott McLaughlin, Center for Constitutional Rights, and Jack Greenberg, former director, Legal Defense Fund.

Although this film was produced in 1988, these individuals' observations ring true today. For example, one contends that only in an expanding economy can Americans accept efforts to assure equality for African Americans. But such an assessment does not explain the racial incidents that occurred in places like Maplewood with their upper-class populations. Another panelist argues that equality can exist only when there is no violence in the cities. To suggest that most blacks live in ghettos or are violent is absurd and, this reviewer asks, what is the correlation between civil liberties and violence? The video explores this notion and other code words that suggest racism—affirmative action, busing, pay equity—but it does not analyze them.

Some panelists call for a reinstatement of such government programs as the Comprehensive Employment Training Act that did train and place young people into responsible jobs. Others discuss the government policies of the Reagan and Bush administrations that reversed many of the gains blacks had experienced since the 1960s. For example, the Office of Contract Compliance has initiated policies that result in 75 percent of businesses not following affirmative action guidelines for hiring or letting contracts to minority firms. For the first time, the Justice Department actually supported voluntarily the defendant in civil rights cases.

Racism in America delineates the major issues that policymakers and the public are discussing regarding race and African Americans in 1992. Yet, it leaves to the viewer to assess the validity of the arguments that are discussed. For example, despite the increase in racial violence and anti-Semitism, studies indicate that most Americans are appalled by such incidents—yet the film does not attempt to explain this apparent anomaly. Therefore, it seems especially useful for introducing the topic of racism.

Companion videotape: *Pockets of Hate* (see p. 153).

Other related published works:

John Hope Franklin. *Race and History: Selected Essays, 1938–1988.* Louisiana State University Pr., 1989.

George Fredrickson. *White Supremacy.* Oxford University Pr., 1981.

Andrew Hacker. *Two Nations: Black & White, Separate, Hostile, Unequal.* Scribner's, 1992.

Kenneth T. Jackson. *The Ku Klux Klan in the City, 1915–1930.*

David Roediger. *The Wages of Whiteness.* Verso, 1991.

Peter I. Rose. *Violence in America.* Random, 1969.

Studs Terkel. *Race: How Blacks and Whites Think and Feel about the American Obsession.* New Pr., 1992.

Lillian S. Williams, Department of Women's Studies

USRACECO

Title:	# A Raisin in the Sun
Producers:	David Susskind and Philip Rose
Director:	Daniel Petrie
Distributor:	Facets Video
Release Date:	c1987
Technical:	128 min. / b&w / English
Purchase Price:	$14.95
Rental:	$10 for members of Facets Video Club
Presentation:	Videorecording of the 1961 screen adaptation of the Lorraine Hansberry stage play, starring Sidney Poitier, Claudia McNeil, Ruby Dee, and Diana Sands; there is also a videorecording of the 1989 televised version of the play starring Danny Glover.
Awards:	Best Play of the Year Award, New York Drama Critics, 1959; ten NAACP Theatre Image Awards for its 1986 revival; Cannes Film Festival Award, 1961; *Raisin*, the musical based on the play, won a Tony Award in 1974

Content: The play was originally presented on Broadway in 1959. It was revived in 1986 at the Kennedy Center in Washington, D.C. Lorraine Hansberry was the first African-American woman to have a play produced on Broadway. The inspiration for the play came from the experience of her own family, which moved in the 1930s to a white neighborhood and fought against the "restrictive covenants" to the Supreme Court and won. The action takes place in the 1950s in the black ghetto of Chicago's South Side and shows the hopelessness that substandard housing and restricted opportunities instill. At the same time, the growing consciousness and affirmation of a black identity rooted in Africa is presented.

The play presents three generations of a black family living in a crowded apartment in a Chicago ghetto. Also shown are the daughter's suitors, both collegians: one, an African American from a well-to-do family, and the other, a Nigerian. In addition, we meet the representative of the white community where the family wants to move.

Lena, the family matriarch, receives $10,000 from her dead husband's life insurance. This money represents hope for each member of the Younger family. Lena and Ruth, her daughter-in-law, want to escape the crowded ghetto apartment and buy a house. Beneatha, the daughter, wants to go to med-

ical school. Walter, the son, wants to invest the money in a liquor store in order to stop working as a chauffeur for white people. The diverse aspirations provoke conflicts among the family members, particularly when the money that Lena has entrusted to Walter is lost through an unwise investment. But the family's dreams do not dry up like a "raisin in the sun." Rather, their courage and vision help them decide to leave their depressing surroundings and face an uncertain future in a home of their own in a white man's neighborhood in which they may have to face great hostility.

Classroom Use: Aside from its potential contribution to the study of theater and drama, *A Raisin in the Sun* can also be useful in courses dealing with black feminism, civil rights, ideology and cultural values, and the effects of prejudice on family life. The central foci of *Raisin in the Sun* are: the struggle for civil rights, identity quests, self-valuation, and societal respect. It also addresses several criteria for human diversity course requirements. For example, it relates directly to contemporary U.S. experiences (students would be able to recognize existing biases affecting housing, jobs, and education); it addresses issue of black self-image in a predominantly white culture (it speaks of standards of beauty, hair, and dress and of a rich African history and culture). Because of the dramatic format of *Raisin in the Sun,* its social and political message has a powerful impact; in addition, the performers' moving and vivid portrayals can help students perceive more readily the effects of racism.

Critical Comments: Inspired by Langston Hughes's poem ''Dream Deferred,'' *A Raisin in the Sun* is about just that: a dream deferred. It is considered one of the great American plays and critics have likened Hansberry's work to that of Eugene O'Neill, Arthur Miller, and Tennessee Williams. The playwright has sometimes been criticized for not being militant enough and for presenting an outdated view of integration, black matriarchy, the emasculation of the black man, and for giving secondary importance to the particular desires and frustrations of the three black women in the play. But it has also been recognized that she was ahead of her time in the way she dealt with the concepts of black beauty, identity, and heritage, and of the despair that exists and the courage that is necessary for black Americans to survive in poverty in an unjust and hostile land. Inspired by Hansberry's own experience with institutional racism in housing discrimination, the film presents a poignant and reliable view of how difficult, if not impossible, the American Dream is for some to realize. The overall effect is powerful and very moving as this accurate picture of a black family's crisis is presented. The play is published by Samuel French and is readily available from libraries and bookstores. Also in print by Hansberry are *To Be Young, Gifted and Black* (S. French, 1971), an autobiography; *The Movement: Documentary of a Struggle for Equality* (Simon & Schuster, 1964), a photo-history of the fight for civil rights; and her plays, such as *Les Blancs* (1972) and *The Sign in Sidney Brustein's Window* (1965). There is also a retrospective assessment of Hansberry published by Freedomways called *Lorraine Hansberry Speaks Out: Art of Thunder, Vision of Light* (1972).

Regina W. Betts, Department of Theatre

GLETHECO

Title:	**Raoni: The Fight for the Amazon**
Producers:	Barry Williams and Michael Gast, a Charter Films Presentation
Director:	Jean-Pierre Dutilleux
Distributor:	Mystic Fire Video
Release Date:	1979
Technical:	82 min. / color / English, Portuguese with subtitles in English
Purchase Price:	$29.95
Rental:	n/a from distributor
Presentation:	Documentary, with some narration
Awards:	The original film (produced by Pierre Louis Saguaz in 1978) on which this video is based won awards for best film, best photography, and best music at the VII Film Festival of Gramado; it was also nominated for an Academy Award as best documentary

Content: This film is about the Mekronoti Indians, a tribe in the Amazon region of Brazil. While the video shows some of their customs, beliefs, and practices, it emphasizes their efforts to protect their lands from the oncoming invasion of white settlers in the Amazon region during the 1970s.

Classroom Use: The film is recommended for use in courses on cultural diversity, Latin-American studies, Brazilian studies, Indians of South America, cultural anthropology, and ecology.

Critical Comments: The initial scene of the video was especially prepared for the present version, in which subtitles in English were also added to the original documentary. It depicts the gathering of some 2,000 Native Americans, representing some 70 Indian nations, in Washington, D.C., on July 15, 1978, following "the longest walk," a trek of more than 3,000 miles from San Francisco to Washington, which took five months to complete. The gathering was to combat anti-Indian legislation which was before Congress at the time. That legislation would have resulted in the closing of all schools and hospitals on the reservations of the Indians, who have both the highest suicide rate and the lowest average income of any group in the United States. This section is narrated by Marlon Brando, who describes some of the misconceptions about the Indians which are common among others in America. He and some Indian leaders discuss problems of Native Americans in this country.

The principal section of the video presents an ethnographic documentary of the Mekronoti Indians of Brazil. In addition to depicting the daily life of the tribe and describing some of its principal customs, beliefs, and practices, this section documents the imminent danger, at the time of filming (1976), of white settlers taking over the Indian lands. The chief of the Mekronoti is Raoni, a remarkable leader who visits other tribes—some of them former enemies—and invites them to discuss what they should do collectively in order to protect their territory. Some of the leaders wish to fight against the white men. (The white women and children are not to be killed, with the women being used for procreation!) As the film crew later learned, part of the discussion among the chiefs deals with a proposal to initiate the war against the whites immediately, by executing the outsiders who are making the documentary, in order to show that the Indians are resolute and will resist intrusion. The proposal is countered by the argument that the crew must be allowed to live, because the film can help others understand the Indians and their problems. Raoni wants to speak with the leaders of other tribes and with the head of FUNAI, Brazil's national agency for assistance to the Indians. This part of the documentary ends with the visit of the Indian chiefs to Brasilia, where they speak with the current head of FUNAI, General Ismarth de Oliveira. The Indians' primary request is simply for delimitation of their lands, which they consider urgent. The general promises to take their proposal to the president; although he does not promise that the proposal will be carried out within a year, he states the belief that the major obstacle to implementation is merely the question of funding.

In the third and final part of the video, Raoni visits São Paulo in the company of Claudio Vilas Boas, who, along with his brother, had worked with Indians for more than 30 years. (The Vilas Boas brothers devoted their lives to preventing extinction of the Indians in Central Brazil. Their work, which began in 1943, led to establishment, by the Brazilian government in 1961, of the Xingu National Park, the country's first national park for Indians. See the book *Xingu: The Indians, Their Myths,* by Orlando and Claudio Vilas Boas (Straus & Giroux, 1973).)

While accompanying Raoni in São Paulo, Vilas Boas speaks of white men and their society; he mentions some ways in which the life of the Indians seems preferable. The two men visit a pathetic group of acculturated Guarani, who live on land owned by a Japanese company outside São Paulo. Raoni tells them that he is fighting for his land, and that they should fight for theirs. Later, as the two friends walk the streets of São Paulo, Raoni says that he does not like the city, that he prefers where he lives, where there is no smoke and no noise. He comments on some of the misconceptions that white men have of Indians (that they are like animals or that they are lazy), and he speaks of what happens to Indians who leave their tribal homes and come to the big cities.

The men return to the shores of the Amazon, where they and the filmmaker look out over the waters. Raoni says he has heard that there are Indians in North America who are fighting for their land. He says this is good, that the whites want to get rid of all of the Indians, and that the Indians all fight the same battle together: "He is an Indian, and I am, too. I am Raoni, a Mekronoti Indian."

As the images fade, Marlon Brando resumes his narration, adding a postscript on what has happened to the Mekronoti Indians following the original filming on which this video is based, and appealing for help in the fight to save the Amazonian rainforest: "What you have just seen in this film is the result of savage ambitions of politics and big business. And since this film was completed, these people have been made to fight for their lives; some were killed: some Indians, and some whites. These people will be made to leave their present life, family after family, tribe after tribe, until the end finally comes for all of them, with nothing left to mark their passage except the jungle vines which will twist their decaying villages into memories.

And all for what? So that we can have a new camper trailer, perhaps an air conditioner, more watches, maybe 100,000 brand new cans of beer for Cincinnati or Budapest. You know, everyone thinks that someone else is helping. Well, it simply isn't true. If not you, who? And if not now, when?''

The video ends by showing the following text:

''In 1989, after 17 years of struggle, Raoni and director Jean-Pierre Dutilleux finally succeeded in drawing worldwide attention to their fight to protect the forest. In a highly publicized world tour they met with heads of state, rock stars and even the Pope, enlisting their support. They started the Rainforest Foundation, which has chapters in many countries. Today Raoni has become a living symbol of the ecological battle to save the last rainforests. His message has been heard by millions of people. It all started with this film, proving that ideas and images are more effective than violence and killing. But for Raoni and Jean-Pierre, this is only the beginning. So much has to be done. They need your support.'' If you want to help, please write to: RAONI, PO Box 1167, Venice, CA 90294 USA.

In sum, this video provides an accurate, moving portrayal of threats to the traditional habitat and ways of life of indigenous peoples of the Amazon region. It exemplifies the conflict between the traditional cultures of primitive societies and the onslaught of modern technology in the service of capitalistic development, while presenting an ethnographic documentary of some of the customs of the Mekronoti Indians and providing insights into the thoughts and acts of their great leader, Raoni. Thus, it can be viewed from the perspectives of both cultural diversity and social anthropology.

Brian F. Head, Department of Hispanic, Italian, and Portuguese Studies

USCULEXP

Title:	**The Ribbon Starts Here**
Producers:	Nigel Noble and Hilary Raff Lindsay
Director:	Nigel Noble
Distributor:	Noble Enterprises
Release Date:	1988
Technical:	45 min. / color / English
Purchase Price:	$25
Rental:	n/a
Presentation:	Documentary with brief excerpts of interviews with project organizers and participants

Content: This video chronicles the development of the August 1985 Ribbon Project, in which over 15 miles of yard-long fabric panels were ceremonially wrapped around the Pentagon and other symbolic structures in Washington, D.C., by some 20,000 participants in order to protest the nuclear arms race that flourished during the Reagan era. It depicts project founder Justine Merritt and other organizers of this grassroots effort as they met with community groups around the country, seeking their participation by making ribbon panels that would be used in the Washington event. There are scenes of local sew-ins and ribbon events in various states prior to the national ceremony.

Although the voices and fabric arts of women are primarily featured, the video does not make a point of identifying this as a women's project. However, it is clear from the medium of expression (fabric and the needle arts) and from the networks of family and friends through which news about the project spread, that the project was predominantly the work of women. Noting that many women are critical of the toll war has taken on their lives and the lives of loved ones, an unidentified participant comments, "You know, women are tired of pushing babies out, spending 18 years gettin' them grown up, and then having them blown away with a gun!" Although white women were the primary participants in and organizers of the Ribbon Project, the video attempts to diversify the voices of panelmakers, particularly by highlighting the African-American and Japanese participants in a dedication service at the Washington Cathedral.

Nigel Noble, an award-winning filmmaker, used his own footage supplemented by videotapes sent to him by dozens of project participants. The video notes how women utilized their traditional fabric arts in unconventional ways to make a public and political statement. He situates the Ribbon Project within the context of related efforts by others to call attention to the arms race, including a ribbon reception for congressional representatives just prior to the 1985 ceremony; anti-nuclear activists who painted human "shadows" on the sidewalks of Washington, D.C., to represent the remains of atomic bomb victims in Nagasaki and Hiroshima when they were vaporized in 1945; and a ribbon ceremony in Hiroshima, which encircled the A-Bomb Memorial Dome in that city.

Classroom Use: *The Ribbon Starts Here* is appropriate for classroom viewing at the university level, both undergraduate and graduate. It accu-rately describes and comments upon the meaning of the Ribbon Project for the participants and the larger society. Although it is not an in-depth analysis, the video provides a useful introduction to and overview of the project.

This video would be of use in addressing diversity issues in a variety of ways. It comments on alternative methods of expression that marginalized groups, particularly women, often use to convey their views when they feel that other avenues are not readily available to them. It also can be used in courses on diversity in the arts, women's studies, peace studies, political science, or concerning gender or folklore.

Critical Comments: It is worth noting that Noble has chosen to emphasize the ways in which the project represented an unusual, beautiful, and critical political commentary on U.S. military policies. This was an aspect of the project that some of the organizers chose to deemphasize, but one which Noble highlights throughout the video.

This video relates directly to the contemporary United States and addresses gender-related concerns (through visual representation but not through the narration—this would need to be brought out by the instructor), but does not speak directly to racial or ethnic diversity. It provides knowledge of diversity as expressed through aesthetic and ideological endeavors and focuses on the dynamics and mechanisms of alternative forms of social and political commentary used by women to express their views and discontent.

Linda Pershing, Department of Women's Studies

GLGENECO

Title:	**The Rice Ladle: The Changing Role of Women in Japan**
Series:	The Human Face of Japan
Producer:	Film Australia Production (Gil Brealey)
Director:	Oliver Howes
Distributor:	Film Australia Production
Release Date:	1981
Technical:	28 min. / color / English
Purchase Price:	$425
Rental:	$50
Presentation:	Documentary filmed in Japan
Study Guide:	''Leaders Guide,'' a one-page review of the film, a set of discussion questions, and a relevant bibliography can be obtained free from the distributor

Content: The focus of the film is on two women in Japan in the 1980s: one a young would-be pop singer (Fumiko) and the other a widow who works as a cook's assistant in a sushi shop (Mrs. Suda). The narrative alternates between the lives of these two women, though there are brief glimpses of the lives of other working women such as Mrs. Suda's daughter who works in a hospital, and young women who are training to be air hostesses for Japan Air Lines. The women are shown to have a variety of attitudes towards work and marriage: from a popular film singer who retires at age 21 to marry, to the cook's assistant who has to work to support herself, to serious women executives and the would-be pop star who are involved in developing their own careers, to women involved in construction and factory work, and others who are only ''seat warmers'' (i.e., waiting to quit work as soon as they get married).

Issues such as wage inequality (women get only 56% of the wages of men in the same job) are discussed. There is also a tongue-in-cheek discussion of the ''culture of cuteness'' that dominates the media portrayal of women in Japan. The would-be pop star's grooming and training and the type of television commercials she does are depicted in detail to give the audience an idea of the social expectations of women. The pressure on Japanese women to be cute and silly and portray themselves as playthings is contrasted with the realistic life of the working woman (like Mrs. Suda) who works ten-hour days with no weekends off.

The term ''Rice Ladle'' in the title of the film comes from the traditional control Japanese women have exercised over family finances after marriage. Japanese women are expected to run all aspects of the home from raising children to determining the monthly pocket allowance of the husband.

It remains to be seen how changes such as the two-income family are going to affect this neatly demarcated sphere of power.

Classroom Use: This reviewer used the video recently for a course on Asian women and society with a class of college seniors, who liked the film and appreciated the look at Japanese popular culture. While Japanese art and literature tended to remain very alien and different from the life experiences of the students, the ice-cream and soda-pop commercials seemed to strike a responsive cord. The film would be useful in a variety of courses on Japan, women in Asia, political science, anthropology, and communications. It might be useful as a discussion tool for exchange students, both Japanese students in English-as-a-second-language classes and students going to Japan.

Critical Comments: To some extent the film succeeds in showing "the human face of Japan." After the American media barrage on Japan and images of grim-faced executives who are all going about destroying the American economy, the somewhat silly activities of the Japanese teenagers engrossed in making it to the top of the pops is a pleasant change.

The film does challenge stereotypes of Japanese men and women. At another level, however, the film does not manage to go beyond superficial depictions of Japanese women and the complexities of contemporary Japanese society are glossed over.

Sucheta Mazumdar, Department of History

USETHPOL

Title:	**The Right to Be Mohawk: The Survival of a People and Their Traditions**
Producers:	George Hornbein, Anne Stanaway, and Lorna Rasmussen, for Sunlight Productions
Distributor:	New Day Films
Release Date:	1989
Technical:	17 min. / color / English
Purchase Price:	$250
Rental:	$50
Presentation:	Documentary

Content: Filmed at the Akwesasne Reservation, which straddles the New York State/Canadian border, this video offers little narration or background information; it primarily presents statements of various Mohawk Indians (Iroquois Indians) confirming in their own words their commitment to Mohawk identity. The opening statement indicates that contemporary Mohawks do not intend to remain static or live as their ancestors did, but that they do believe in their rights to live according to their traditional Mohawk values. This theme is reiterated by other speakers. Interspersed among the statements is footage from the reservation and elsewhere, including scenes of pollution, wampum belts, classes held at the Akwesasne Freedom School, and the presence of state troopers on the reservation during a conflict. These scenes and the statements by Mohawks are generally organized around three issues, presented in sequence: Iroquois attitudes toward the land, Mohawk sovereignty, and education of the younger generation.

Classroom Use: The video is appropriate for undergraduate classes at all levels. It represents the views of traditionalist Mohawk Indians, rather than of all Mohawks, on the reservation. Thus it would be useful for viewers to be aware of the ongoing conflicts at the Akwesasne Reservation. Viewers should, for instance, be made aware prior to seeing the film that there are competing governments on the reservation; that while most Mohawks agree with the general statements about Mohawk identity and concepts of land, some may not hold to the views expressed by speakers about the lack of jurisdiction of the New York State and federal governments over Indian land; and that not all Mohawks choose to send their children to the Akwesasne Freedom School. Showing the film in class offers an excellent opportunity to raise the issue of both controversy and agreement among native peoples over how best to maintain their identity within the larger society. It also suggests some of the forces working against the survival of Mohawk identity. The video would be particularly appropriate for diversity courses in the disciplines of anthropology, history, political science, and education.

Critical Comments: The video assumes the value of maintaining cultural identity rather than a strategy of assimilation for Indians. One speaker identifies as genocide anything that threatens the land base, language, or cultural identity of Indian peoples. The central focus here is on what we might call ethnicity. The video has the advantage of presenting very eloquent and articulate Indian people; it makes the distinction nicely between what students may often define as Indian identity (i.e., clothing, lifestyle, etc.) and what Mohawks themselves use to define their Indianness (i.e., their set of values). Because Mohawks speak for themselves here, students are exposed to Indian intellectuals, leaders, and teachers who may challenge their stereotypes of Indians as either frozen in time or as passive victims of poverty and despair. They also offer their own analyses of Mohawk life in contemporary America.

The video compares aspects of Mohawk life to the contemporary U.S. experiences of students. It explicitly raises aspects of ethnic and racial diversity, as well as the issue of nationalism for Mohawks. The film offers examples of Mohawk political activism, efforts by Mohawks to create their own educational system, and statements of ideology. It explicitly discusses conflicts in cultural values (especially those of land and community) arising from human diversity, and allows for discussion of diversity within an ethnic group. By focusing on the contemporary Mohawk experience, the video addresses the results of social diversity.

Gail H. Landsman, Department of Anthropology

USRACSOC

Title:	**The Rise in Campus Racism: Causes & Solutions**
Series:	Black Issues in Higher Education
Producer:	Cox, Matthews & Assoc., Inc.
Director:	Wally Ashby
Distributor:	Cox, Matthews & Assoc., Inc.
Release Date:	1991
Technical:	120 min. / color / English
Purchase Price:	$325
Rental:	n/a
Presentation:	Teleconference held February 20, 1991, on issues of racism on campus, moderated by Julian Bond
Participants:	Michael Williams, Office for Civil Rights, U.S. Dept. Education; Jawanza Kunjufu, President, African American Images; Howard J. Ehrlich, Director of Research, National Institute Against Prejudice and Violence; Mary Ellen Ashley, Vice-provost, University of Cincinnati; Reginald Clark, Professor of Afro-Ethnic Studies, California State University, Fullerton; Na'im Akbar, Psychologist and Educator, Florida State University; Richard Rubenstein, Director, Center for Conflict Analysis and Resolution, George Mason University; Susan Weidman Schneider, Editor-in-Chief, *LILITH*, Jewish Women's Magazine; Raynard Davis, Executive Director, Students Against Apartheid and Racism (SCAAR)

Content: Four incidents or issues are presented in the video: a false report in a student newspaper of assault and rape; institutional racism at Harvard; separatism on the campus of the University of North Carolina at Chapel Hill; and diversity in the student body at the University of California at Berkeley. Each issue is preceded by a short prepared presentation of circumstances, followed by panel discussion, comments from administrators and others on the campuses involved, and questions from the audience or from teleconference sites. Following the four subjects, three sets of recommended solutions for students, faculty, and administrations are presented and discussed.

The groups involved in the incidents are primarily white and African American, although the segment on diversity of the student body includes comments by Asian-Americans, Native Americans, and Hispanics. In the false report incident, a woman representing herself as a rape counselor told a student newspaper about a rape incident involving two African Americans and a white woman. The newspaper published the report, including statements using negative stereotypes. The report was false. Panel discussion centers on how students reacted to the report and why they were willing to believe it, the freedom of the student newspaper to report such incidents, and the historical background to the relationship between sexism and racism.

The second discussion, concerning institutional racism, centers on why minority faculty are important, and the role of educational institutions in perpetuating racism.

The third discussion, on separatism on campuses, looks at why African Americans often stay together in cafeterias or dormitories, and whether this behavior is the same as whites in seeking to keep to themselves. The problems that groups face when they are the minority at an institution are discussed.

The fourth discussion centers on the difficulties of increasing the diversity of the student body on campus, white reactions to those policies, and the situations of individuals who are brought onto campus by such policies.

Classroom Use: The video is appropriate for all levels of students and is useful to faculty as well as administrators. On any given issue, the video presents viewpoints from a wide range of individuals who bring different perspectives to the questions. Discussion is informed and no one person dominates. The video can be broken up into four parts, one shown on each day, followed by class discussion.

Critical Comments: As far as I can see, there are no hidden theoretical assumptions in the video. Each person's point of view is fairly easy to identify (e.g., university president, student, psychologist). The video is very well-suited to diversity classes. It directly addresses major questions about race relations on campus and multicultural problems of diversity. It does not approach these questions from the point of view of a single academic discipline but from psychology, sociology, and Africana studies. Further, there is ample opportunity for faculty members to contribute to the discussion from the point of view of their own disciplines.

The use of this video has the advantage that it covers many topics that ought to be discussed in a course on diversity, and the panel members make many excellent points regarding racism on campus. The disadvantage is that there are so many issues covered. Much more needs to be said about any one issue. The video doesn't build to make a single large point about racism, one that will be remembered by students. The video definitely needs to be broken up into four half-hour segments and discussed in class. Used in this way, it is bound to generate substantial and meaningful class discussion.

Michael J. Sattinger, Department of Economics

USETHEXP

Title:	## Ritual Clowns
Producer:	Victor Masayesva Jr.
Distributor:	IS Productions
Release Date:	1988
Technical:	15 min. / color, b&w still photos and film clips / Hopi with English translation
Purchase Price:	$75
Rental:	n/a
Presentation:	Experimental documentary and video art

Content: Produced by a Native-American Hopi filmmaker, *Ritual Clowns* is a short piece that was shown not long ago at the Whitney Biennial as video art. The voice—in Hopi, then in English—that recounts the story is that of a tribal storyteller explaining the ritual of clowns and their interaction with katchina spirits in ceremony. The specifics of what might simply be a documentary about religious beliefs and practices are expanded in Masayesva's hands to encompass the world and the cosmos. The film constantly shifts back and forth from the microcosm of the plaza and the ceremony to the creation and life plan of the universe. Human's disruption of the natural plan and the consequences become a central matter of concern. A variety of film techniques highlight the narrative progression including landscape shots, animation, scenes of outer space, and scenes within symbolic geometric configurations.

At a critical point about halfway through the video, it becomes clear that humankind must be disciplined and corrected for abuse and pollution of the environment. The social criticism here aimed at war and nuclear weapons primarily targets countries of the world whose flags are prominently displayed. However, the presentation is predicated upon the idea that the world community is a larger extension of the Hopi tribal community, meaning that all of humanity is united in responsibility for mistakes and the ability to rectify them. At this point, voices and images begin to multiply as cultural differences and stereotypes are exposed. Expressing disgust and superiority, the voice of a German anthropologist accompanies slides of a Hopi dance ritual.

Children in animal masks expound unintelligibly in the language of philosophy and anthropology. A woman's voice comments upon the obscenity and immorality of Hopi dances. Finally, circus music accompanies images of Charlie Chaplin and rodeo clowns as the narrator comments on the importance of the clown. In Western culture the clown merely entertains, but in native culture the clown also instructs and admonishes. A child's voice warns of the inevitable approach of Judgment Day when every soul will be revealed. A note of hope is accentuated at the end when the child assures us that if only one individual survives, the information to start again will be given to him.

Critical Comments: Victor Masayesva is again pushing through the medium of film and the documentary genre to find new forms of native self-expression. A strikingly beautiful view of the importance of ceremony and its connection to the world at large is available in *Ritual Clowns* for anthropology students and sociologists alike. Environmental concerns and religious tenets intertwine.

Another very important part of this film is the presentation of material in a humorous way. Many have said that the key to native survival has been a sense of humor. The complex power of humor and the clown as its propagator is given depth and complexity in the context of this video. Any class concerned with oral tradition or narrative voices will find materials for consideration.

Jeanne Laiacona, Department of Art

USRACLAW

Title:	**The Road to Brown: The Untold Story of "the Man Who Killed Jim Crow"**
Producer:	William A. Elwood, for the University of Virginia
Director:	Mykola Kulish
Distributor:	California Newsreel
Release Date:	1989
Technical:	48 min. / color, b&w archival footage / English
Purchase Price:	$295
Rental:	$75
Presentation:	Documentary; written by Gary Weinberg, narrated by Steven Anthony Jones

Content: This excellent film traces the story of the campaign by the National Association for the Advancement of Colored People (NAACP) to end school segregation in the South, focusing on the role of one lawyer, Charles Hamilton Houston. It begins by showing a Chester County (S.C.) high school that in 1989 has a black principal and equal numbers of black and white students. After showing the students at various activities, it makes the point that only 35 years ago, before the Supreme Court's Brown decision, such scenes were both unthinkable and against the law. The film then flashes back to a 1934 black-and-white video showing separate schools, no school buses for black children, and separate drinking fountains.

The first section of the film, entitled "Prologue to Brown," traces the history of blacks in the United States beginning in Jamestown, Va., in 1619 up to the Civil War. It emphasizes the legal underpinnings of segregation and discusses the 13th, 14th, and 15th Amendments, *Plessy* vs. *Ferguson,* and the thousands of lynchings in the South in the early part of the century.

The second part gives a brief biography of Charles Hamilton Houston, a northern black, the child of a lawyer and a teacher, who graduated summa cum laude from Amherst College in 1915 with no plans for activism. He volunteered to serve in World War I and, as an officer in the army, he encountered Jim Crow for the first time and confronted a lynch mob of white soldiers in France. He returned to go to Harvard, where he edited the *Law Review.*

At this time there were only 100 black lawyers serving the 9 million blacks living in the South. In 1934 Houston was appointed special counsel to the NAACP and began to examine the weaknesses in the schools as a violation of the 14th Amendment. To have separate but equal schools would have been prohibitively expensive, given the 7 to 1 white to black ratio in teacher's salaries and the 10 to 1 ratio in expenditures per pupil. His first case involved a student named Murray who was admitted to the University of Maryland Law School. But the environment of a law school is much different from that of a rural southern school system. He eventually left the NAACP and focused on cases involving transportation, housing, and labor, but not before he had involved Thurgood Marshall (later the first black Supreme Court justice) in continuing the cause of equal schooling. He died in 1950, four years before the Brown decision.

The third part of the film recounts the actual events leading up to the Brown case, named after seven-year-old Linda Brown. On May 17, 1954, the Supreme Court unanimously passed the Brown decision declaring that separate is not equal in American education. The film then moves to a consideration of the aftermath, the massive resistance to enforcement of the Brown decision in the South, and the role of the Ku Klux Klan and George Wallace in Alabama. It quickly summarizes the many protests leading up to the 1964 Civil Rights Act and the 1965 Voting Rights Act. In the end, it returns to contemporary high school life.

Classroom Use: The film will be useful in any class that touches on any of the many issues it covers: school quality, African-American history, civil rights, integration, etc. It provides a context for all these issues and can be used as a starting point for a more in-depth discussion of any of them, depending on the actual subject matter of the class and the interests of the faculty.

One of the film's main benefits is that it requires very little setup by the instructor. It is extremely well-done and appropriate for all students. If they know little they will get a broad overview; if they know the outlines they will learn details. Relating the story through the eyes of Houston makes it seem new since his is not a household name to many students. The use of some film footage he shot to reveal the inequalities in southern schools and the linking of present and past combine for an interesting viewing experience, even if

one is well-versed in the issues. The music is also extremely effective and it is possible to understand the words to the songs. In addition to good sound and visual quality, the video moves along quickly and holds the viewer's attention very well.

Critical Comments: Intellectually, the film is celebratory of black progress in the United States while promoting the cause of school integration. It also reminds viewers of the current plight of African Americans in terms of poverty, high school graduation rates, and political representation. It ends with a very effective quote from Houston which points out that, while equal rights have been won, more is still to be done to ensure that the system guarantees justice and freedom for everyone.

Nancy A. Denton, Department of Sociology

USETHCUL

Title:	**Running on the Edge of the Rainbow: Laguna Stories and Poems with Leslie Marmon Silko**
Series:	Words & Place: Native Literatures of the American Southwest (Program no. 6)
Producer:	Larry Evers, for the University of Arizona and its Radio-TV-Film Bureau
Distributor:	Norman Ross Publishing
Release Date:	1981
Technical:	28 min. / color / English
Purchase Price:	$175
Rental:	n/a from Norman Ross
Presentation:	Storytelling performances and voiceover narration by Silko
Study Guide:	Guides for the Words & Place videos are available from the distributor

Content: The social group represented in the video is Laguna Pueblo, one of the Keresan-speaking matrilineal societies of eastern New Mexico. Leslie Marmon Silko is a member of the Laguna and an acclaimed writer and storyteller, author of the novel *Ceremony* (1977) and the autobiographical *Storyteller* (1981). Her work is especially noted for bridging the gap between oral tradition and contemporary written literature.

The context is the economically marginalized society of a Native-American community still residing on its traditional territory. These Pueblo communities have been among the Native-American groups most successful at surviving culturally under Spanish and then U.S. domination. Social life remains communal, kin-based, and gynocentric.

The video alternates between scenes of the pueblo and its natural setting and scenes of Silko telling stories and reading poems—poems incorporating some of those stories—to two other Laguna women and, in one scene, to two small children. Settings are casual; performances do not appear staged. Silko's voiceover provides context for the poems and stories and explains the importance of oral tradition to the community and the continuities between the old stories and her contemporary versions. Readings include three poems from *Storyteller:* "Storytelling," "Toe'Osh: A Laguna Coyote Story for Simon Ortiz," and "Indian Song: Survival."

Classroom Use: In regard to classroom study of diversity, the video fits several disciplinary contexts: anthropology, literature, folklore, Native-American or U.S. ethnic studies, and women's studies. The type of diversity represented is cultural and artistic, concerning ethnic identity and the adaptation of traditional expressive culture to contemporary life. The poems and stories are very funny so there is a potential application to ethnic humor.

For classroom use, I recommend having students first read Silko's "Storytelling" and/or "Toe'Osh: A Laguna Coyote Story," poems which she reads in the video. Both poems are in her book *Storyteller;* both are humorous; both combine traditional oral stories with parallel happenings in contemporary life. Students can then discuss how Silko establishes these continuities, and how cultural traditions shape understanding of the present.

Critical Comments: The video is appropriate for any undergraduate level, but does require some introduction. It does not explain who Silko is nor what and where Laguna is. Introductory comments to establish this context would be needed for viewers unfamiliar with the geographic distribution and general characteristics of Native-American peoples. One should note that this is a traditionally sedentary society of matrilineal descent, with a social life organized around groups of related women having considerable authority and autonomy. Another Laguna writer, Paula Gunn Allen, refers to this lifestyle as "gynocentric" or woman-centered, to avoid the misconception, common especially in feminist circles, that matrilineal societies are matriarchal or ruled by women. For many Americans, the prevailing image of Native-American society is that of the 19th-century Plains Indians (e.g., the Lakota of the film *Dances With Wolves*); videos set in contemporary Native-American communities such as this could help to correct this narrow stereotype.

The video is a personal statement by a Native-American woman writer about her art and her people; it does not fall into any particular theoretical category. The content is not overtly political—she does not speak directly about conflict between Indians and white America. But in a more subtle way, perhaps more effective because it is not simply confrontational, Silko conveys some of the dilemmas of being Indian in today's America. She tells of how anthropologist Elsie Clews Parsons in the 1930s declared Laguna a "lost cause" because it no longer had a *kiva* (the Pueblo underground ceremonial chamber). Silko says that anthropologists ("anthros and people like that") always made her feel that to be a "worthy" Pueblo person she should tell stories the way they are in the Bureau of American Ethnology reports. She could never identify with those stories because they were cut off from actual experience; instead, she found continuities with the old tales in the stories and gossip she heard around her every day. The tendency of Anglo-Americans to place value upon an earlier "authentic" Indian culture at the expense of living people (as in *Dances With Wolves*) is a major grievance of Native-Americans today.

Another issue she deals with, again subtly and indirectly, is that of mixed ancestry. Many Native-Americans have partial white or African ancestry and must come to terms with this in establishing their identity. Silko's great-grandfather Robert Marmon was a white man who married into the Laguna community. The video shows the Marmon family's store and houses, while Silko observes that the buildings are on the edge of the village by the river because the family itself is marginal. Instead of causing alienation, this became a source of creativity: the river is a place where things happen that would not happen in the middle of the village. It is where, in a favorite traditional story that Silko has retold in prose and poetry, a married woman named Yellow Woman was abducted by a supernatural being. For Lagunas this is the prototype for all tales of unfaithful wives.

The video's principal focus is the vital social role of storytelling: because of the stories people tell about each other, everyone knows who they are. No matter what one does, somebody sometime will have done something similar; one's own experience becomes a new version of an old story. Individuals learn to see their personal situations in relation to the group: "your story's gonna be right there with all the others." This conveys an aspect of self-construction in a communal society—something difficult for individualistic westerners to comprehend.

Louise Burkhart, Department of Anthropology

GLGENECO

Title:	**Selbe: One among Many**
Producer:	Safi Faye
Director:	Safi Faye
Distributor:	Women Make Movies
Release Date:	1983
Technical:	30 min. / color / Wolof, French with subtitles
Purchase Price:	$225
Rental:	$60
Presentation:	Ethnographic documentary with narration

Content: *Selbe* is the story of a Senegalese rural woman and life in her village. Its focus is primarily upon women's work activities and their family roles. It describes the extraordinary economic contributions that women make to their families and communities. The film examines the conflicts and dilemmas women face when tradition confronts modernization.

Classroom Use: This film is appropriate for college students in history, African-American studies, and women's studies courses.

Critical Comments: *Selbe* examines the nature of women's lives in this West African village and the forces that shape them. Through the account of Selbe's daily life, viewers experience women's enormous capacity for work. Women assume responsibility for the economic survival of their communities in the absence of their husbands. While they are potters, peddlers, and domestics, they also fish, mine salt, and engage in agricultural production. Selbe performs all of these tasks.

This film also delineates a number of important themes that should be explored in greater depth to understand West Africa: gender roles and their effect on women's ability to seek self-actualization; migration and urbanization; and the relationship between the city and its hinterland. And finally, it raises questions, but does not explore, the effect on village life when the traditional encounters modernization.

Selbe is quite compelling in its exploration of rural Senegalese women's lives as workers and mothers. The film, however, presupposes that one has knowledge of their culture. This viewer would like to have seen an exploration of the support networks that women are able to access in order to complete their duties—female relatives, benevolent societies, etc. To fully appreciate Selbe's experiences, one has to understand the Senegalese traditional cultures. Roles between men and women are clearly defined. For example, in many West African societies women wield significant economic power as market women, farmers, etc. Men perform different, but equally important, tasks in their communities. It is not enough for Safi Faye, an anthropologist, to tell us that "men are rendered helpless and deprived of their dignity." Colonialism challenged, if not destroyed, the ways in which villagers organize their lives. Selbe's life has to be placed within this historical context so that viewers will be able to appreciate more fully her reality.

Lillian S. Williams, Department of Women's Studies

GLGENCLA

Title:	**Simplemente Jenny**
Producers:	Jane Stubbs, Latin American production; Melanie Maholich, U.S.A. production
Director:	Helena Solberg Ladd, for The International Women's Film Project
Distributor:	Cinema Guild
Release Date:	1975
Technical:	33 min. / color / narrated in English; Spanish dialog has voiceover translation and subtitles in English
Purchase Price:	$295
Rental:	$55
Presentation:	Documentary
Award:	Blue Ribbon, American Film and Video Festival

Content: Filmed in Latin America, this documentary exposes the extreme poverty and few alternatives available to women in these societies.

Critical Comments: Although this documentary focuses on the condition and roles of women in Latin-American societies, it also offers a critical view of the highly stratified class structure and mass poverty that dominates these countries by attempting to capture the feelings and survival struggles of those who live at the margins of society.

The linkages between patriarchy and the class system and how it affects the daily lives of the poor are emphasized through interviews of both young and elderly women. They express the many burdens they face both in the household and as workers in the informal sector of the economy. The roles of the church, the family, and the media in perpetuating women's oppression are also explored.

The film includes the voices of Latin-American women from Bolivia, Mexico, and Argentina, from various social and racial groups. Jenny, the name mentioned in the title, is a young woman now confined to a reformatory. Her life experiences as an abused unwed mother represent the grim future of many Latin-American youth. Poverty, exploitation, crime, and domestic, social, and political violence are the overwhelming realities of the daily existence of young women like Jenny, limiting their possibilities for a better life.

In its attempt to denounce the general problems of extreme poverty, sexism, racial prejudice, and political violence that plague most Latin-American nations, this documentary becomes too diffused and fails to establish effectively the intended links between class, sexual, and racial exploitation, and the control and influence of foreign (primarily U.S.) capital in this region.

The title of the film is a parody of *Simplemente Maria*, a very popular Latin-American soap opera. In Latin America, soap operas (both on TV as well as in the printed fotonovelas) are a common and popular entertainment medium for escaping the harsh realities of daily survival.

This documentary is useful for discussions about women's roles and stereotypes in Latin America and to illustrate the conditions and effects of poverty in this region.

Edna Acosta-Belen, Department of Latin American and Caribbean Studies

USETHSTE

Title:	**Slaying the Dragon**
Producer:	Deborah Gee, for Asian Women United
Director:	Deborah Gee
Distributor:	National Asian-American Telecommunications Association/CrossCurrent Media
Release Date:	1988
Technical:	60 min. / color, b&w footage / English
Purchase Price:	$225
Rental:	$50; preview available
Presentation:	Documentary with cinema film clips, archival footage, interviews with Asian historians, sociologists, actors, actresses, and broadcasters
Award:	Finalist for American Film and Video Festival Award

Content: The film traces the stereotypical and one-dimensional portrayals of Asian and Asian-American women in Hollywood. Three basic categories seemingly evolved: the evil and manipulative Dragon Lady, the subservient and demure Geisha Girl, and the seductive Suzy Wong. The film surveys media representations over the last 60 years. Beginning with a discussion of the early (19th-century) history of Asian immigration, the film moves on to delineate the passage of anti-Asian legislation and how this shaped media depictions of Asians. The focus is primarily on Chinese-Americans and Japanese-Americans in this part of the video.

The video also shows how the American political climate and U.S. foreign policy has been reflected in the portrayal of Asians by Hollywood. Initially, the Chinese were depicted as "the enemy." Then, after 1937 and the alliance between the United States and China during World War II, the Japanese emerged as the "devils." The "cruel and lustful" Japanese men were contrasted with the "helpless and innocent" Chinese women in many of these forties productions. After 1949 and the victory of the Chinese Communists, Hollywood rediscovered "the enemy," and the portrayal of Chinese and Chinese-American women and men began to range from the sly and shrewd Charlie Chan types to the malevolent empresses who were inciting the Mongols (the yellow races) to conquer the world. The portrayal of Japanese women (in *Tea House of the August Moon,* for example) reverted

to one of the "passive" Asian female stereotype, ever-willing to please her man.

The video then moves to a more contemporary period, including that of the Vietnam War era, and examines the stereotypes that emerged. In conclusion, the film explores how these Hollywood stereotypes may be changing as politically conscious Asian-American film directors begin to make films about their own communities.

There are extensive interviews with Asian-American women who reflect on how these stereotypes have affected their lives. Some of the interviewees feel that the sexism and racism of Hollywood combined to limit the types of roles available, so that the actresses who wanted to work had little choice but to "play along." Other interviewees disagree and say their roles were not necessarily derogatory.

Classroom Use: The film is suitable for an upper-division course, in which there has been some prior discussion of Asian-American history or racism and sexism. I would not plan on using this film in isolation without a lecture and some supplementary reading. It certainly meets criteria for human diversity courses and should be useful in sociology, communications, history, and women's studies courses.

Critical Comments: The film is well-made, though there are some sexually explicit clips which may divert attention from the issues being discussed. More broadly, the film enables a discussion of how the American media has played a major role in shaping perceptions of Asians, perceptions which have had little to do with reality. It also shows the extent to which the American media is quick to reflect the policy decisions emanating from Washington and uses very little critical judgment of its own.

Sucheta Mazumdar, Department of History

GLGENECO

Title:	**Small Happiness: Women of a Chinese Village**
Producers:	Carma Hinton and Kathy Kline; executive producer, Daniel Sipe
Directors:	Carma Hinton and Richard Gordon
Distributor:	Long Bow Group
Release Date:	c1987
Technical:	58 min. / color / English
Purchase Price:	$325
Rental:	$75
Presentation:	Documentary, including individuals' stories; originally shown on PBS
Awards:	Blue Ribbon, American Film and Video Festival and several other awards
Study Guide:	Transcript available

Content: Part of the three-part film series ''One Village in China'' made in the 1980s, *Small Happiness* deals with the life of women in Low Bow village, 400 miles southwest of Beijing; a village where William Hinton went to work and study in 1947 and wrote the classic work in Chinese ethno-history, *Fanshen*. Producer Carma Hinton was born there and grew up in the village and its environs. *Small Happiness* is a unique and intimate look at the lives of Chinese women telling their own stories to an American, but one who is also an insider. As a result, this is a more intimate look than would have been otherwise possible.

The film focuses on a mother-in-law and daughter-in-law and, through their life histories, looks at questions of marriage, treatment of women in society, access to education, birth control, and the role of women in farm work. The mother-in-law, born around World War I, was sold by her father to her husband for 200 yuan so that her natal family could buy grain and survive during a lean year. Footbinding is discussed in terms of how society inflicted it on women and how the women in pre-1949 China had no options but to go through this painful process. After marriage numerous pregnancies were also inevitable due to the high rate of infant mortality.

This absence of choice, either in terms of the marriage partner or in terms of the pattern of life, is contrasted with a contemporary wedding in the village. The bride and groom had met, dated, and decided to get married. Similarly, the daughter-in-law had also met and married her high-school sweetheart despite parental opposition. There is considerable discussion in this segment on women's views of marriage, birth control, the need for labor on the farm, and the resultant need for children, as well as the official birth control policy. Clearly, the lives of women improved significantly after the Chinese Revolution.

The inequalities experienced by women in the post-1949 period are also discussed, particularly the inequalities in wages received by women versus men. The last segment of the film shows the 1980s and the impact of the economic liberalization policies under Deng Xiao-ping. Now the farm work is being done almost entirely by women as the men increasingly take up jobs away from the farms. The possibilities for women to work outside the farm are shown to have increased in this period. Some young women from the village work in a saw-blade workshop. The film also shows the continued inequalities as the manager of the workshop is an older male official, while the workers are younger unmarried women whose demands for better working conditions are dealt with in a paternalistic manner.

Classroom Use: This is one of the best films available for providing American students with a glimpse of life and the status of women in China and,

by extension, in a Third World country. It is very well-made and accessible to all university levels. It is also useful as a discussion tool because the film raises so many questions. It would be useful in courses in sociology, Asian history, women's studies, anthropology, cultural geography, political science, and women and development.

Critical Comments: My only quibble with this excellent film is that the specificity of the location of the village in north China is not fully explained. Even in the early 20th century there were sharp differences in the social conditions between north and south China. Women in the South had a somewhat higher position and footbinding was not as common. The film should not be taken as typical of all of China.

Sucheta Mazumdar, Department of History

USGENCOM

Title:	**Still Killing Us Softly: Advertising's Image of Women**
Producer:	Margaret Lazarus
Director:	Margaret Lazarus
Distributor:	Cambridge Documentary Films
Release Date:	1987
Technical:	32 min. / color / English
Purchase Price:	$385 (or more, depending on restrictions)
Rental:	$46 for one day; $106 for one week
Presentation:	Update of a film produced in the late 1970s of a lecture given at Harvard by Jean Kilbourne; interspersed in her lecture are examples of commercial advertisements that contribute to sexism and patriarchal cultural patterns
Awards:	First Place, National Council on Family Relations Film Festival; National Educational Film Festival; First Place, Chicagoland Educational Film Festival

Content: Professor Jean Kilbourne makes the point that media advertising places an important role in the social construction of women's roles in our culture. Speaking from a feminist perspective, Kilbourne argues that advertising constructs women as weak, ineffectual sexual objects; conversely, she

argues that advertising constructs men as hard, unfeeling sexual machines. While her argument is basically problematic (that advertising effects our attitudes about self and others and, in this way, affects our behavior), her analyses of advertisements themselves are very interesting and politically provocative: women appear in the ads in ways that demonstrate how they are constructed as sexual objects; Kilbourne's analysis goes on to show how violence against women is advocated through the ads. Throughout the lecture, Kilbourne uses statistics to support her claims that women's interests are subverted through advertising. For example, she notes that in a survey of women across multiple ages, 80 percent reported that they were overweight; she notes that this statistic speaks not to the shape of women across the country, but to the consensus on "thin" engendered by advertising. Although this film has not received any major awards, it has been updated which speaks to its ongoing resonance in our culture.

Classroom Use: This video is very appropriate for undergraduate students. It provokes thoughtful reflection about the role of the media in the social construction of gender and fosters discussion on the ways both men and women experience themselves as gendered through ad campaigns. The film is also appropriate for graduate students; but because I expect graduate students to have more familiarity with the theme, this film would be useful and interesting as an example of content analysis: ads are analyzed in terms of their meaning, and thus the video reports on a good example of qualitative research.

I recommend that this video be used early on in a diversity course as it is a useful tool to begin discussion about gender. As discussions about feminism must necessarily flow from discussions of gender, this tape is a good forerunner to a more politicized view of gender.

Critical Comments: Because the ads that are highlighted in the video are central advertising campaigns of major corporations, Kilbourne's analysis can be widely recognized by the general public. This contributes to the reliability of her sample; also the fact that she discusses ads that feature both men and women increases the validity of her claim that ads contribute to the construction of gendered roles.

However, as I mentioned, her claim that ads shape attitudes and, in that way, shape behavior, is methodologically flawed. Media studies have shown that viewers appropriate "messages" from the television in unique ways that reflect their own culture, family patterns of interaction, and individual interpretative frames. Therefore, it is exceedingly problematic to argue that ads are interpreted uniformly by viewers. Despite this limitation, Kilbourne's analysis is valid because she draws similarities across ad campaigns.

This film uses "cultivation theory," developed in media studies, to make the claim that culture is both reflected and constructed in the media, specifically on the television. Therefore, ads are a reflection of how (male-dominated) corporations both create and appropriate cultural symbols to shape gender identities for men and women alike.

The study of gender cannot be complete without systematic attention to the role of the media in the social construction of gender. Differences in roles, professional opportunities, and sexual behavior, for example, are not established via some genetic programming; gender differences are created, maintained, and altered through communication processes. Analyzing and reflecting upon gender must therefore include a focus on the role that communication plays in our culture, television being a central medium for the transmission of culture.

Certainly, this film relates to the analysis of gender in contemporary American culture as it focuses on the role of current ad campaigns in our experience of gender. Because this film is political without arguing that women are victims of men (both men and women are portrayed as victims of ad campaigns), it would foster discussion of both male and female gendered roles. This kind of examination contributes to students' understanding of the politics of gender in our culture and is a useful tool to favor reflection on the ways our lives are gendered.

Sara Cobb, Department of Communication

USCLAEXP

Title:	**Style Wars!**
Producers:	Tony Silver, Linda Habib, and Henry Chalfant, for Public Art Films
Director:	Tony Silver
Distributor:	New Day Films
Release Date:	1984
Technical:	69 min. / color / English
Purchase Price:	$487
Rental:	$15
Presentation:	Documentary with short excerpts of interviews and actual footage of graffiti artists at work
Awards:	Blue Ribbon, American Film and Video Festival; Grand Prize, U.S. Film Festival; Best Television Documentary, National Black Progressive Consortium; Ciné Golden Eagle; PBS National Primetime Special

Content: *Style Wars!* examines the subculture of graffiti art by young men living in New York, who risk injury and jail to paint on the sides of subway trains. They discuss their aesthetics, the informal transmission of style and technique, and the meanings their work has for them. These graffiti artists are Hispanic, African American, and white, but most come from working-class or lower-income families, and their art gives them a sense of self-worth and recognition. Former New York mayor Ed Koch and the transit authorities go to enormous lengths to try to stop them, but the youths inevitably find ways to subvert the system. Groups of graffiti artists sometimes compete for territory and fame. The high art world makes them celebrities and displays portions of their work in a gallery. The video raises fascinating questions about popular art and contestation, the economics of art, and racial, class, and gender dynamics of artistic expression.

Classroom Use: *Style Wars!* is a splendid and carefully crafted documentary, appropriate for classroom viewing at the university level, both undergraduate and graduate. This reviewer uses the video in a course entitled "Issues and Images of Diversity in the Visual Arts." It would also be effective in other courses dealing with the arts, popular culture,

sociology, American life, issues of censorship and free expression, and urban anthropology.

It does not require any special introduction but is most effective when time is left for substantive discussion afterwards. Since it is a long video, I suggest showing half of it during two different class periods in order to allow discussion after each showing. Students in my course found *Style Wars!* very compelling, and there was lengthy and heated discussion afterwards.

Critical Comments: This film carefully contextualizes graffiti within the lives of the artists and as one of many aspects of a larger subculture that incorporates other forms of expression, such as break dancing and rap music. It addresses important issues concerning how class, race, and/or gender identity may entail certain privileges and social recognition, and how these spill over into claims about "legitimate" forms of self-expression. At the center of the video are questions about what is considered "real" art and who defines social categories. These questions are raised for the viewer, but they are not answered definitively, leaving the viewer to draw his or her own conclusions. The video presents a collage of different viewpoints, including those of the graffiti

Winner of numerous awards, *Style Wars!* explores the sub-culture of young graffiti ''artists'' through interviews and actual footage of the (illegal) art in progress on New York's subway trains. Among the issues that have given rise to heated classroom discussion are the boundaries of art and the dynamics of race, class, and gender in artistic expression. (Courtesy New Day Films)

artists, their apprentices, their parents, governmental authorities, patrons of the fine art world, and the general public.

Linda Pershing,
Department of Women's Studies

USETHSTE

Title:	**Sun, Moon, and Feather**
Producer:	Metropolitan Arts
Directors:	Bob Rosen and Jane Zipp
Distributor:	Cinema Guild
Release Date:	1989
Technical:	30 min. / color, b&w footage from home movies and classic American films / English
Purchase Price:	$250
Rental:	$55
Presentation:	Combines documentary with singing, dramatization, and narration by an ensemble of three sisters who collectively call themselves Spiderwoman Theatre
Award:	Special Jury Prize, USA Film Festival, 1989

Content: The three sisters who wrote the script are related through their mother to the Rappahannock Nation (Virginia) and through their father to Cuna Indians of Sand Blas Islands (Panama). The three sisters—Muriel Miguel, Gloria Miguel, and Lisa Mayo—reminisce about their childhoods and reenact their memories of growing up in an Italian section of Brooklyn during the 1930s and 1940s. The sisters use the rituals of their working-class family as means of calling attention to the stereotyping, commercialization, and marginalization of Native-American cultures. Some of their dialog is adapted from Anton Chekhov's *Three Sisters.*

Background reading: Regina Betts of the University at Albany Theatre Department suggests the following for background on the mission and theories of Spiderwoman Theatre and of other feminist theater:

Linda Jenkins. "Spiderwoman." In *Women in American Theatre*, ed. by Helen Krich Chinoy and Linda Walsh Jenkins. New York: Theatre Communications Group, 1981. 303–5.

"The Dynamics of Desire: Sexuality and Gender in Pornography and Performance." In *The Feminist Spectator as Critic* by Jill Dolan. Ann Arbor: UMI Research Pr., 1988. 59–81.

"Women of Colour and Theatre," in *Feminism and Theatre* by Sue-Ellen Chase. New York: Methuen, 1988. 95–111.

Rayna Green. "The Pocahantas Perplex: The Image of Indian Women in American Culture." In *Unequal Sisters: A Multicultural Reader.* New York: Routledge, 1990.

Classroom Use: This video is appropriate for viewing by a college or university audience. The humor and inventiveness of Spiderwoman Theatre are an advantage, for the coalition raises issues of racism and sexism that students sometimes find embarrassing, painful, or otherwise uncomfortable to discuss. I suggest that instructors precede a screening of this video with some discussion of the genocide of Native-Americans in this country, and of recent efforts by Native-American nations to reclaim their lands, revive their language, and return to traditional ways of life.

The video offers many applications to courses on human diversity, literature, women's studies, oral history, popular culture, and theater studies. Most relevant to human diversity courses is the focus on the commercialization of Native-American culture and the pressures upon Native-American communities to discard their traditional ways of life and assume the trappings of the dominant white culture. (This video may also have potential use in social science courses interested in issues of human diversity, although students need to be oriented to the medium of drama and satire.)

Critical Comments: Throughout their film, the sisters of Spiderwoman present skits that challenge whether or not we can assume that all Americans participate in a "universal" all-American culture. In my own classes, white students often punctuate discussions of cultural diversity or racism with the exasperated wish that "everyone should be the same," that "everybody should be like everybody else and we won't have any problems." In the film, Spiderwoman exposes the covert meaning of this "same": in American culture, the white European male. The sisters recreate childhood scenes that make students of all races and ethnic backgrounds nod with knowing understanding: a toddler having a party for her invisible friends, two teenagers who discover that "men have hoses." Set against such experiences that we share, however, are the recollections of adjustments to white culture that Native-Americans face. The sisters show a picture of a party for their father at his place of work. The father stands, smiling, in a sweat-dampened T-shirt and apron. To his left—sinister, smiling, passing a "gift" of a gallon jug of booze—is the father's white employer in a tie and three-piece suit.

Spiderwoman has centered many performances on radical feminist theories, and this film is no exception. With their girlhood wishes for rich husbands and lovers who will whisk them away, the sisters call attention to the messages women receive of their helplessness and of their need to adhere to strict definitions of beauty. The sisters demonstrate radical feminism's commitment to art as a force for social change and to the potential for collective healing and transformation.

The issues of commercialization of Native-American culture and pressures to assimilate are shown most powerfully when the sisters reminisce about their father's traveling "snake oil" shows through the white communities of Brooklyn. Charging a modest admission fee, the father and his friends dressed as Winnebago war chiefs (they were not Winnebagos), invent their own "native" language, and stage inauthentic hunters' dances spiced by chicken feathers, whoo-whoo-whooping, bows and arrows, stolid squaws, and a taxidermist's wolf! Their father and his friends would profit from the whites' crass stereotypes of Native-American peoples, stereotypes that "the Injun" was savage, impulsive, magical, feral, and loud.

It proved difficult for the three daughters not to take these stereotypes to heart and not to wish that they themselves could change into something more assimilated, more American, more white. They show this self-hate that hate produced during a skit based on the 1936 film *Rose-Marie*. One daughter plays the blonde, blue-eyed heroine (Jeanette MacDonald); the other plays the white-horse-riding cavalryman who ostensibly rescues blondie from the "savages" and saves the day (Nelson Eddy). As the dreamy-eyed daughters perform their roles for a make-believe matinee black-and-white clips of Native-American dancers and musicians are interspersed. It is their own culture and history, enduring thousands of years, that Native-Americans are pressured to devalue and despise. This the daughters demonstrate by ignoring the scenes of their people and by assuming the gestures and features of the white couple only.

Barbara McCaskill, Department of English, now at the University of Georgia, Athens

GLCULREL

Title:	**Teotihuacán: City of the Gods**
Producer:	Educational Video, written by Sidney and Mary Lee Nolan
Distributor:	Educational Video
Release Date:	c1987
Technical:	29 min. / color / English
Purchase Price:	$49.95
Rental:	Free 30-day preview only
Presentation:	Still slides of the Teotihuacán site in Mexico translated into video format with narration
Study Guide:	Book by the same title by Eduardo Matos Moctezuma

Content: The video provides considerable coverage of the total Teotihuacán site in central Mexico, insofar as it is visible today. The archaeological history of the site is briefly summarized, and alternative interpretations are provided of the Teotihuacánal Indians and their culture. The history of the site is interpreted from the first century c.e./a.d., to the modern period. There is fairly extensive coverage of Aztec culture as a successor culture with affinities for the Teotihuacánal peoples, but the primary focus is upon the significance and function of this site during the eight centuries when it was integral to Teotihuacánal cultural life. The narrator draws upon diverse archaeological and anthropological scholarship which is seeking to render intelligible the visible remains of the site.

Classroom Use: Perhaps there are some advantages to this type of material, assuming instructors do not have slides of their own making. The quality of these stills is excellent. Compared with the somewhat similar video *Machu Picchu*, the coverage of Teotihuacán is more inclusive and enough interpretive material is provided to challenge the student to weigh its evidential merits, or explore further its interpretive power. A verbatim transcript of the narration accompanies the video and can be used independently by students to review important features of the site and to engage significant issues in the hermeneutics of its religio-cultural import. Narration returns to some slides allowing the viewer to integrate new data and new issues.

Critical Comments: Substantial interpretations are offered of the site, of its varied histories, and of its alleged meanings over time for a variety of peoples. There is some discussion of alternative views, and the brevity of the presentation lends itself to supplemental interpretation and discussion. An imaginative instructor can make good use of this tape in any number of courses, such as Meso-American histories, the ethnology of religions, American religions, Pre-Columbian cultures, and the ethnology of art.

Robert M. Garvin, Department of Philosophy

USETHEXP

Title:	**That's Black Entertainment**
Producers:	Norm Revis Jr., Davis Arpin, et al., for Skyline/T.B.E. Ltd.
Director:	William Greaves, William Greaves Productions
Distributor:	Video Communications
Release Date:	1989
Technical:	60 min. / color, b&w film clips / English
Purchase Price:	$19.95
Rental:	n/a
Presentation:	Documentary with clips of films made by blacks in the 1930s and 1940s
Performers:	Paul Robeson, Bessie Smith, Lena Horne, Cicely Tyson, Ethel Waters, Spencer Williams, and many other black entertainers

Content: Narrated by African-American actor and director William Greaves, *That's Black Entertainment* reveals the largely unknown fact that during Hollywood's heyday there also existed an underground industry of films directed and acted by blacks for black audiences. It notes that 500 such films were made, but only 100 have been preserved to the present day. During the 1930s and 1940s, African Americans were often denied access to theaters where "regular" movies were being shown; movies in which blacks were frequently stereotyped, and in which positive images of blacks were rare. Hollywood's products, destined for a mainstream market, were directed by whites and featured mostly white performers who often played African-American characters in blackface. The few representations of blacks were frequently as servants, entertainers, exotics, rapists, etc; they were portrayed as dim-witted objects of derision, "primitive" objects of fear, or one-dimensional "noble savages." The examples given in *That's Black Entertainment* of films intended for blacks and featuring blacks show that they gave a realistic picture of the persona of black Americans, their family life, their religious beliefs, their fears in living in white society, and the injustice of their plight.

Classroom Use: The video can be used in Africana studies, social sciences, and film studies. However, the video's numerous citations may be a disadvantage in a general education course. Some prior exposure to American film history and some familiarity with the contributions of the great black artists of the past is necessary to make *That's Black Entertainment* truly meaningful. A knowledge is needed of the stilted and undignified presentations of blacks in films made by whites, in order to contrast them with freely acted performances. Extensive explanations and discussions are needed to make the video useful in a human diversity course.

Critical Comments: *That's Black Entertainment* gives a revealing glimpse at the distorted manner in which black Americans were used and represented in made-for-whites entertainment, contrasted with the way they presented themselves to each other. For example, the video contrasts the violence attributed to the black characters, played by whites, in *Birth of a Nation* by D. W. Griffith, with the devoutness and dignity of the family members in *Juke Joint,* directed by the black director Spencer Williams. It shows how the great Stephen Perry's creation of Stepin Fetchit was appropriated, further distorted, and conventionalized to become, for many whites, the only representation of a black person.

That's Black Entertainment juxtaposes the offensive and inane appearance by Bing Crosby (wearing black makeup) in *Crooner's Holiday* with Paul Robeson's moving performances. Even when the great and iconoclastic singer had to portray a "primitive" in *Sanders of the River*, or when he was shown yearning for Africa in *Song of Freedom*, while ironically contemplating a map of South Africa, Robeson was moving. The video gives us a privileged view of great black performers in made-for-blacks "underground" movies: an immensely talented and vivacious 16-year-old Lena Horne in *Boogie Woogie Dream*, before she crossed over to the white show-business world; a young Ethel Waters proudly watching a tap-dancing eight-year-old Sammy Davis Jr. in *Rufus Jones for President;* virtuoso piano playing by Nat King Cole in *Killer Diller;* and moving song renditions by Bessie Smith in the 1929 *St. Louis Blues. That's Black Entertainment* presents works by black artists which are a far cry from the ones in which they appeared under white aegis; they did not play servant roles as rolling-eyed mammies like Hattie McDaniel or as flighty as Butterfly McQueen in *Gone With the Wind. That's Black Entertainment* creates an awareness of an area of

American film history which is, for the most part, unknown, and in which the stereotypical and defaming characterizations of blacks were offset by realistic and dignified portrayals.

A good companion piece to *That's Black Entertainment* is the videotape *Ethnic Notions* (see p. 76) which more fully explores the stereotypical ideas that whites have about blacks. In addition, the following books about African Americans in films and the entertainment industry would also be useful:

Donald Bogle. *Brown Sugar.* Harmony Books, 1980.

—— *Toms, Coons, Mulattoes, Mammies, and Bucks: An Interpretive History of Blacks in American Films.* Viking, 1973.

Langston Hughes and Milton Meltzer. *Black Magic: A Pictorial History of the Negro in American Entertainment.* Prentice Hall, 1967.

Regina W. Betts, Department of Theatre

USRACCUL

Title:	**To Kill a Mockingbird**
Producer:	Alan Pakula
Director:	Robert Mulligan
Distributor:	Ztek
Release Date:	c1962, 1987
Technical:	131 min. / b&w / English
Purchase Price:	$19.95
Rental:	n/a
Presentation:	A video copy of the 1962 motion picture based on the Harper Lee novel of the same title; screenplay by Horton Foote; performers include Gregory Peck, Brock Peters, and Robert Duvall; music by Elmer Bernstein
Awards:	1961 Pulitzer Prize to Harper Lee for her novel; 1963 Academy Award for Best Actor to Gregory Peck for his performance as Atticus Finch

Content: *To Kill a Mockingbird* was Harper Lee's first novel. Written in 1960, it is a somewhat autobiographical account of her early years growing up in a small southern town in the early 1930s. A generally faithful rendering of the book, the Hollywood movie is set in Alabama during the Depression. Placed in a world where the segregation of the races is the established rule, the events and characters are seen through the perceptions of the main character's six-year-old daughter. Atticus Finch, a white lawyer, is raising his two children with the help of a black servant. He is shown to be a man of integrity who often represents the area's poor farmers pro bono. His generally uneventful life in the somnolent southern town is soon disturbed when he is asked to represent Tom Robinson, a black man falsely accused of rape. While there is no doubt in anyone's mind that the accused is innocent, there is also no doubt that he will be found guilty. Peripheral to the main characters are various members of the black community. Also represented are racist, poor southern whites. All along the lawyer faces castigation by the white community, but gains the added respect of his children and the segregated blacks. Through a twist of poetic justice, the black man's death is avenged when the father of his accuser is killed by the children's mentally unstable neighbor.

Classroom Use: *To Kill a Mockingbird* may be useful in film studies and literature courses. For human diversity study, it has some values, though limited because of the obsolete manner in which the subjects of racism, classism, and sexism are treated. The following are some of the ways in which the movie may be used:

1) as an illustration of the effects of the segregation that existed in the South, where blacks were only permitted to sit in the balcony of the courthouse;

2) as a comparison of the unequal administration of justice for African Americans, both as illustrated in the movie and as evident from current events.

Aside from the novel itself, the following works may be used in conjunction with the film:

Amiri Baraka. *Home: Social Essays.* Morrow, 1966.

Donald Bogle. *Toms, Coons, Mulattoes, Mammies, and Bucks: An Interpretive History of Blacks in American Films.* Viking, 1973.

Ralph Ellison. *The Invisible Man.* Random, 1965.

Critical Comments: Many of the issues touched upon in *To Kill a Mockingbird* were as relevant in 1962, when the movie was made, as they were in 1932, when the action is set. However, the film was written and directed as a wistful period piece, in spite of the momentous events which had already taken place in the South: the Emmet Till tragedy; the Montgomery bus boycott; the bombing of the Birmingham church where black children were killed; and the height of the civil rights movement and the work of Martin Luther King Jr. in Alabama. The film has a self-serving and paternal tone, and the trial of the black man becomes an excuse to adorn the character of the white lawyer. Unlike the accused, the other members of the black community—including the accused's wife, the minister, and Finch's lifelong servant—are treated as if invisible and in a one-dimensional manner befitting the cast of a sit-com. Furthermore, the virulent expressions of racism are mostly ascribed to poor white ''trash,'' which includes the alleged victim, who is herself at the mercy of parental abuse and shown to be crazed and illiterate.

It is ironic that the leaders of the town, including the sheriff and judge, are shown to be benevolent figures. If there is a redeeming feature in *To Kill a Mockingbird,* it is the trial scene with Atticus Finch's final injunction to the jury and Brock Peters's performance as the accused. These scenes make evident the racism, humiliation, and injustice blacks have had to suffer.

Regina W. Betts, Department of Theatre

USGENSOC

Title:	**Torch Song Trilogy**
Producer:	Howard Gottfried
Director:	Paul Bogart
Distributor:	Columbia Pictures Home Video
Release Date:	c1989
Technical:	120 min. / color / English / close-captioned
Purchase Price:	$89.95
Rental:	n/a
Presentation:	Videorecording of the film based on the Harvey Fierstein play which opened on Broadway in 1983; starring Harvey Fierstein, Anne Bancroft, and Matthew Broderick
Award:	Fierstein received a Tony Award for his portrayal of Arnold on Broadway.

Content: The central characters in this film are homosexual, mostly white, men. Also represented are members of the heterosexual world, including the protagonist's Jewish mother and "gay bashers." Harvey Fierstein, the playwright, is himself a white, homosexual, Jewish male; *Torch Song Trilogy* is largely autobiographical. The film presents aspects of the gay world as it intersects with "straight" society. In addition, it introduces the subculture of drag queens and gay "pick-up" bars and, more generally, the world of alienated individuals who strive for some degree of acceptance in a hostile world.

When we first meet Arnold, he is working as a torch-song performer in a gay nightclub which caters largely to the heterosexual tourist trade. On one occasion when he is in a bar looking for a sexual encounter, he meets Ed and they become steady lovers. But the new-found friend cannot quite accept his own homosexuality and marries a woman whom he has known for sometime. Eventually, Arnold meets Alan and establishes a long lasting loving relationship with him. But one night, Alan is attacked by some gay bashers and dies as a result of his injuries. After a time, Arnold decides to adopt the child that he and Alan had wanted. He confronts his mother with the facts of his homosexuality and, at the end of the film, he hopes to establish a permanent relationship with Ed, whom he has found again.

Classroom Use: This reviewer presented the video in a course, "Voices of Diversity in Contemporary Theatre and Drama." At the same time the play was assigned for reading. Some of the students, at first, had homophobic reactions owing to a lack of exposure and to misconceptions about gays; but the film helped them gain a clearer understanding and they no longer looked upon Arnold merely as a "queer." Aside from its value to the study of theater and drama, *Torch Song Trilogy* can also be useful in gender studies, sociology, and psychology.

In human diversity courses, the video can be used to discuss the issues of gender categories and sexual preferences. It can show how the dominant society sometimes uses racial, sexual, and ethnic typifications to control categories of people economically and politically. It can give the students an opportunity to study the contributions to the American theater and other arts by gays and other groups which are not considered part of the mainstream and are omitted from the aesthetic canon.

Critical Comments: *Torch Song Trilogy* is an appropriate and reliable presentation of the struggle for acceptance by a gay individual in a society which has stereotypic gender conceptions. It shows the difficulty those who profess unconventional sexual preferences have in their quest for love and stable relationships. It deals dramatically with issues of sexual promiscuity, of child adoptions by gays, of guilt by straight parents, and gay-bashing. Written as it was in the late 1970s, the work does not address the problems of AIDS. Therefore, discussions of the epidemic as it has affected gays would have to take place in order to offset the omission. Students are likely to be amused by Arnold's humor, his campiness, singing, and his transvesticism, but they are also apt to be moved and to understand his frustrations, his sorrows, his successful parenting, his assertions of individuality, and his confrontation with his mother.

The play *Torch Song Trilogy* is published by the Gay Presses of New York. Other plays written by Harvey Fierstein are: *Spookhouse, Flatbush Tosca, Freaky Pussy,* and *Cannibals Just Don't Know No Better.* The following will also provide added background:

Stefan Brecht. *Queer Theatre.* Chapman and Mall, 1985.

Kaier Curtin. *We Can Always Call Them Bulgarians.* Alyson, 1988.

David Halperin. *One Hundred Years of Homosexuality.* Routledge, 1989.

Regina W. Betts, Department of Theatre

GLCULEXP

Title:	**Touring Mexico**
Producer:	Albert Nader, for Encounter Productions
Distributor:	Facets Video
Release Date:	1988
Technical:	60 min. / color / English
Purchase Price:	$39
Rental:	$10 for members of Facets Video Club
Presentation:	Narrated travel documentary

Content: The video encapsulates five centuries of cultural history encoded in ancient ruins. It refers to the mathematical and astronomical skill of ancient Mayan civilization, still evident in residual structures at Uxmal and at Chichen-Itza; the pyramid of Tijan in Vera Cruz; the Toltec empire of Tula; the Olmec civilization at La Venta; and the greatness of the Aztecs, builders of Tenochtitlan, which is now called Mexico City. The magnificent Stone of the Sun, once unearthed from the Zocalo and now housed in the city's anthropological museum, contrasts with scenes of everyday life in the present-day metropolis. Similarly, the sequence on Zapotec culture, as seen in the ruins of the sacred city of Monte Alban, prefigures a rapid display of images of modern Indian political heroes who were also born in the Oaxaca region.

Shots of colonial cities, such as Guadalajara and Taxco, combine with sequences on contemporary cultural centers, such as Puerto Vallarta and Baja, where involvement with contemporary English-speaking giants of the film industry and literary tradition complete the Mexican cultural mosaic. Occasional shots show contemporary Mexican residents and foreign tourists of diverse backgrounds at major cultural and social centers. Editors focus on the architectural and cultural greatness of Mexico's pre-Columbian and colonial heritage, and give scant attention to the nation's modern political history. The inclusion of rare historical films of two folk heroes, Emiliano Zapata and Pancho Villa, and a dramatized episode of the miracle that took place at the Shrine of Guadalupe, greatly vivify the colorful travelog.

Classroom Use: Any viewer who seeks a general introduction to Mexican history and culture will find this video to be appropriate. In addition, the video vivifies cultural allusions used by such writers as Julio Cortazar, Jorge Luis Borges, and Gonzalez Prada. Arturo Uslar Pietri's thesis that links the economic dependency of ''Third World'' societies and declining cultural creativity builds on a substratum of pre-Columbian greatness for its strongest support. The video potentially lends itself to applications of this kind.

Critical Comments: Given the commercial motive that underlies its production, the video highlights the most favorable aspects of Mexico's rich heritage. Explicitly, the narrator explains the power of the Quetzalcoatl myth in establishing conditions that led to the facile conquest of the Indian majority by the minority of Cortez and the Spanish conquerers. He expresses the great pride that Mexicans feel in their Aztec heritage and in the confluence of Spanish and Indian currents in their cultural past. He implies that a great past suggests a promising future.

A limitation is the presentation of the miracle at the Shrine at Guadalupe as if it were an isolated event. A broader contextualization would reveal that visitations by indigenous virgins at pre-Columbian religious centers formed a part of the evangelizing project of the Church, which fostered religious syncretism in the worship of the Virgin and of saints just as the state erected colonial cities on the structures of indigenous settlements with a pre-established Indian work force combined with imported African labor.

Another limitation is the excision from history of a rather ample African presence that began when Hernan Cortez introduced several hundred ladino or Spanish-speaking slaves who were involved in the various activities essential to the construction of colonial settlements. Given the broad base of Indian labor that was already organized and available to colonists, Africans were principally involved in mining and textile production and Indians performed most of the urban domestic services. By the middle of the 17th century more than 35,000 slaves were reported in official census records. Countless others had escaped to maroon settlements or palenques, which were isolated communities governed in accordance with African traditions. Occasional treaties between palenque heads and rulers of the Spanish Crown stipulated agreement to cease resistance and to return future runaways in exchange for ending attacks on the maroon communities. By 1810 the number of slaves had dropped to 10,000, but census data also include more than 70,000 free coloreds. The presence of African descendants, especially in the area of Vera Cruz, had an impact on the music and folklore of that area and of other regions of Mexico.

Edith M. Jackson, Hispanic,
Italian, and Portuguese Studies

GLRACCOM

Title:	**Town Meeting in South Africa**
Producer:	ABC News Nightline: The Koppel Report
Distributor:	ABC Distribution Co.
Release Date:	1990
Technical:	123 min. / color / English
Purchase Price:	$89.95
Rental:	n/a
Presentation:	Panel discussion with live audience, taped on Feb. 14, 1990; some background segments
Study Guide:	Transcript available

Content: Television newsman Ted Koppel moderates a panel forum among South African politicians from the Conservative Party, the National Party, the African National Congress (ANC), Inkata, and the Pan-African Congress (PAC) in the auditorium of The University of Witwatersrand in Johannesburg, South Africa, in front of a racially mixed audience.

The discussion is explicitly about apartheid and its reform. Between the audience and the six panel members in front of the audience, a variety of political groups and positions are displayed. These groups include the ruling white majority party, the conservative white Dutch faction, the ANC, the PAC, and Inkata. Panel members include Kous van der Merwe, Stoffel van der Merwe, Helen Suzman, Musa Zondi, and Allan Boesak.

In order to clarify the participation of the various groups, the moderator cuts to two segments of tape: the first shows everyday scenes from a black township and includes an interview with a member of that community; the second offers a description of the political groups involved in the struggle in South Africa, including the issues and concerns central to each group. This presentation was the first time that there had ever been a public forum in front of a live audience, televised internationally. For this reason, this program has contributed to the creation of a context for discussion and debate between and among political groups.

Classroom Use: This video is appropriate for both undergraduate and graduate classes. Under-

graduates can gain an understanding of a culture in which oppression and racism are the norm (although comparison between the United States and South Africa are limited in the video, there are similarities across cultures in the discourses of oppression). Graduate students can use this tape to analyze the role of the media with issues related to diversity; and to analyze the interaction between conservative and liberal discourses, the social construction of racism, and the social construction of the "other" in the resistance to racism.

Students of communication will find this tape very interesting. Those interested in media will be able to address questions concerning the role of the media in the reduction (and maintenance) of racism. Those interested in discourse/rhetoric can study the various arguments advanced in defense of racism and the struggles of the opposition to gain legitimacy and credibility. Those interested in social processes can study the interactional patterns between groups and thereby develop sophisticated descriptions of how racism is maintained. Finally, those interested in power and ideology can examine processes related to colonization and marginalization in the meeting, as dominant (white) groups maintain dominance in this conversational setting.

I recommend that this tape be used early in a diversity course, as it offers an extreme example of racism and can be used to generate discussion and reflection. The transcript is available for class projects which may involve in-depth analysis. In this reviewer's conflict resolution class (communication), students were asked to view the tape and write about their responses using questions such as the following:

(1) Assuming that South Africa is different for each group—that South Africa is a function of membership in a particular community—identify the different South Africas that you hear described and discussed.

(2) What is the problem or conflict that is being addressed in this tape? Back up your answer with specific examples.

(3) Which of these versions of South Africa are legitimated or delegitimated by the moderator? Back up your answer.

(4) Which of these South Africas has a plan for action that is articulated by the group members? Which group has the most articulate plan?

(5) Summarize your reaction to this tape; be sure to use first person singular so your opinions remain your own.

Critical Comments: Because the various groups in the video are representing themselves, there is a high degree of reliability in the presentation of each group's political position and history. Nelson Mandela is not in this tape, which may account for the limited platform articulated by the ANC during the forum. But given that this tape appeared in a given historical moment in the move to dismantle apartheid, it stands as an empirical evidence of the arguments, political positions, and histories advanced by all the groups involved. Clearly, this tape, produced by an American media corporation, is exploring issues of racism as if the American public shares the ideological position that apartheid is immoral, and (therefore) the move to overthrow apartheid is moral. Nowhere in the tape is the American audience asked to question the ways in which racism flourishes in this country. In this way, racism is portrayed as "over there," in South Africa. The danger in this approach is that viewers can then displace responsibility for racism in this country by distancing themselves from the political situation in South Africa. Paradoxically, it is also by looking at a political context other than our own that we have the opportunity to examine racism in our own culture.

There are implicit assumptions in the design of this program that conflicts are resolved through negotiation and debate. Thus, some fundamentals of the American political process are manifested—fundamentals related to representation, freedom of speech, and equality.

This film is about racism; racism is a part of our lives in the United States. Discussion about racism where we live is often difficult and requires a classroom context in which people can raise concerns and issues and discuss their experiences. This tape would be an excellent way to develop such an atmosphere precisely because it is about racism in South Africa; students would have a chance to look at the tape and discuss feelings, responses, and experiences as the tape relates to their lives. Also, the tape gives viewers an opportunity to examine cultural differences between and among the groups in South Africa and, in that way, provides an opportunity to identify cultural differences as such.

Sara Cobb, Department of Communication

GLRACREL

Title:	**Triumph of the Spirit**
Producers:	Arnold Kopelson and Shimon Arana
Director:	Robert M. Young
Distributor:	Zenger Video
Release Date:	1989
Technical:	124 min. / color / English
Purchase Price:	$97.95
Rental:	n/a
Presentation:	Dramatized feature film account of a true story

Content: *Triumph of the Spirit* is a dramatization of the true story of Salamo Arouch, a Greek Jew who became a victim of the Holocaust in World War II. Arouch had been the middleweight boxing champion of the Balkans before the war, and when he is sent with his family to Auschwitz by the Nazis, he is recruited to fight for the entertainment of his captors. While others in his family perish, he survives and eventually moves to Israel.

Classroom Use: Advanced high school and college students would certainly benefit from seeing *Triumph of the Spirit* as it is one of the best dramatic feature films on the Holocaust. The video would benefit from some introduction to the historic context of the Holocaust but could be appreciated without any such introduction. It would be appropriate for special showings to students outside of the classroom, since it has only limited classroom use as a full-length feature film. Though it received excellent reviews, the film has very strong language and was rated accordingly.

Critical Comments: *Triumph of the Spirit* is among the most effective films on the Holocaust because of the quietly moving way it shows how the lives of individuals were affected by the events it describes. Well-acted by a cast headed by Willem Dafoe and Robert Loggia, it only occasionally sensationalizes its material or allows its characters to become stock villains. It never tries to shock with graphic violence, but still manages to stay very close to the facts in showing how Auschwitz functioned. Its account of how the selection process worked, for instance, is one of the best on film.

Donald S. Birn, Department of History

USRACCLA

Title:	**Trouble Behind: Roots of Racism**
Producer:	Robby Henson, for Cicada Films
Director:	Robby Henson
Distributor:	Resolution, Inc./California Newsreel
Release Date:	1990
Technical:	56 min. / color / English
Purchase Price:	$250
Rental:	$75
Presentation:	Documentary, with interviews and narration
Awards:	1991, American Library Association *Booklist* Editor's Choice; Red Ribbon, American Film and Video Festival

Content: This is a film about a small town of 8,000 people called Corbin, located in Kentucky. It begins with some older white men talking about the "good old days" of minstrel shows and why they want to live in Corbin. Despite being famous for the race riots in 1919, Corbin is described as one of the finest communities in the United States to live in. There are no blacks in Corbin, a fact explained by the words "they have chosen to live elsewhere." The men claim no knowledge of the reason. A white woman then recounts how the railroad hired blacks and how much "rhythm" they had. It is okay with residents for blacks to fill in labor gaps but not to take someone else's job. The bottom line is a concern for maintaining Corbin as the whites have known it.

The film then recounts the history of Corbin in some detail, including the presence of the Ku Klux Klan (KKK), and how blacks were run out of town. KKK members formed a band, beat drums, marched to the black's house, knocked on the door, took all the men, marched them to the train, and shipped them out of town. When newspaper clippings of events like this were shown to residents, they claimed they were lies and said, "Negroes aren't discriminated against here." The film makes clear that those who were run out of town had been working on the railroad for the previous ten months. Their crime appeared to be that they had fun and enjoyed their new-found money. There is a discussion of whites feeling "walked on," Negroes being high and mighty ("uppity"), and the need for people to know their place.

The past is explained as "we had a problem one night and it stayed with us forever because the blacks didn't choose to come back." The film then shows college students talking about blacks at a party and the fears of the high school students when they play teams from nearby high schools that have black members. It talks about how church-oriented Corbin is, and then shows a black person shopping on Corbin's main street. Pointing to the African American, a small white child asks "what's that?" and is told by his mother "shh—they git you." There is a discussion of language and the use of Nigger Creek Road as a street name, which whites resolve not by changing it but by saying "it's always been called that." Someone comments: "I don't hate blacks, but 90 percent of the blacks who come to Corbin screw up shit."

In 1982 Corbin High School had its first black football player on the team and there were death threats. McDonald's hired a black manager and a cross was burned in front of the store. People explained that they were not going to put up with it, saying the manager tried to boss people. Corbin appears like a ghost town in the final scene.

Critical Comments: The film strongly makes the point that you can't go on believing you're a better American if you've completely missed a whole segment of the U.S. population. It is powerful because it blatantly shows the ignorance upon which many of the statements are based, as well as the contradictions present in the attitudes and opinions of the townspeople. One possible drawback is that students from sophisticated urban backgrounds may find it very hard to identify themselves with the whites in the film. Put another way, the racism may be dismissed as being caused by the small-town ways of the residents. But this is speculation; the film might well be tried with students of various backgrounds. It should provide much to discuss because so many of the commonly heard statements about why African Americans do not get ahead are clearly portrayed here. The chance to listen to these statements from individuals we don't know and with whom we perhaps do not identify, may make it easier to see the underlying assumptions and silliness of racism.

Nancy A. Denton, Department of Sociology

USETHGEN

Title:	**Two Dollars and a Dream**
Producer:	Stanley Nelson, for PBS
Director:	Stanley Nelson
Distributor:	Filmakers Library
Release Date:	1989
Technical:	56 min. / b&w with color / English
Purchase Price:	$495
Rental:	$85
Presentation:	Documentary with archival footage, interviews, and narration
Awards:	Ciné Golden Eagle, 1988; Best of the Decade, Black Filmmakers Foundation, 1989; Bronze Apple, National Educational Film Festival, 1989

Content: Through archival footage, stills, and interviews, *Two Dollars and a Dream* documents the extraordinary life of Sarah Breedlove Walker, better known as Madame C. J. Walker. She was born of slave parents in 1867 and later built a successful cosmetology business and became the first self-made woman millionaire in the United States. Her life spanned half a century, and the documentary chronicles Madame C. J. Walker's influence upon the times and the social history of African Americans as they adjusted to freedom.

Classroom Use: This film is appropriate for high school and college students. It is useful for classes in U.S. social history and literature, African-American studies, and women's studies.

Critical Comments: This film places in historical perspective the life and deeds of Madame C. J. Walker. Widowed at a young age, Walker found herself restricted by the same job limitations that most black women faced at the turn of the century in both North and South. Most black women could find employment only as domestic workers or in agriculture because of gross discrimination. Besides paying minimal wages, these jobs frequently placed African-American women in hostile environments where they experienced sexual exploitation.

Walker, imbued with the contemporary black ideology of self help and racial solidarity, determined that only through independent business enterprises would black women find access to liveable wages and respectability. She developed a hair-care system and devised a unique marketing and advertising strategy that not only removed her from the washboard, but also enabled scores of her sisters to follow suit. Through interviews with Walker's contemporaries, viewers share the significance of the Walker system for their own lives. Her system of door-to-door sales was highly successful and was adopted by a number of modern corporations with equal success.

Walker is renowned, not only for her seemingly Horatio Alger success story, but more importantly for her philosophy regarding business in the black communities of the nation and her commitment to social change. In an age that can be characterized by entrepreneurship and its emphasis on substantial economic margins, Walker bucked the trend and distributed two-thirds of her profits to the African-American community and charities. Thus, in tangible ways, she was able to implement the self-help ideology that undergirded black community activism. She donated funds to several black colleges and established beauty culture schools to provide blacks with an education for life. Walker was a staunch supporter of the National Association for the Advancement of Colored People and fought the inimical effects of racism wherever they manifested themselves. She supported the National Association of Colored Women's Clubs (NACW) and was the largest contributor to the Frederick Douglass Memorial and Historical project that NACW President Mary Burnett Talbert directed. Walker also was a patron of the Harlem Renaissance literati and other artists. The eminent black architect Vertner Tandy designed the plans for her Hudson River estate, Villa Lewaro, named in honor of her daughter A'Lelia Walker Robinson.

Her daughter inherited Walker's empire and her commitment to philanthropy, epecially in the African-American community. The film also documents A'Lelia Walker Robinson's promotion of Dark Tower, the Harlem nightclub that symbolized the cultural movement of the 1920s. While this film depicts the life and deeds of the Walker family, it is important because it chronicles the history of an era—1867 through the 1930s—and its impact upon African Americans.

The following videos are companion pieces to this history:

Freedom Bags documents the experiences of African-American domestic workers who migrated to Washington, D.C., from 1911 to 1960.

A Passion for Justice depicts the life of Walker contemporary Ida B. Wells-Barnett, a leading supporter of anti-lynching campaigns, women's suffrage, and other human rights issues.

Other related published works include:

Ida B. Wells-Barnett. *Crusade for Justice.* University of Chicago Pr., 1970.

Elsa Barkley Brown. ''Womanist Consciousness: Maggie Lena Walker and the Independent Order of St. Luke.'' *Signs* 14 (Spring 1989): 610–33.

Paula Giddings. *When and Where I Enter.* Morrow, 1984.

Darlene Clark Hine, Lillian S. Williams, Elsa Barkley Brown, and Tiffany Patterson. *Black Women in United States History.* 10-vol. series. Carlson, 1990.

Mary Church Terrell. *A Colored Woman in a White World.* Ayer, 1986.

Juliet K. Walker. *Free Frank.* University Pr. of Kentucky, 1983.

Lillian S. Williams, Department
of Women's Studies

USGENEXP

Title: **Variety Is the Spice of Life**

Producer: Lyn Blumenthal

Director: Lyn Blumenthal

Distributor: Video Data Bank

Release Date: 1987

Technical: 75 min. / color, b&w stills / English, some German subtitles

Purchase Price: $59.95

Rental: n/a

Presentation: A series of very short films: cartoon, dramatization, even several shorts that resemble slide presentations, with voiceovers supplied by director Blumenthal

Content: This video is a compilation of short works, for the most part, by women working in film, video, and the visual arts. It uses contemporary settings to examine issues of gender: gender roles, the relationships between gender and social institutions, the influence of gender upon conversation and language, representations of gender in television and advertising, and how our conception of gender shapes public policies directed toward birth control and pornography. And these are but a few of the topics raised. The film does not purvey unflinching judgments on any of these issues. Instead, it provokes discussion by presenting situations—such as two young women flamenco dancing—that challenge conventional notions of how men and women must behave. The film does not judge what is right and what is wrong. Instead, it facilitates discussion so that students may realize that constructing notions of gender are tasks that are not as easy as they might seem.

Classroom Use: I very much recommend this film for its challenging level of difficulty, and I very much advise preliminary discussion of some of the film's issues. This film is particularly suited for discussion of gender-related concerns in human diversity courses. An excellent background source is *The Gender Reader,* edited by Evelyn Ashton-Jones and Gary Olson (Boston: Allyn and Bacon, 1991). See especially these essays:

(1) ''The Dangers of Femininity'' by Lucy Gilbert and Paula Webster, pp. 39–55;

(2) ''Emotion'' by Susan Brownmiller, pp. 126–37;

(3) ''Awakening and Revolt'' and ''Birth Control'' by Margaret Sanger, pp. 225–36;

(4) ''The Contrived Postures of Femininity'' by Susan Brownmiller, pp. 542–46;

(5) ''Racism and Feminism'' by Bell Hooks, pp. 549–56.

In addition, I highly recommend it for use in human diversity courses which include a focus on art.

Critical Comments: College-level viewers should keep in mind that the film intends to call into question the reliability of the various perspectives and experiences it represents. It intends to spark argument, for example, about what constitutes a real man and a real woman, what advertisers really sell—products or sex—and to what extent love and marriage are economic and political transactions. Blumenthal is careful to balance the perspectives so that both stereotypical and realistic portrayals of men and women, gays and straights, are shown. Also, viewers should be prepared for the abstract forms of presentation that Blumenthal introduces. For example, she displays a series of pictures—lightning, roller coasters, fireworks, airplanes, Elvis Presley, ships on turbulent seas—accompanied by a soundtrack that features top-40 voices singing about romance and courtship. Or, between the film shorts, she flashes, boldface and capitalized, words such as ''doublecross'' and ''sex,'' or questions such as ''What does she want?''

These techniques are similar to those of many contemporary American artists who use collage, graffiti, and neon signs to call attention to the cynicism, loneliness, violence, and commercialism of urban life. Viewers' understanding of the film will be much enhanced if they possess some prior familiarity with these techniques. There are many visual artists who explore aspects of racial and ethnic diversity by using techniques similar to those in this film: Edgar Hachivi Heap-of-Birds (Native-American), Juan Sanchez (Puerto Rican), and Adrian Piper (African American), to name a few.

It is evident from the film that Blumenthal has drawn from feminist literature and even adapted her dramatizations quite closely from particular feminist poetry and fiction. One of the final shorts, for instance, presents a woman being interrogated in a police station, ostensibly for a criminal offense such as illegal possession of narcotics or guns. However, once we viewers overhear the dialog, we learn that the woman is being charged for possession of a diaphragm. In this way, the short forces us to consider how laws that control women's access to contraceptives curtail women's freedom and legal rights. To fully appreciate this segment, viewers might engage in prior discussion of Judy Grahn's poem ''A Woman Is Talking to Death,'' in which she presents similar interrogations that expose sexism and homophobia. This and other useful material can be found in *The Work of a Common Woman: The Collected Poetry of Judy Grahn, 1964–1977* (St. Martin's, 1977).

Blumenthal's dramatizations confront bigotry and prudishness head-on and are intended to engender discomfort on the part of viewers. I suggest instructors bear in mind that she also uses humor liberally throughout. She portrays a macho male named Lenny, for example, who brags about picking up the babes while he dials on a pink Princess telephone. But the touches of humor and surprise do not undermine the video's serious intentions. What they do accomplish is not only to suggest a critique of sterotypical attitudes, but also to underscore a celebration of difference.

Barbara McCaskill, Department of English, now at the University of Georgia, Athens

GLRACREL

Title:	**Weapons of the Spirit**
Producer:	Pierre Sauvage
Director:	Pierre Sauvage
Distributor:	Friends of Le Chambon
Release Date:	1987
Technical:	28 min. (classroom version) / color, b&w photos / English, French with subtitles
Purchase Price:	$50 (classroom version)
Rental:	n/a
Presentation:	Documentary with interviews, descriptive commentary, and archival movie footage
Awards:	Full 90-min. version: 1987 Belfort (France) Film Festival; Gold Hugo at the 1987 Chicago Film Festival; Documentary Award, 1988 Los Angeles Film Critics Association; Red Ribbon, 1988 American Film and Video Festival
Study Guide:	Comes with video

Content: *Weapons of the Spirit* describes the remarkable events that occurred during World War II in a small French village, where some 5,000 Jewish refugees were sheltered from the Nazis and possible extermination. The village is Le Chambon-sur-Lignon in central France some 350 miles southeast of Paris, a largely Protestant farming community. Residents of this mountainous region of France kept alive memories of their own centuries-old persecution in predominantly Catholic France. Under the leadership of their pastor, Andre Trocme, the people of Le Chambon refused to cooperate with the Vichy regime of Marshal Petain which collaborated with the Nazis in persecuting Jews.

What made the events in Le Chambon remarkable was that the entire community participated in the effort, making it an almost unique "conspiracy of goodness." Initially they sheltered only French Jews who had previously vacationed there. But gradually Jews from Germany and elsewhere were hidden and schools were set up for the many children given shelter in the village. Here was an example of passive resistance to Nazi persecution, but it did not escape notice from the authorities. Pastor Trocme was imprisoned briefly by the Gestapo in 1943, but after his release he did not curtail his rescue work. His example proved contagious, and there is some evidence that it spread to Vichy and even some German military occupation authorities who were reluctant to intervene.

Classroom Use: The classroom version of *Weapons of the Spirit* could be used by high school or college classes, but it requires some preparation. The context of the Holocaust, the fact that some 75,000 French Jews were deported and killed by the Nazis, and the broader picture of collaboration and resistance in Nazi-occupied Europe during World War II, should be described to make the story of Le Chambon more meaningful.

Critical Comments: This video assumes that the viewer is aware of the horrors perpetrated by the Nazis during World War II but does not explicitly represent them. The awareness of this evil becomes a kind of unstated backdrop to the simple faith of the villagers and their pastor in their desire to do good. The filmmaker, Pierre Sauvage, was born to Jewish parents who were taking shelter in Le Chambon in 1944. A French-Canadian, he makes the film partly a rediscovery of his own family's history as he revisits the peasants who gave his family refuge during the war.

The focus of human diversity courses on ethnic and religious diversity can be admirably illustrated by this video. In the example of the people of Le Chambon we have Christians who drew on their own distinctive religious and historical background of oppression to find the strength to reach out and protect another people.

Weapons of the Spirit is directly appropriate to the classroom study of diversity in several ways. This reviewer used it together with the companion book *Lest Innocent Blood Be Shed,* in a history class where it provided a stirring example of rescue work. It raises important questions about intergroup relations, about the power of nonviolent resistance to unjust authority, and about the key leadership role women played in organizing the efforts in Le Chambon.

The prize-winning book, Philip Hallie's *Lest Innocent Blood Be Shed* (Harper & Row, 1979) describes the events in Le Chambon. It is available in a paperback edition and makes an excellent accompaniment to the film.

Donald S. Birn, Department of History

USETHIMM

Title:	**West of Hester Street**
Producers:	Allen Mondell and Cynthia Salzman Mondell
Directors:	Allen Mondell and Cynthia Salzman Mondell
Distributor:	Media Projects, Inc.
Release Date:	1983
Technical:	58 min. / color, b&w footage and stills / English
Purchase Price:	$79.95
Rental:	$50
Presentation:	Documentary which combines contemporary scenes, considerable archival film and photos, and dramatizations of historical events
Awards:	Ciné Golden Eagle; Filmex Golden Athena, Athens International Film Festival; Best of Category in Hemisfilm International Film Festival; American Film and Video Festival; Educational Film Library Association

Content: *West of Hester Street* is concerned with one episode in the history of the Jewish immigrant experience in America: the Galveston Movement. Between 1906 and 1916, the Galveston Movement brought 10,000 Jews from eastern Europe to the port of Galveston, Texas, and settled them throughout the Midwest and Southwest of the United States. The movement was a reaction to the brutal pogroms against Jewish communities in Russia which reached a peak in 1906, following Russia's defeat in the Russo-Japanese War. The founders of the movement, a diverse group, were also disturbed that most Jewish immigrants were settling in their northeastern ports of disembarkation, particularly New York City, and forming new ghettos in tenement slums. Thus, the movement helped Jews become more widely scattered in the United States. Their goals were to rescue Jews from abysmal conditions in eastern Europe as well as to dissipate the anti-Semitism that they feared was generated by the Jewish ghettos of large cities.

The film features the reminiscences of a 75-year-old man who came to America under the auspices of the movement as a youth in 1907. Interspersed with this individual's memoirs are historical segments which make use of black-and-white film footage and still photographs to detail the violent persecution and economic insecurity Jews left behind in eastern

Europe and the poverty and hardship they found in the big northeastern cities of America. Also interspersed in his memoirs are dramatizations of various events in the history of the Galveston Movement, including the process of immigration from Russia to Galveston, passing through immigration inspection in the United States, and the difficulties of settlement in Texas. The good-humored narrator describes his progression from peddler to prosperous storekeeper, including his friendly relations with non-Jews, his marriage, his memories of religious life, educational and social events, and communal tensions between German and eastern-European Jews, and his current pride in his successful children and grandchildren.

A less upbeat sub-theme of the film is the growth of isolationism and anti-immigrant feeling in the United States before World War I. *West of Hester Street* details, through dramatization and narration, how this isolationism, combined with documented anti-Semitism by immigration officials in Texas, led to the end of the Galveston Movement.

Classroom Use: This is an historically accurate, richly documented, and entertaining film which has obvious uses in courses about the Jewish experience in America, immigration history, and the history of the western United States. The film assumes some

The Galveston Movement, which brought some 10,000 Jews from Eastern Europe to Galveston, Texas, from 1906 to 1916, developed as a response to pogroms in Russia and the clustering of Jewish refugees in the northeastern U.S. port cities. *West of Hester Street* documents the movement through the reminiscences of one immigrant, with historical footage and still photos. (Courtesy Media Projects)

familiarity with Jewish history and Jewish social life, and uses some Yiddish terms without translation. Its narrow focus also limits its accessibility.

Critical Comments: It is regrettable that the film details the life of only one immigrant family; it would have been enriched by more information on what Galveston and Texas were like in the early 20th century, as well as more exploration of the fates of the 10,000 immigrants who arrived in America via this movement. How many stayed in the West? Where are their descendants today? Similarly, the film has a rather sentimental tone which is not always appropriate in a documentary presentation.

Judith Baskin, Department of Judaic Studies

USETHSTE

Title:	**When You Think of Mexico: Commercial Images of Mexicans in the Mass Media**
Producer:	Yolanda M. Lopez
Director:	Carl Heyward
Distributor:	Piñata Publications
Release Date:	1986
Technical:	28 min. / color / English
Purchase Price:	$60
Rental:	n/a
Presentation:	Narration over images from the mass media (advertising, television, etc.), and of objects such as food packaging, books, and clothing.
Awards:	Honorable Mention, Guadalupe Arts Film Festival, 1987

Content: The video shows a variety of images of Mexicans as they are represented in U.S. advertising, food products, and other electronic and print media. Writer/producer Yolanda M. Lopez is a Mexican-American artist from California who describes her work as "driven by love, rage, and a sense of irony." In the video, she and a second narrator demonstrate and comment on how Mexicans are portrayed in advertising and food products, on television and in film, on clothing and other common objects such as dishes, napkin holders, and lamps, and in newsmagazines. The video is meant to raise viewers' consciousness regarding the racism contained in these images and their potential effect on Chicanos in the United States.

Critical Comments: *When You Think of Mexico* presents a broad-ranging look at symbolic images of Mexicans in such diverse areas as food products and packaging, travel posters, dishes and coffee mugs, restaurant names and advertisements, billboards, film and television, children's clothing, and newsmagazine covers. The print and television advertisements, the home and food products, and the film clips presented in the video do provide a sense of the types of crude, overused, and demeaning images of Mexicans that pervade U.S. popular culture. This should make Lopez's video a useful complement to courses that seek to explore stereotyping in general or of Latinos in particular.

The video can be used in a broad range of courses to illustrate how groups of people can be caricatured and stigmatized in subtle and not-so-subtle ways. Alone, each image can seem relatively inconsequential; displayed together, the set of images gives the viewer a better sense of the general pattern of stereotyping of Mexicans by non-Mexicans in the United States.

An important shortcoming of the video that will place much of the analytic burden on the instructor, is its somewhat haphazard and jumpy quality. While the images displayed are powerful and provocative, the narrative analysis and the way the images are organized in the video are disappointing. The video jumps from travel posters to the Frito Bandito, from news articles and photographs to restaurant advertisements, from children's clothing to Granny Goose "Tortillos," from household products to El Zorro, from dishware to Freddy Prinze, and from images of women in liquor billboards to news clips of the Immigration and Naturalization Service, without clearly demarcated transitions and without an obvious structure or organizing principle. This makes it difficult to see which are the major and minor points.

Beyond displaying how stereotypes of Mexicans have been incorporated into and disseminated in the popular culture, *When You Think of Mexico* seeks to indict the mass media and corporate interests for their insensitive and exploitative use, and indeed their fabrication, of these images. However, in its attempt to go beyond the images into an analysis of their sources and their effects, the video's power is greatly diluted. These are representative statements made by the narrators which seem unsubstantiated in the video:

> It is the nature of suppressed racism to reduce the cultural traits, symbols and values of another culture to its simplest and most simplistic form. It is the nature of U.S. cultural imperialism to reduce another culture to the level of popular entertainment. —[referring to El Pollo Magico] . . . subtle slander of Mexican masculinity.

> . . . the media is equally brutal in its depiction of ''all'' women.

> Corporate manufacturers . . . are in the process of reinventing Mexican food. They are redefining Mexican traditions and culture for corporate profit.

This at best is a corruption of Mexican cuisine and character.

It is these images people carry in their minds when you go to apply for housing, jobs, and money.

While it may be that these are accurate statements or justifiable positions, the video itself does not provide adequate backing for them: they are simply asserted as facts. Ultimately, the choppy editing combined with this type of general and unsubstantiated commentary led me to experience the video as somewhat shallow. But it was precisely because of the potency and offensiveness of the many images presented that I was left with a desire for more incisive and studied analysis. Thus, I believe that the weaknesses of the video do not rule out its potential usefulness in the classroom context.

A film that comes to mind when watching *When You Think of Mexico* is Marion Riggs's *Ethnic Notions,* a powerful and much better analysis of stereotypical images of African Americans over the course of U.S. history. *Ethnic Notions* dramatically shows the contrast between stereotypes and reality, something that this video does not adequately accomplish. Nevertheless, *When You Think of Mexico* might be especially useful if used in conjunction with other videos such as *Ethnic Notions*. I recommend use of the video as a stimulus for classroom discussion and for provoking additional exploration and analysis by students, if these are combined with appropriate readings and with adequate framing and analysis provided by the instructor.

Bernardo M. Ferdman, Departments of Psychology and of Latin American and Caribbean Studies

USGENCLA

Title:	**With Babies and Banners: Story of the Women's Emergency Brigade**
Producer:	Lorraine Gray, Women's Labor History Film Project
Distributor:	New Day Films
Release Date:	c1979
Technical:	46 min. / color, b&w sequences
Purchase Price:	$295
Rental:	$50
Presentation:	Documentary, with interviews and period footage

Content: As one of several late-1970s genre films about the lost history of American militants, *With Babies and Banners* is outstanding for its solid treatment of women's issues and for its technical virtues. The action of this film occurs in Flint, Michigan, in the great General Motors (GM) sit-down (factory occupation) strikes of late 1936 and early 1937.

Critical Comments: In a milieu filled with elderly talking heads reminiscing about the good old days before Taft-Hartley, the Palmer Raids, or the McCarthy era, this film offers a welcome relief. More than the usual edifying study that demonstrates the dignity of a now-dying generation of militants, placing their story in a sleepy pocket of quaintness, *With Babies and Banners* uses the past to grapple with current issues of women's struggle for fair treatment on the job.

This film surprises the viewer with its direct look at women's working conditions and the injustices suffered, yet in many ways the story is a current one. A voiceover, for example, notes that employers were only interested in hiring two kinds of women: diligent workers and easy sexual partners. It even recounts that in an age when syphilis plagued many in American society, the sex-for-jobs practices of one employer meant that in one plant, all of the women were infected. For those not granted certain latitude as compensation for their sexual services, the jobs

were tough, replete with draconian surveillance and rapid, shoulder-to-shoulder handwork on moving production lines. In trying to give a sense of the oppression all workers experienced on the job in the interwar period, however, this film comes perilously close to justifying violence against women. Conditions were so bad for male workers, it argues, that it was no wonder they sometimes came home and beat their wives. (One must wonder, by this logic, whom the women had a right to beat in this environment of compensatory violence.) In such desperate conditions, men found solace in drink, women found it in church.

As a study of the collective wisdom of the working class and its ability to learn from others, this film is a large zero. We are led to imagine that GM workers invented the sit-down strike when, indeed, it first appeared on a wide scale in Italy in 1920 (the Turin occupations), simmered in Europe in the 1920s and early 1930s, and broke out as a massive wave—millions of strikers—in May–June of 1936 in France (where it was termed the ''Polish strike'' in recognition of Polish workers' use of it). American exceptionalism again carries the day.

But the story gets murkier. As the plants were occupied, male union leaders, in their collective brilliance, concluded that if women were to stay in the plants they would be accused of sexual lassitude, and thus, the occupied factories would have to be all-male citadels of workers' justice. The film allows this decision to be reported flatly and without any comment either from voiceovers or women interviewees about alternatives to bourgeois morality, new social standards, or defiance of conventions.

Editor's note: Though the reviewer judged this video, on balance, unsuited to the particular diversity courses at the University at Albany, I have included it in the guide as worthy of consideration for use elsewhere, depending on local needs, audience background, and options. Three such videos appear in the guide.

These men might have been militant, but they were socially conservative.

The film does mention that male unionists' sexism was such that women activists were discouraged from going to the union hall, which itself was designated as a testosterone zone. This exclusion pushed women to the margins of the struggle, as supporting actresses in the great male drama of GM. To this, they heroically adapted, docilely cooking meals for the strikers, ensuring the delivery of supplies into the plants and, in a crucial turning point of the strike (one which this reviewer would not dare to minimize), creating a diversion at the factory gates as the Chevy engine plant was successfully closed down. One is led to believe that this action, the work of the Women's Emergency Brigade, saved the day for the Flint strike and hence, for the American labor movement as a whole. It might not be good history, but it is politically exciting.

The film does warrant considerable positive comment, however. It shows the fascinating reinvention of women's classic domestic support role into that of strike supporters. Without much comment, it shows the changes in purpose, using similar skills and technology, in the shift in activity from cooking for the nuclear family to collective cooking. Unfortunately, the film lets this subtle redefinition of social roles and technological applications pass without comment. Similarly, it offers an interesting recounting of the story of a woman who protested the union's efforts to get women back into the home or into subservient roles as strike supporters. In response, she began to organize children's pickets, but the film misses the political import of the irony.

It would be a pleasure to be able to give this film a strong endorsement for adoption in the university diversity program. Its heart is in the right place, and its attitudes toward women workers and unionists are certainly right on—too right on to be credible, and a bit naive as well. Only one of the interviewees is African American and, as with a number of films in this genre, it wants us to believe that the notion of double oppression—by race and class—suffices to explain the plight of people of color, and that the path to liberation is with the labor movement as a whole. At the end of the film, it is suggested that working women can only liberate themselves if they stay in the mainstream union movement and prevail upon male union leaders to (paternalistically) recognize their contributions and their rights. Slender as this reed is, it is more than the film offers for people of color. The debate itself is not even posed squarely, and for a film which so consciously wears its politics on its sleeve, this kind of burying of issues is disturbing. It is a film produced for preaching to the convinced. Within the context of the fate of industrial America, it could be fruitfully paired with the recent documentary about Flint called *Roger and Me* (hence offering a tale of the rise and fall of American labor), but alone it is simply weak.

Robert L. Frost, Department of History

USETHGEN

Title:	**With Silk Wings**
Series:	Talking History (program no. 4)
Producer:	Spencer Nakasako, for Asian Women United
Director:	Spencer Nakasako
Distributor:	National Asian-American Telecommunications Association/CrossCurrent Media
Release Date:	1982
Technical:	30 min. / color / English
Purchase Price:	$160 (each program)
Rental:	$50
Presentation:	Combines oral histories, interviews, and historical documentary footage

Content: This film is fairly comprehensive in its coverage of all the major Asian-American communities: Japanese, Chinese, Filipino, Korean, and Hmong women are interviewed. There is historical documentary footage on the Chinese and Japanese immigrant women as well.

The film begins with the late-19th century, and follows the story of a Chinese immigrant woman to San Francisco's Chinatown. It shows her immigration through Angel Island and the limited opportunities available to her as a result of the legislation which prevented Chinese from buying homes and living outside of Chinatowns.

The scene then moves to the story of Japanese immigration, and a Japanese-American woman gives her life story. She worked as a maid and was later held in an internment camp during World War II. In this way, her particular story is a common one from the Japanese-American community, where a very large number of women worked as domestic maids since few employment opportunities were open to them.

The life of a Filipina farmworker forms the third segment of the film. This depicts life in central California's small agricultural towns and semirural areas and what it meant to grow up there. It gives the viewer some idea of rural poverty and struggles of everyday life.

The next segment focuses on a Korean woman who has emerged an active union organizer for the hotel and garment workers unions in the San Francisco Bay area. In a thoughtful interview, the segment covers the life of garment workers and shows their working conditions. Many of the workers are shown to have had professional training in Korea, but because of the language barrier they find themselves doing unskilled or semiskilled work.

The last segment in the film includes interviews with a Hmong-Lao woman who came as a refugee after 1975 and the end of the Vietnam War. Initially, this woman and her family were resettled in Minnesota as part of the Refugee Resettlement Program. But later they moved to California, where they are shown operating a small farm growing Asian vegetables for the ethnic market. Her hope, however, is that her children will not end up in back-breaking farmwork and will be more comfortable than she is.

Classroom Use: This film is suitable for both lower-division and upper-division courses and should be of interest not only in women's studies courses but also in sociology, history, and anthropology courses.

Critical Comments: In these various life histories the strength and resilience of Asian-American women is highlighted. The film does assume a certain knowledge of Asian-American history, so the instructor may have to use some additional reading materials or give a lecture to place these women and their experiences into a broader context. It is a good film for challenging racial and sexual stereotypes of Asian and Asian-American women, for these women are anything but quiet and passive. The film, because of its wide coverage, also introduces the audience to the diversity of Asian-Americans. Asian-Americans are shown to come from a variety of backgrounds, and the film shows that not everybody grew up in Chinatown. The focus of the Talking History series is "women and work," so the different types of work done by Asian women is also discussed.

Sucheta Mazumdar, Department of History

GLRACREL

Title:	**Witnesses: Anti-Semitism in Poland, 1946**
Director:	Marcel Lozinsky
Distributor:	Filmakers Library
Release Date:	1990
Technical:	26 min. / b&w / English, Polish with translation
Purchase Price:	$295
Rental:	$55
Presentation:	Documentary with interviews and archival movie footage
Award:	American Film and Video Festival, 1990

Content: *Witnesses* describes a horrifying set of events which occurred in the aftermath of the Holocaust in war-torn Poland. In the village of Kielce, a group of Jewish survivors who have returned from Nazi concentration camps attempt to rebuild their lives. However, when the rumor of a "blood sacrifice" of a Christian child by some Jews begins to spread, the townspeople set upon them and massacre them. Forty-two innocent people who had survived the Holocaust are murdered and many others wounded in a terrible episode of ancient hatreds.

After initial documentary footage on the background of the end of the war and the plight of Jews returning to their homes, the video consists of interviews with several surviving Polish witnesses of this modern-day pogrom. Some recall the events with vivid expressions of shock and horror; others appear unmoved or unsympathetic to the victims, even at times justifying the actions of the mob. With telling detail, they help the filmmakers (who film on location in Kielce) reconstruct this almost-forgotten episode in history.

Classroom Use: This video is suitable for classroom use at the college level, although its effectiveness

without a great deal of introduction is questionable. It consists chiefly of very slow-paced interviews which will probably bore to distraction all but the most patient and well-prepared viewers. The events did occur, and warrant the attention the video tries to give them. But they might leave ill-informed viewers without an understanding of the way the Polish-Catholic people, themselves victims who suffered terrible oppression under Nazi occupation, fell prey to ignorance and superstition. The video is limited in the time it can devote to the historic context in which the perpetrators acted, and might leave viewers without an understanding of their situation.

Critical Comments: The film is of limited value in teaching concepts of diversity, except in a classroom setting that can provide very extensive supplementary reading and discussion of the historic context. The film can be easily misunderstood. If used with this sort of extensive introduction, it would allow students to understand the sources and manifestations of controversy and conflicts which arise between ethnic groups.

Donald S. Birn, Department of History

USCLAECO

Title: **The Wobblies**

Producers: Stewart Bird and Deborah Shaffer

Distributor: First-Run

Release Date: 1979

Technical: 89 min. / color / English

Purchase Price: $490

Rental: $150 video or 16mm

Presentation: Documentary; narrated by Roger Baldwin, founder of the American Civil Liberties Union; music by Utah Phillips singing old Industrial Workers of the World songs

Content: The film features former members of the Industrial Workers of the World (IWW) revealing their feelings, motivations, beliefs, and actions. It uses union songs, posters, paintings, archival stills, and newsreel footage to trace the impact of the big industrial union.

Critical Comments: This video represents part of the wave of "People's History" films of the 1970s. As the movement of the New Left declined after 1973, many radicals turned to making historical films in an effort to connect their collective discovery and experience of radicalism to deeper historical roots. These efforts met with mixed success. Many such experiments overblew the influence of radical movements and presented the past as a series of elderly talking heads. *The Wobblies* is typical of the genre, as well-meaning as it might be.

At the outset, the promise of the IWW was considerable. As an anarcho-syndicalist union, it directly confronted and opposed the largely unrestrained power of a WASP bourgeois elite. Promising "One Big Union" in which the organized force of the working class would become the embryo for a liberated social order—one which would overturn both the exploitative capitalist system and the repressive state with which capitalism has a symbiotic relationship—and citizenship would be defined as simply the status of

Editor's note: Though the reviewer judged this video, on balance, unsuited to the particular diversity courses at the University at Albany, I have included it in the guide as worthy of consideration for use elsewhere, depending on local needs, audience background, and options. Three such videos appear in the guide.

productive worker. This collective identity would, the Wobblies claimed, transcend traditional differences in race and gender. Though the film undoubtedly minimizes internal IWW conflicts over race, gender, and ethnicity, it does seem clear that the Wobblies successfully bridged such divisions. In particular, the IWW succeeded in integrating many women and new immigrants into the movement; it seems to have had less success, though, in dealing with a Deep South plagued by the introduction of Jim Crow.

In their time (1905–1920), the Wobblies did, however, confront the major tribulations of the northern working class, from the introduction of speeded-up "scientific" Taylorist production methods to the lure of class collaboration (Jay Gould, the famous robber baron, claimed that he could hire half of the working class to kill the other half). The Wobblies also confronted the divisive character of skill among workers and the exclusionary and nativist ends to which it was used by the American Federation of Labor (AFL). Not unlike Karl Marx a half-century earlier, the Wobblies predicted that the working class would be reduced to an indiscriminate army of unskilled laborers, united in the commonality of their oppression and wage slavery. Neither Marx nor the Wobblies seem to have comprehended that over time, skills are recomposed as well as degraded, and that the workers who have the newer skills tend to see their deskilled comrades as simply the passive victims of "progress." That is, Marx and the Wobblies seem to have believed that over time, economic evolution would tend to make uniform rather than differentiate the working class. This observation might help to explain the Wobblies' decline, freeing the film of having to account for the eclipse as simply the result of the Red Scare repression of the Palmer Raids (1920).

This film does indicate how the IWW's willingness to cross racial and ethnic lines and to challenge the skill elitism of the AFL gave it a respectably plucky public image. It tellingly reproduces a clip of the crude "liberty vs. anarchy" imagery—Lady Liberty as a virginal WASP and Anarchy as a swarthy, unwashed immigrant toting a bomb—peddled for propaganda purposes. It similarly shows clips of Samuel Gompers (AFL) denouncing the IWW. Through such devices, the film depicts the IWW's inclusive character, implying that simply opening the doors to all comers as workers, regardless of race, was enough of a strategy to combat racism. It indicates few explicitly anti-racist (or anti-sexist—the IWW viewed the suffrage movement as a species of silly bourgeois reformism) actions taken by the IWW. Indeed, it shows that the IWW sought to resist racism and sexism merely by organizing all the oppressed peoples as workers dedicated to a revolution which, in constructing an anarchist-communist society, would of necessity preclude racist and sexist activity. Worse, the film discusses an Elizabeth Gurley Flynn (an early 20th-century American Communist) speech in which soft hands on women are presented as a sign of bourgeois decadence; yet also in which women were urged to oppose capitalism as a way to liberate femininity from the shackles of oppression. The film tries to have it both ways, and ends up only confusing issues. It similarly offers lit-tle critique of the tensions between individual acts of propaganda by the deed and the need for organizational discipline.

The balance of the film maintains a heroic, romantic air as it discusses major strikes, protest strategies, and the like. It does a respectable job of documenting the IWW's opposition to World War I and the price paid for such opposition, as well as the Wobblies' tortured ambivalence about the revolution(s) in Russia.

As a film for possible inclusion in the university's diversity agenda, *The Wobblies* falls far short of what one might wish. It reflects the almost naive simplicity of both the IWW itself and of the New Left in the 1970s, in that both seem to have imagined that organizing the workers as a class for a socialist revolution would suffice as a strategy to combat racism and sexism. Neither offered specific strategies to deal with the very real and deeply felt oppression experienced by women and people of color. This problem is implicitly underlined in the film by the near-absence of African Americans (except for a precious few western miners) and the incomprehensible confusion over the question of femininity depicted in the Flynn speech. In short, this film might entertain students as a dreamy and heroic reconstruction of the past, and it might make students view the capitalist system a bit more skeptically, but it would do little to open up or shed new light upon genuine issues of human diversity.

Robert L. Frost, Department of History

GLCULEXP

Title:	**Yanco**
Producer:	Producciones Yanco
Director:	Servando Gonzalez
Distributor:	Facets Video
Release Date:	1989, 1964
Technical:	85 min. / b&w / mostly silent, with sparse dialog in Nahuatl; subtitles not provided (or needed)
Purchase Price:	$29.95
Rental:	$10 for members of Facets Video Club
Presentation:	Dramatization originally produced as a film
Awards:	Winner of sixteen awards at film festivals

Content: The context in the film is the Mexican Indian village of Mixqui. This remarkably beautiful, sensitive film dramatically depicts misunderstanding due to false interpretation of cultural differences.

Classroom Use: The film is recommended for introductory general courses on cultural diversity, as well as courses on cultural anthropology, folklore, Mexico, and Latin-American studies.

Critical Comments: The opening scene shows a young Indian boy named Juanito besieged and tormented by various noises which surround him in the village: hammering on anvils, ringing of church bells, squeaking wagon wheels. He flees from them by taking a boat out to a marsh, where he lies down on the ground and takes delight in listening to the sounds of nature and playing a primitive, home-made one-string violin.

When Juanito returns from the peaceful setting, the other boys of the village make fun of him; some of them tie tin cans to numerous stray dogs and release them all at once near him, while others beat noisily on larger cans. Realizing that her son's hearing may be abnormally sensitive, Juanito's mother takes him for treatment to a kind of witch doctor who attempts to cure him by mixing potions, fanning smoke on his ears, and using incantations.

At the end of the school year, Juanito receives recognition for being one of the best students, while several of the rowdy boys who tormented him receive failing grades. His proud mother takes him to town, buys him a hat, and has his picture taken. While in town, Juanito hears the sound of a violin. When he goes looking for the source, he meets an old man and the two become friends. Juanito begins going to the home of the old man, who is a former musician of European descent. There, he begins to learn to play the old man's violin, which bears the name "Yanco." Juanito learns quickly, and soon his playing starts to produce beautiful music.

When Juanito's mother becomes ill, he stays home to care for her. He also calls a medical doctor, who drives the false healers from her, throws away the things they are using for medicine, and gives the sick woman an injection. As soon as she has recovered, Juanito hastens back to the home of his old friend, who has died since the last time the youth visited. Juanito is greatly grieved.

One day, when Juanito goes with his mother to the shop where she sells the fabrics that she weaves on her loom, Juanito sees the violin named Yanco hanging on the wall of the store. His mother attempts to buy it for him, but the shopkeeper offers to sell her a cheap toy instrument instead. Juanito discovers a way to take the violin from the wall through a window, and soon he begins to remove it, play it out at the marsh, and return it later every night.

When the superstitious villagers hear the sounds of the violin coming from afar, they believe that it is the deceased musician who is playing, and they become frightened. Their fright later leads to panic, and they begin to attribute deaths (actually due to disease) and other misfortunes to the effects of the phantom-like music. Juanito's playing of Yanco ultimately leads to his own death.

Brian F. Head, Department of Hispanic, Italian, and Portuguese Studies

Directory of Distributors

ABC Distribution Co.   (212) 456-1725
825 7th Ave. / New York, NY 10019

Baker & Taylor Video   (800) 435-5111
501 S. Gladiolus / Momence, IL   (708) 965-8060
60954

Broadway Entertainment   (800) 924-9490
1650 Broadway / New York, NY
10012

California Newsreel
(see Resolution, Inc.)

Cambridge Documentary Films   (617) 354-3677
P.O. Box 385 / Cambridge, MA
02139

CBS/Fox Video   (212) 819-3200
1330 Avenue of the Americas /
5th Floor / New York, NY 10019

Center for New American Media   (212) 925-5665
524 Broadway, 2nd Floor /
New York, NY 10012

Cinema Guild   (212) 246-5522
1697 Broadway / New York, NY
10019

Clarity Educational Productions   (201) 891-8240
P.O. Box 315 / Franklin Lakes, NJ
07417

Columbia Studios, Division of   (818) 954-6000
Warner Bros.
3400 Riverside Dr. / Burbank, CA
91505

Corporation for Public Broadcasting   (800) LEARNER
P.O. Box 2345 / So. Burlington, VT
05407-2345

Cox, Matthews, & Assoc., Inc.   (703) 385-2980
10520 Warwick Ave. / Fairfax, VA

Direct Cinema   (310) 396-4774
P.O. Box 10003 / Santa Monica, CA
90410

Educational Video Inc.   (409) 295-5767
1401 19th St. / Huntsville, TX 77340

Electronic Arts Intermix   (212) 966-4605
536 Broadway, 9th Floor / New York,
NY 10012

Encounter Productions   (503) 241-8663
2267 N.W. Pettygrove / Portland, OR
97210

Encyclopaedia Britannica   (800) 554-9862
Educational Corp.
310 South Michigan Ave. / Chicago,
IL 60604

Ergo Media, Inc.   (201) 692-0404
P.O. Box 2037 / Teaneck, NJ 07666

Facets Video   (800) 331-6197
1517 W. Fullerton Ave. / Chicago, IL
60614

Film Australia   (612) 413-8777
P.O. Box 46 / Lindfield, NSW 2070
Australia

Filmakers Library Inc.   (212) 808-4980
133 East 58th St. / New York, NY
10022

Films for the Humanities and   (800) 558-6968
Sciences   (609) 452-1128
P.O. Box 2053 / Princeton, NJ 08540   (800) 257-5126

First Run/Icarus   (212) 243-0600
153 Waverly Place / New York, NY
10014

Friends of Le Chambon   (213) 650-1774
8033 Sunset Boulevard #784 /
Los Angeles, CA 90046

Hearts and Hands Media Arts
(see New Day Films)

Home Vision/Public Media Video (312) 878-2600
5547 N. Ravenswood Ave. / Chicago, (800) 826-3456
IL 60640-1199

Indiana University Audio Visual (812) 855-8087
Center
Bloomington, IN 47405

Intellimation (800) 968-2291
P.O. Box 1922 / Santa Barbara, CA (800) 443-6633
93116-1922

International Film Exchange/ (212) 582-4318
Ifex Films
201 W. 52nd St. / New York, NY
10019

International Video Network (510) 866-1121
2242 Camino Ramon / San Ramon,
CA 94583

Jacka Photography (602) 944-2793
P.O. Box 9043 / Phoenix, AZ 85068

KAMU-TV, Texas A&M University (409) 845-5611
College Station, TX 77843-4244

Kino International Corp. (212) 629-6880
333 West 39th St. / New York, NY
10018

Light-Saraf Films (415) 469-0139
131 Concord St. / San Francisco, CA
94112

Lorimar Home Video (714) 474-0355
10202 W. Washington Blvd. / (800) 345-1441
Culver City, CA 90232

Long Bow Group (212) 724-9302
617 West End Ave. / New York, NY
10024

Malofilm Video (514) 844-4555
3575 St. Laurent / Montreal, Quebec
H2X 2T7

MCA Home Video (818) 768-3520
11312 Penrose St. / Sun Valley, CA
91352

Media Basics (203) 458-2505
705 Post Rd. / Lighthouse Square /
Guilford, CT 06437

Media Guild (619) 755-9191
11526 Sorrento Valley Rd., Suite J /
San Diego, CA 92121

Media Home Entertainment Inc. (310) 216-7900
5730 Buckingham Parkway / (800) 421-4509
Culver City, CA 90230

Media Projects, Inc. (214) 826-3863
5215 Homer St. / Dallas, TX 75206

Merco International Films (805) 484-2213
Box B / Somis, CA 93066

Minnesota American Indian Aids (612) 870-1723
Task Force
1433 E. Franklin Ave. / Minneapolis,
MN 55404

Mystic Fire Video (212) 941-0999
Box 1090 Cooper Station / New York, (800) 999-1319
NY 10276

National Asian-American (415) 552-9550
Telecommunications
Association/CrossCurrent Media
346 9th St., 2nd floor /
San Francisco, CA 94103

National Film Board of Canada (212) 586-5131
1251 Ave. of the Americas, 16th
Floor / New York, NY 10020

Native American Public (402) 472-3522
Broadcasting Consortium
P.O. Box 83111 / Lincoln, NE 68501

New Day Films (212) 645-8210
121 W. 27th St. / New York, NY
10001

New Yorker Video (212) 247-6110
16 West 61st St. / New York, NY
10023

Noble Enterprises (718) 369-2181
53 Cheever Place / Brooklyn, NY
11231

Norman Ross Publishing, Inc. (800) 648-8850
330 West 58th St. / New York, NY (212) 765-8200
10019

PBS Video (703) 739-5380
1320 Braddock Pl. / Alexandria, VA
22314-1698

Pennsylvania State University (814) 865-6314
Audio Visual Services
University Park, PA 16802

Piñata Publications (510) 444-6401
200 Lakeside Drive / Oakland, CA
94612

Prism Entertainment (213) 277-3270
1888 Century Park East, Suite 1000 /
Los Angeles, CA 90067

Rediscovery Productions (203) 226-4489
2 Halfmile Common / Westport, CT
06880

Resolution Inc./California Newsreel
149 Ninth St., #420 / San Francisco, CA 94103   (415) 621-6196

SKC Media Center, Salish-Kootenai College
Box 117 / Pablo, MT 59855   (406) 675-4800 ext. 285

Teatro Campesino
Box 1240 / San Juan Bautista, CA 95045   (408) 623-2444

University of California-Berkeley, Extension Media Center
2223 Fulton St. / Berkeley, CA 94720   (415) 642-0460 / (415) 642-5578

University of Washington, Instructional Media Services
Kane Hall DG-10 / Seattle, WA 98195   (206) 543-9909

Video Communications, Inc.
6539 E. Skelly Drive / Tulsa, OK 74145   (918) 622-6460 / (800) 331-4077

Video Data Bank, Art Institute of Chicago
Columbus Dr. and Jackson Blvd. / Chicago, IL 60603   (312) 443-3793

Vidmark Entertainment
2901 Ocean Park Blvd., Suite 213 / Santa Monica, CA 90405   (310) 399-8877

Warner Home Video, Inc.
4000 Warner Blvd. / Burbank, CA 91522   (818) 954-6266

Western Film and Video, Inc.
30941 Agoura Rd., Suite 302 / Westlake Village, CA 91361   (818) 889-7350

WETA-TV
3620 27th St. / Washington, DC 20013   (703) 998-2713

William Greaves Productions
230 West 55th St. / New York, NY 10019   (212) 246-7221

Women Make Movies, Inc.
225 Lafayette St., Suite 206 / New York, NY 10012   (212) 925-0606

World Video
P.O. Box 30469 / Knoxville, TN 37930-0469   (615) 691-9827

Zenger Video
10200 Jefferson Blvd. / Culver City, CA 90232   (800) 421-4246 / (310) 839-2436

Ztek
P.O. Box 1055 / Lexington, KY 40201-1055   (800) 247-1603

Gregory I. Stevens is assistant dean, College of Humanities and Fine Arts, University at Albany, State University of New York, where he also teaches classics and humanities. He earned a Ph.D. in comparative literature from the University of Michigan and taught there and at the University of Texas/Dallas and Auburn University before joining the University at Albany as executive director, Capital District Humanities Program. Stevens has distinguished himself as a leader in state and national humanities projects, earning numerous awards from the University and professional communities.

73 152NJD FM 6059
04/94 36591

DATE DUE

GAYLORD			PRINTED IN U.S.A.